PERSPECTIVES ON AUSTRALIA

PERSPECTIVES
ON AUSTRALIA

Essays on Australiana in the Collections of the
Harry Ransom Humanities Research Center

Edited by Dave Oliphant
With an Introduction by Thomas F. Staley

Harry Ransom Humanities Research Center • The University of Texas at Austin

Illustrative materials in black and white were photographed by Patrick Keeley of the HRHRC; color reproductions were photographed by George Holmes of the Archer M. Huntington Art Gallery with the exception of the cover illustration, which was photographed by Patrick Keeley.

Cover illustration: *Queensland Landscape* by Henri Bastin, watercolor on paper, 1965. 21¼ x 29⅝ inches. Archer M. Huntington Art Gallery, The University of Texas at Austin, Gift of the Mertz Art Fund, 1972.

Contents

AUSTRALIA

Chapters by K. H. Bailey, F. A. Bland, E. H. Burgmann, Herbert Burton, S. J. Butlin, Colin Clark, H. C. Coombs, John G. Crawford, R. M. Crawford and G. F. James, K. S. Cunningham, Sir Frederick Eggleston, A. P. Elkin, L. F. Fitzharding, Brian Fitzpatrick, Ross Gollan, C. Hartley Grattan, H. M. Green, Gordon Greenwood, J. Macdonald Holmes, T. H. Kewley, Gavin Long, Eris O'Brien, Vance and Nettie Palmer, Lloyd Ross, Bernard Smith, Clive Turnbull, E. Ronald Walker, John M. Ward

EDITED BY C. HARTLEY GRATTAN

UNIVERSITY OF CALIFORNIA PRESS
BERKELEY AND LOS ANGELES · 1947

Title page of C. Hartley Grattan's *Australia* (University of California Press, 1947). *HRHRC Grattan Collection.*

Introduction

The essays in this volume collectively reflect the richness and range of the literary and historical materials that constitute an archive of Southwest Pacificana in the Harry Ransom Humanities Research Center at The University of Texas at Austin—a holding complemented by the Mertz Collection of Australian Paintings in the University's Huntington Art Gallery. The contents and significance of the Mertz Collection are characterized by John Clarke in his essay, "Australian Painting of the Sixties." Within the HRHRC's archive of Southwest Pacificana, the collection of manuscripts and books forming what is commonly referred to as the "C. Hartley Grattan Collection" is regarded as the most substantial gathering of Australian materials outside of the country itself. In addition to the Grattan Collection, the HRHRC holdings also contain other important collections of Australian books and manuscripts.

In the year of Australia's Bicentennial, and more immediately the announcement of the establishment of a center for Australian Studies at The University of Texas at Austin, it is appropriate that this volume appear. These essays offer not only a partial description of the collections held by the HRHRC, they afford scholars an opportunity to learn of the vast resources available for study of the art, literature, history, and culture of Australia as it emerged into a modern and vital country located in a crucial part of the world where the meeting of East and West is still to be defined.

On 24 June 1988, the Honorable R.J.L. Hawke, prime minister of Australia, and Dr. William H. Cunningham, president of The University of Texas at Austin, jointly announced the creation of the University's Center for Australian Studies. The endowment of this Center will assure the academic community at large of the sustained commitment of the University to the support of research and study of a country with which the University has maintained long and close ties. The establishment of the Center was the natural outgrowth of many academic connections between the University and Australia, beginning with the work of Professor Emeritus Joseph Jones of the University's Department of English. As early as 1959 the University of Texas Press published Jones's *The Cradle of Erewhon: Samuel Butler in New Zealand*, which was printed in Australia in 1960 by Melbourne University Press. In 1962 he edited a special number of *The Texas Quarterly*, entitled "Image of Australia." Jones's interest in the field of World Literature in

English has continued to the present and has attracted many Australian writers and scholars to the University, among them Robert D. Fitzgerald, whose volume of poems, *Of Some Country*, was published by the Humanities Research Center in 1963. The cornerstone of the University's relationship with Australia remains, however, the C. Hartley Grattan Collection, which has been held in the HRHRC since 1964 when Grattan arrived here at the behest of Harry Huntt Ransom, then chancellor of the University of Texas.

As Frank B. Poyas's essay makes clear, Hartley Grattan was a man with many interests, but foremost among them was his enduring professional and personal attachment to Australia. He traveled its terrain extensively, wrote about it exhaustively, and promoted its culture and promise relentlessly. His knowledge of the country, his important contacts with its political and literary figures, and his penchant for collecting anything written by Australians, all resulted in his amassing the finest individual collection of Australian materials ever assembled outside Australia. In articles describing the collection that Grattan brought with him and added to for the University, Sudhakar R. Jamkhandi suggests the research opportunities that exist for scholars who work with the books in this collection, while Laurie Hergenhan in his "critical introduction" gives a thorough account of the full range of subjects covered by the Grattan archive of manuscript materials.

Essays by Jill Roe and Desley Deacon elucidate Grattan's role not merely as a commentator but as a key figure deeply involved in the Australian literary world who tried to promote Australian writers and writings in America. More importantly, the correspondence reviewed in these essays reveals much about life in Australia during the thirties. Roe's article on the Miles Franklin ("Brent of Bin Bin") correspondence not only offers a fascinating portrait of an important Australian author but reflects Grattan's concern with intellectual issues and the place of Australian literature in the larger context of world literature. Likewise, Desley Deacon, who with John Higley of the University's Department of Government will direct the Center for Australian Studies, discusses Grattan's part in encouraging the publication of the memoirs of Alice Henry, whose involvement with women's trade unions in America had been informed by her Australian background and experience.

The HRHRC's Iris Milutinovic archive described in John McLaren's essay is a separate acquisition that affords a valuable historical record of domestic life during the period when European emigration reached its peak and transformed the singularity of British settlement, with its outpost mentality, to a more diverse and ethnic culture. At the same time that Milutinovic's observations represent the difficulties of settlement, her sensitive understanding of the changing patterns in Australian life adds historical resonance to her writings.

Another important HRHRC acquisition is the correspondence between the Australian novelist Christina Stead and Stanley Burnshaw, along with other

8

related Stead materials, all of which are discussed by Robert L. Ross. Ross's essay traces fully the importance of Randall Jarrell's introduction not only to Stead's novel, *The Man Who Loved Children*, but to her literary career generally. Ross also uses materials from the R.G. Howarth Collection in the HRHRC to chart Stead's difficult struggles and later success with the novel. Ross's essay, together with Robert Zeller's, which discusses more fully the Howarth Collection as it relates to the published and unpublished writings of Joseph Furphy, reveals the interconnections that are already being discovered among the manuscripts and letters in the various Australian collections at the HRHRC.

Although anchored by the richness of the Grattan Collection, the archive of Southwest Pacificana at The University of Texas at Austin is a diverse and growing collection offering boundless opportunities for study, and one that forms a vital core for the University's Center for Australian Studies as well as a research holding that will serve scholars from all over the world.

—Thomas F. Staley
Director, HRHRC

Photograph of C. Hartley Grattan by the Blackstone Studios, New York, 1936. *HRHRC Photography Collection*.

C. Hartley Grattan: The Man and the Collection

BY FRANK B. POYAS

Since 1964, the Harry Ransom Humanities Research Center at The University of Texas at Austin has been the home of one of the largest and most comprehensive collections of Australian-related materials outside of Australasia. Officially titled the "University of Texas Collection of Southwest Pacificana," this resource is more commonly referred to as the "Grattan Collection," after C. (for Clinton) Hartley Grattan (1902-1980), who by any measure was an intriguing figure. When the man and his collection came to Texas a quarter of a century ago, the University immediately became a vital center for Australian studies. In this year of the Australian Bicentennial, it is both timely and significant to undertake a fuller appreciation of this collection and of the man who created such an invaluable archive.

For the first sixty-two years of his life, Hartley Grattan was a free-lance writer and in many ways a free-spirit. "In my own eyes," he once reported, "I'm simply a fellow who has made a desperate effort to understand the world in which we live."[1] For many valid reasons, Grattan is remembered today and will be remembered in the future as the first and foremost American expert on Australia, a fact that his permanent collection at the HRHRC will ensure. However, Grattan was many other things that at times in his life were of greater importance to him. In earning his livelihood as a free-lance writer, he was compelled to produce a massive amount of "copy" in whatever field he was able to market his writing at the moment. Fortunate in having the ability to read rapidly, to absorb vast quantities of material, and to put his thoughts quickly into words, Grattan was able to develop his expertise in a variety of subject areas. At various times and to various people, he was known as an economist, literary critic, educator, philosopher, critic of government policy,

---

[1]From an undated (circa 1948) draft entitled "What am I?," Box 27F/file 2. This and the following references to papers in the Grattan Manuscript Collection follow the current (May 1988) numbering sequence as it appears on the collection's 74 uncatalogued boxes. Within each box is a set of file folders, usually, but not always, numbered. As pointed out below, the manuscript collection is in no particular order. Permission to quote from unpublished writings by C. Hartley Grattan has been given by Mrs. Marjorie Grattan.

and historian. Although Grattan never became a novelist (claiming "I have always written non-fiction; I have never knowingly written fiction"),[2] on one occasion he did consider writing an historical novel about a prisoner escaping from Botany Bay.[3] Most of his publications were on American topics and appeared in the United States in what he termed "quality" magazines, such as *Harper's* and *The American Mercury*. Although he acknowledged that he had "mostly written for the middle-brow audience," Grattan was proud of having what he considered "strong high-brow proclivities."[4]

To date there is no complete bibliography of Grattan's writings, which number in the hundreds both for published articles and book reviews. One bibliography was attempted about 1966 by Jack Healy—a handwritten copy of which is in the HRHRC—and includes works by Grattan through that time, but the effort was abandoned in part because Grattan considered it an almost impossible task.[5] In his preface to Healy's bibliography, Grattan hoped that someone would write his biography, but he doubted that it would ever be done because "nobody has ever been prepared to struggle through all the printed matter I have produced."[6] Indeed, to see Grattan whole would be a formidable task. His reluctance to write his own autobiography stemmed from a feeling that he was able to "exhaust the autobiographical impulse in talk with my family and friends."[7] There does exist in the HRHRC some evidence that in 1977 he intended to start writing the story of his life, but apparently he did not progress beyond a few brief paragraphs.[8] If he had completed the task, there is no doubt that it would have made for most interesting reading.

Apart from the Australian connection, Grattan was noted primarily for several early books. In 1929 he published *Why We Fought* (reprinted in 1969 by Bobbs-Merrill), which was one of the earliest and most respected Revisionist histories of the United States entry into the First World War. Biog-

---

[2]Letter from Hartley Grattan to Professor Wilbur R. Jacobs, Chairman, Department of History, University of California at Santa Barbara, 17 January 1961, Box 22A/file 2. In this lengthy letter Grattan summarizes his career in support of his request for employment.

[3]The reference to a novel is found in Box 17. During 1963, Grattan gathered data on the First Fleet and the escape of "Bryants" in 1791. Other than some tentative rough drafts and correspondence with prospective publishers, not much remains of this idea.

[4]Letter from Grattan to Jacobs, 17 January 1961, Box 22A/file 2.

[5]The 200-page handwritten bibliography is shelved in the Center's reading room. A long preface by Grattan to the bibliography contains many valuable insights and is considered by his wife the best statement he ever made about himself. The complete preface is located in Box 12A. Grattan refused to allow the bibliography to be published since he saw it as incomplete and because he expected to add to it over the next few years. See also Box 27H/file 2 for a letter from Grattan to then HRC director Warren Roberts, 23 March 1967.

[6]Ibid., p. 2.

[7]Ibid., p. 1.

[8]Among a brief listing of his own works, contained in Box 24A/file unnumbered, Grattan included a 1977 work entitled "View from the Periphery: An Autobiography." An undated draft of a preface, which was quite likely intended for an autobiography, is found in Box 27E/file 4. Also, Gift Box 1513 holds a series of Grattan's notes on his early childhood and family background.

raphy interested Grattan from his earliest days of writing, and in 1932 he published *The Three Jameses: A Family of Minds.*[9] He also contributed respected chapters to biographies of William Jennings Bryan and Mark Twain.[10] In part, as a result of the need to seek employment, Grattan became actively involved in the field of adult education, and his book, *Quest of Knowledge*, published in 1955, was recognized as a standard in the history of this field.[11]

Grattan always found it difficult to characterize himself, especially in job applications. He worried about not being appreciated because of a "fragmenting of my reputation. In the vernacular, I am aware that I do not readily add up."[12] In 1963 he wrote that "anybody wanting to be nice to me . . . can call me a man-of-letters, modern style. On my passport I am described as an 'author-journalist'."[13] This lifelong inability to fit nicely into a specific category caused Grattan considerable personal and financial difficulties, but it also resulted in a far-ranging career that in turn produced an immense archive of American and Australian materials.

A case could be made that Grattan was genetically predisposed to become involved in Australian affairs. His father, a descendant of French-Swiss stock, emigrated with his family to Nova Scotia in the late eighteenth century, and his mother's family left Scotland for Canada early in the nineteenth century. While his mother later became a naturalized United States citizen, his father retained his Canadian citizenship, and even though shortly before Hartley was born, on 19 October 1902, his parents moved to New England, Grattan was himself eligible for British citizenship deriving from his Commonwealth parents. As he recalled with apparent pride, "the British element in my heritage is colonial British, not metropolitan British."[14] Following an apparently normal childhood in Wakefield, Massachusetts, Grattan entered New Bedford High School with every intention of becoming a certified public accountant. However, after his "commercial course" led to graduation in 1920, Grattan—at the urging of his high school English teacher—enrolled at Clark College in Worcester, Massachusetts, where he studied and developed a lifelong friendship with Harry Elmer Barnes. Although he did poorly in

[9]C. Hartley Grattan, *The Three Jameses: A Family of Minds* (New York: Longmans, Green, 1932; reprinted by New York University Press, 1962).

[10]C. Hartley Grattan, with Paxton Hibben, *The Peerless Leader: William Jennings Bryan* (New York: Farrar & Rinehart, 1929); "Mark Twain," in *American Writers on American Literature*, ed. John Macy (New York: Liveright, 1931).

[11]C. Hartley Grattan, *In Quest of Knowledge: A Historical Perspective on Adult Education* (New York: Association Press, 1955).

[12]Letter from Grattan to Professor Wilbur R. Jacobs, 17 January 1961, Box 22A/file 2.

[13]Draft of unpublished article from 1963, Box 22A/file 3.

[14]From an undated draft of a preface for an autobiographical work, Box 27E/file 4. The concept of "colonial British" fits well with Grattan's Canadian roots and his Australian studies. While never openly anti-British, Grattan was often pro-"colonial British."

French and Latin, Grattan received his Bachelor of Arts degree with honors in 1923. Immediately afterwards, he set to work at one of his few "real" jobs— teaching English Literature and composition at Urbana Junior College in Ohio. It was a rather marginal job, since the student body consisted of only nine students, six of whom were at the high school level. While teaching in Ohio, Grattan received a fateful letter from H. L. Mencken inviting submission of an article for *The American Mercury* magazine. Apparently it was Grattan's old professor, Harry Elmer Barnes, who had instigated the request. In any event, the article, on James Russell Lowell, was published in May 1924, and in June 1925 Grattan quit the teaching profession to move to New York City as a "writer."

On discovering at once that the income of a free-lance writer did not go far toward paying New York City rents, Grattan started looking for salaried employment, a quest that was to preoccupy him for the next forty years. He worked briefly as a private secretary and a book reviewer for several magazines, but with no degree of permanency. In the meantime, he was also pursuing the one great and true romantic interest of his life, having maintained from July 1923 a very warm correspondence with a former student, Miss Marjorie Campbell. Grattan's letters to Marjorie reveal his strong desire to get married and settle down; they also clearly show his driving motivation to be a successful writer. On 3 August 1925 Grattan explained to Marjorie that "either I can take a job that will absorb all my energies and earn a commonplace salary, or I can scrape along for a year or so and get a reputation." He wanted to be a noted writer but wondered, "Is a reputation worth the sacrifices I'll have to make to get it?" Even at age 23, Grattan feared poverty, writing in this same letter to Marjorie that "I have no desire to be a poverty stricken person, even for a few years."[15] This was not the last time Grattan expressed this aversion to being poor.

By March 1926, Grattan was working as a secretary, noting in a letter to Marjorie that he was sharing offices with the sister of a Broadway stage manager.[16] In April his marriage proposal was rejected by Marjorie and he exploded in a letter to her that "I care damned little about people who are mere friends. . . . It is either everything or nothing. You have made your choice."[17] Almost exactly six months later, on 22 October 1926, Grattan married actress Beatrice Kuper in a New York Unitarian Church. Beatrice Kay, as she was known to her public, later became a popular singer with a radio show of "Gay 90s" music and her own recorded albums. As it happened, Beatrice was under contract to play in the road company of the musical *Sunny* in Sydney and Melbourne. Grattan went along "for the ride" to Australia from February through October 1927. He explained that "having little to do I

[15]Letter from Grattan to Marjorie Campbell, 3 August 1925, Box 27B/file 3.
[16]Letter from Grattan to Marjorie Campbell, 14 March 1926, Box 27B/file 3.
[17]Letter from Grattan to Marjorie Campbell, 15 April 1926, Box 27B/file 3.

14

Henry Elmer. Barnes, from *The Clark Year Book* (1922), Clark College, Worcester, Massachusetts. *HRHRC Photography Collection*. Courtesy of The Clark University Archives.

Passport photograph of C. Hartley Grattan and his first wife, actress Beatrice Kay, for their 1927 trip to Australia. *HRHRC Grattan Collection*.

turned my attention to trying to make sense of the country in which I so inadvertently found myself."[18] Even before arriving he was, through good fortune, drawn to an interest in Australia while sharing activities on board ship with then Prime Minister of Australia S.M. Bruce, who was returning home from the Imperial Conference. Because of this chance meeting with Bruce, and even more as a result of Grattan's attempts to understand the Prime Minister's country, his powerful interest in things Australian lasted considerably longer than his involvement with the actress who was the direct cause of his first visit to the Antipodes, for Beatrice and Hartley were divorced in 1934. However, had it not been for his first and unsuccessful marriage, it is entirely possible that Grattan never would have become involved with Australia.

Whatever the details of Grattan's first marriage may be, they do not appear in any form within the boxes of letters held at the HRHRC. What does surface is the resumption of letters to Grattan's original interest, Marjorie Campbell. As early as March 1929 he was directing his publisher to send her copies of his writing. Six years later he wrote to her an account of some of the personal events of the last decade, concluding that "except in chance moments of exhilaration my life seems hopelessly dull and uninteresting, barren of significant accomplishment, lacking in stability, sense and direction."[19] Possibly with this as motivation, Grattan applied for and, with the help of his mentor, Harry Elmer Barnes, obtained a significant Carnegie Corporation grant that allowed him to return to Australia. This trip lasted from December 1936 through September 1938, for what was to be his longest and most productive visit. Upon leaving New York City, in 1936, Grattan quarreled with Marjorie, so that it would be another three years before the two finally got together on a permanent basis, when Hartley Grattan married Marjorie Campbell on 3 June 1939. Although Marjorie was concerned about catching him on the rebound, Grattan reminded her that "in 1926 I rebounded into disaster."[20] The records show that this second "rebound" was a success, ending only with Grattan's death in 1980.

On his return to New York from Australia in 1938, Grattan's interest in Australia was well established. He started work on two books about the country; frequently wrote articles for a Sydney newspaper explaining American foreign policy; and maintained a considerable correspondence with important Australian figures. During this time, shortly after the outbreak of war in Europe, Grattan was sent again to Australia by the Institute of Current World Affairs (the Crane Foundation), this time to assess the impact of the war

[18]Draft of article entitled "Five Journeys to Australia and What I Found There," p.1, written after 1971, Box 8-8A/file 2. Pages 2-6 are located in Box 8B-C/file 1.

[19]Letter from Grattan to Marjorie Campbell, 19 February 1935, Box 27B/file 3.

[20]Letter from Grattan to Marjorie Campbell, 27 April 1939, Box 27B/file 3.

in that part of the world. The result of his two-month stay, between August and October 1940, was a paper privately circulated within the U.S. government.[21] Although Grattan was known as something of an "isolationist" ("non-interventionist" would probably be more accurate), this position, which he maintained to various degrees throughout his life, was largely set aside in December 1941. The day following Pearl Harbor, Grattan wrote to Marjorie of his immediate views: "War is miserable business for which I am not well fitted. But I do think that Japan asked for it and should be thoroughly whipped." He demonstrated his understanding of the situation when he went on to suggest that "it will be a long, hard, costly war, probably three to five years."[22]

On 14 December 1941, Grattan wrote to the United States Government offering himself for employment, preferably related to Australian affairs. However, he did have some reservations, stating in his request for a job that he could not, "for reasons of conscience, put my slight talent as a writer at the unlimited disposal of the government." But Grattan added that he would be delighted to "place my knowledge of Australia at its disposal, and accept service either in this country or abroad."[23] It happens that sometimes one's patriotism and financial needs coincide, and on 12 January 1942, Grattan was appointed as the "Principal Economic Analyst, British Empire Division, Section of Economic Warfare Analysis, Board of Economic Warfare." Taking an apartment in Washington, he settled in for the duration of the war. But one of the problems involved in being such a prolific writer—to say nothing of being a financially needy prolific writer—can be the loss of control over one's writings. In 1940 Grattan had accepted payment for an article that appeared, unknown to him, as the introduction to a "German White Paper" on Poland issued by the Reich Propaganda Ministry. By 1942 Grattan's article was viewed by some as not being sufficiently supportive of the British and French governments. As a result, Grattan was accused by the Dies Committee of disloyalty toward the United States. On 3 April 1942, he resigned from his government job "without prejudice," because of "reflection on the Board in view of charges made by Congressman Voorhis of Fascist sympathies."[24] Even the direct appeal of the Australian Minister of External Affairs to the United

[21]This monographed report about the Australian and New Zealand reaction to the outbreak of war is probably among the mass of published and unpublished articles in the manuscript collection, but it is difficult to determine which piece of work Grattan is referring to when he mentions it in a letter to Professor Wilbur R. Jacobs, 17 January 1961, Box 22A/file 2.

[22]Letter from Grattan to Mrs. Marjorie Grattan, 8 December 1941, Box 27F/file 1.

[23]Letter from Grattan to "Mr. Biddle," 14 December 1941, Box 27G/file 5.

[24]Resignation letter from Grattan, 3 April 1942, Box 26/file 45.

States Vice-President failed to gain more for Grattan than an after-the-fact apology.[25]

Grattan was again unemployed and broke, and his wife was expecting twins. He wrote in May 1942 that "I fear poverty with all my mind and emotions. . . . I'm just weary, tired, disgusted with the whole damned mess. I want to get clear of it, once and for all."[26] Although Grattan never again worked formally for the government, throughout the war he was occasionally called on by various branches to provide information and maps about Australia.[27]

Following Grattan's departure from Washington, and until his move to Austin in 1964, he and his family lived in a large white house in Katonah, New York, 44 miles by train from Grand Central Station. One can imagine Grattan entertaining visitors, many from Australia, in this old house wedged in between two churches and across the street from the village library. The cost of putting his three daughters through college while providing special care for his handicapped son contributed greatly to Grattan's chronic financial difficulties. Never really a typical member of the community, Grattan refused to learn to drive an automobile and once, during the early 1950s, was accused of Communist sympathies by the American Legion when he sponsored the showing of a controversial film at the library. In addition to having foreign visitors appear on a regular basis, Grattan often received large shipments of books either through the mail or on loan through the library; this, combined with the fact that he was active on the library committee, must have contributed to a view of Grattan as different, even alien.

It was during this period after his difficulty with the government that Grattan again turned to Australia as a possible escape from his immediate problems. However, he quickly ran into obstacles in obtaining either financing or a visa for the trip—in part, he believed, because "I am poison to the Roosevelt crowd."[28] His depression and anger showed through in December 1942 when he complained about a lack of respect for his Australian writings and his inability to secure an honorary degree. While he continued to

[25]Letter from H.V. Evatt to "Dear Mr. Vice-President" [Wallace], 9 June 1942, marked "Confidential," Box 30/file 1. Evatt, "speaking quite unofficially," notes that "Mr. Grattan is well and favourably known in Australia and is a recognised authority on the economic organisation of our country." Evatt goes on to state that "his integrity is beyond question . . . his status in Australia is of the highest. . . ."

[26]Letter from Grattan to Bill Stone, 23 May 1942, Box 27G/file 6.

[27]Letter from Dean Rusk, Capt., Inf., "Mil Intel War Dept Gen Staff," to Grattan, 7 April 1942, Box 37/file 1. The letter mentions returning "packages of materials which you loaned to the New York office of Military Intelligence." Rusk includes the following note: "I was sorry to read of the recent incident which led to your withdrawal from the Board of Economic Warfare. I trust that the allegations made will throw no further obstacles in your way." A letter from the U.S. Army Map Service of December 1943 asks for maps or guides on Australia and New Zealand, Box 21/file 3.

[28]Letter from Grattan to "Stone," 13 April 1944, Box 27D/file 2. In this letter, Grattan claims to "accept war as part of the social weather," but adds that "I'm damned if I'll ever be associated with a pro-war policy of any kind whatever."

write articles about Australia, his attention turned more toward compiling information for a postwar book describing the cost of the war. He wrote more "commercial" pieces and took part-time employment teaching a few courses and writing on adult education. Had the war not created an increased American interest in Australia, it is possible that Grattan might have turned away from Australian affairs to devote himself to more financially rewarding pursuits.

Becoming the earliest and perhaps the only authority in any subject brings with it certain responsibilities. As postwar graduate students began to focus on a study of Australia, it was natural for them to call on Grattan for advice. If a new book relating to Australia or the Pacific required reviewing, it was also natural to send it to Grattan for review. And if a magazine wanted an article about Australia, or for that matter if an Australian magazine wanted an article about the United States, Grattan was the logical source. Throughout the 1940s and '50s, while mostly trying to make a living in more profitable ways, Grattan was continually drawn back to Australian matters. In 1960, returning for the first time in twenty years to Australia, he renewed personal contacts, talked with students, gave numerous radio talks, and continued his quest for an honorary degree from an Australian university. Even with an honorary Doctorate presented by Clark University in 1953, Grattan still felt that he lacked the credibility he should have.

Grattan's search for permanent employment and his constant striving for acceptance as an "academic" or "scholar," rather than merely as a "journalist," largely governed his life from early on through the time of his arrival at the University of Texas in 1964. He clearly saw himself as an intellectual and resented the fact that he lacked the higher academic degrees to prove the point. As he stated on one occasion, "My dilemma is that of a private scholar without a private income to sustain him."[29] In 1957, Allan Nevins, whom Grattan had known since 1926, convinced the Australianist to undertake the writing of a volume on the Southwest Pacific for the University of Michigan History of the Modern World Series. For the better part of six years, Grattan devoted most of his productive time to this task. In 1963 he published a scholarly success, but found himself close to financial disaster. More and more he realized that his finances were intolerable, and by the end of 1963 he was nearing desperation when he summed up the situation: "I totally lack an income to cover continued living expenses and have failed in every effort I have made to find remunerative work. . . ."[30] The time had arrived for Hartley Grattan to make a final effort to obtain that one elusive goal in his life: professional academic acceptance and its accompanying financial security. This last all-out effort would lead him, and his collection, to Austin, Texas.

[29]Letter from Grattan to "Mr. Evans," 8 September 1955, Box 27D/file 1.
[30]Draft of letter from Grattan to the University of Michigan Press, 11 December 1963, Box 22A/file 3.

On arriving in Australia for the first time in 1927, Grattan had already established something of a reputation in New York City for his many articles, mostly on American literature. During his first visit to the Antipodes, he used the experience as an opportunity to collect information for more articles, chiefly on literary subjects. After returning to New York he corresponded frequently with such literary figures as Nettie Palmer, K.S. Prichard, Alice Henry, and Miles Franklin. These writers encouraged Grattan to return and helped maintain his early interest in Australia.[31] Partly as a result of numerous articles and a 1928 booklet he published on Australian literature, Grattan achieved a considerable reputation as an American authority on Australia.[32] His second visit, in 1936-38, brought him into contact with a wide range of political and academic figures, one of whom was Dr. H.V. Evatt, then on the High Court of Australia and later to become Minister of External Affairs and Leader of the Australian Labor Party, as well as President of the United Nations' General Assembly in 1948. In October 1939, Dr. Evatt sent Grattan a letter of reference in which he said that Grattan was "well and favourably known to the jurists, historians and scholars and writers of the Commonwealth of Australia."[33] Written in aid of Grattan's search for an academic appointment, this letter did not have its intended result, yet Evatt was probably not exaggerating when he concluded that "broadly speaking, I should describe him as the one non-Australian in the world today who is able to speak and write authoritatively on Australian literature, history and economics." In 1939 there were really no other American authorities on the subject, so that Grattan saw the opportunity of moving into the area of Australian Studies and set out to write a book which would give "some promise of enhancing my reputation as student of the country."[34]

[31]In 1965, Grattan recalled that "If any Australian is to be credited with keeping me interested in Australia 1928-1936 it is Nettie Palmer." See "A Garrulity About Australian Literature Since 1927," *Meanjin Quarterly* 24, no. 103 (1965): 409.

[32]C. Hartley Grattan, *Australian Literature*, Foreword by Nettie Palmer (Seattle: University of Washington, 1929). During this period, even Australia did not have much in the way of authorities on the country. In "A Garrulity" from 1965, Grattan noted that "This was my first publication about Australia that achieved so-called permanent form. It brought me about as much grief as pleasure." In part this might have been due to his rather critical appraisal in *Australian Literature* of the state of Australian writing in the late 1920s: "Contemporary Australian literature is not impressive. It is perhaps creditable, but even that is doubtful." Grattan even claimed that "The truth is that Australia does not want literature." It should be noted with great appreciation that this pamphlet has been reprinted in *Antipodes* 2, no. 1 (Spring 1988): 20-24.

[33]"To Whom It May Concern" letter given to Grattan by Dr. Herbert Vere Evatt, 12 October 1939, Box 30/file 1. Quotations from this letter were repeated by Grattan in his own correspondence and writings.

[34]From an undated (circa 1939 or 1940) letter from Grattan, entitled "Plans for Work," probably intended for a publisher or corporate sponsor, Box 12E/file unnumbered.

In 1942 Grattan published *Introducing Australia*, which at once became a standard work and moved him beyond being just a writer of free-lance magazine articles "and other fugitive pieces [that] are no substitute for a substantial book."[35] Five years later, Grattan edited *Australia* for the University of California United Nations series, which firmly established his reputation both in the United States and in Australia.[36] Although widely respected, the first of these two works was not universally praised in Australia. In some of the more conservative circles it was claimed that Grattan was overly ambitious in his praise of the Australian labor movement. The criticism hurt Grattan, who admitted that he did "have labor sympathies, but I am not a labor propagandist."[37] He believed that the criticism was injuring his reputation in the United States and wrote in late 1942 that an honorary degree from an Australian university would help to ease his discomfort. This request, along with numerous attempts over the next thirty-five years, was tactfully rejected.

Although Grattan did not visit Australia from 1941 to 1959, he continued his correspondence, writing, and general interest in the subject and thereby maintained his standing as the foremost American expert on Australia. In 1952, Allan G.B. Fisher, then with the International Monetary Fund, wrote to Grattan in praise of his writing (and in support of Grattan's efforts to obtain an honorary degree from the Australian National University—ANU). Fisher told Grattan that "you know more about Australian literature than any but half a dozen people in Australia, and quite probably in a broad sense more about its history and social development than any single person there."[38] In 1956, James McAuley, who was starting the Australian literary journal *Quadrant*, wrote to Grattan asking him for a contribution to the publication, claiming that "your name means a great deal in Australia because of your intelligent, informed and liberal comment on Australian matters, and to have you as a guest in our pages at an early stage of the magazine would be very helpful to it."[39] In 1959, Grattan was invited to return to Australia to address the Australian Institute of Political Science (AIPS) and to spend a few weeks as a Visiting Fellow at the ANU, for which he was again able to acquire partial funding from the Carnegie Foundation. Grattan was proud of the fact that he thus became the first American to address the AIPS twice, having spoken there previously in 1938.

From 1957 through 1963, Grattan devoted most of his time to writing books on Australia. In 1961, Harvard University published Grattan's *The United*

[35]C. Hartley Grattan, *Introducing Australia* (New York: John Day, 1942, revised and republished 1947; Sydney: Angus and Robertson, 1942, revised and republished 1949); "Plans for Work," Box 12E/file unnumbered.

[36]C. Hartley Grattan, *Australia* (Berkeley: University of California Press, 1947).

[37]Letter from Grattan to "Boyer," 20 December 1942, Box 27F/file 2.

[38]Letter from Allan G.B. Fisher to Grattan, 4 March 1952, Box 36/file 5.

[39]Letter from James McAuley to Grattan, 31 May 1956, Box 37/file 1.

States and the Southwest Pacific,[40] but the highlight among his many published materials is the massive two-volume set on *The Southwest Pacific* (volume one to 1900 and volume two since 1900), published in 1963 by the University of Michigan at Ann Arbor in its series on the "History of the Modern World." The reviews of this latter work were uniformly favorable. R.M. Harney of the ANU, writing in the *Australian Book Review*, claimed that "as far as the Australian section is concerned, this book is the only thorough and competent general history of the period we have."[41] However, even though Grattan at this point was firmly established as the primary American authority on Australia, the years 1963 and 1964 were to be for him a critical and confusing time.

Early in 1963 Grattan could observe that "the Southwest Pacific has been part of my life practically all my active life. If a haunt can be pleasant, I've been pleasantly haunted by it for over three decades."[42] Yet in 1964 he resisted returning to Australia, feeling at times that he was still not sufficiently appreciated there, and was considered a "journalist" rather than a scholar. When Allan Nevins suggested that he seek help in gaining either an academic job or at least an honorary degree by working through W.K. Hancock, the great scholar of the British Commonwealth, who was then at the Australian National University, Grattan recalled what he viewed as an insult at the hands of Hancock in 1960. By introducing Grattan as a "journalist," Keith Hancock "rather absurdly patronized me in the presence of his students and I resent it."[43] Grattan would not allow Hancock to assist him, although it is clear that the latter was unaware of any insult or any bad feelings and continued to write approvingly of Grattan and his work. In explaining his many reasons for not wanting to return to Australia, Grattan wrote to Nevins that "I don't regard Australia as solving anything but rather as complicating my affairs."[44] The depression and frustrations then being experienced by Grattan came through plainly when he described Australia as "an incubus which got on my back years ago and has inexorably ridden me to exhaustion. It has distorted my life and I don't think it exactly wise to strive to get it to finish me off."[45]

The depression and resentment brought on by financial need and the drive for professional recognition were resolved later in 1964 when Grattan and his collection were brought by Chancellor Harry Ransom to the University of Texas. In spite of any dissatisfaction experienced in later years with the University, Grattan was at last able to enjoy his status as acknowledged

[40]C. Hartley Grattan, *The United States and the Southwest Pacific* (Cambridge: Harvard University, 1961).

[41]Dr. R.M. Harney, Dept. of Political Science, ANU, in *Australian Book Review*, June 1964. See Box 22B/file 9 for copies of numerous reviews.

[42]From the draft of a 1963 article, Box 22A/file 3.

[43]Draft of a letter from Grattan to Allan Nevins, 1964, Box 27G/file 2.

[44]Ibid.

[45]Ibid.

academic authority on matters concerning Australia. In June 1964 he attended a White House dinner with President Johnson and Robert Menzies, then Prime Minister of Australia, and during this period Grattan was consulted frequently about United States-Australian relations. In 1968 Hancock wrote to say that "of course I have read all your books about Australia" and to conclude that "you more than anybody else have been my country's interpreter."[46] In the same year, when Kylie Tennant took on the task of writing the "official" biography of Dr. Evatt, she asked, and received, considerable assistance from Grattan. After Menzies, who had retired from politics, visited the University of Texas in 1969, he wrote to Grattan that "never was an old acquaintance more happily renewed."[47] Grattan recalled that during the visit Menzies had asked, "Hartley, you are one of us, aren't you?"[48] In 1970 Grattan was chosen by the Council on Foreign Relations to write reviews of fifteen Australian books for their fifty-year Bibliography in Foreign Affairs. He accepted, pointing out that he had known most of the major figures in recent Australian history, as well as the authors of most of the works to be reviewed. He added that "what many readers will regard as the important part of the story has been transacted, so to speak, under my eyes."[49] No other American could convincingly make such a claim.

By 1970 Grattan considered making "a final, or penultimate, visit to Australia as a DUTY I owe Australia and myself."[50] But even at this time he still had some doubts as to his professional regard within Australia. He did make a trip in mid-1971, giving numerous lectures, radio broadcasts, and speeches. While there he was interviewed by the ANU *Reporter* magazine, in which he is described as "the man who was largely responsible for making Australia known to the Americans." In the article he is quoted as observing that his involvement with Australia was so great that "many Americans think I am Australian by origin, finding it impossible to understand how I could have written such a vast amount about Australia without being Australian. 'Who else would bother?' they ask."[51] That others did not "bother" to write about or to understand Australia accounted in large part for Grattan's success. However, throughout over fifty years of close involvement with the country, Grattan never lost sight of the fact that he was not an Australian. When, in 1938, Dr. Evatt suggested that Grattan accept British citizenship, he refused, since it would require the renunciation of his United States citizenship. At the

[46]Letter from W. Keith Hancock to Grattan, 28 January 1968, Box 27J/file 2.

[47]Letter from Robert Gordon Menzies to Grattan, 12 December 1969, Box 27I/file unnumbered.

[48]Quoted on page 6 of the draft of "Five Journeys to Australia," Box 8B-C/file 1.

[49]Letter from Grattan to Council on Foreign Relations, 15 January 1970, agreeing to do fifteen reviews, Box 19A/file 1.

[50]Letter from Grattan to Jack Crawford, 20 October 1970, Box 27A/file 5.

[51]*ANU Reporter*, 23 July 1971, p. 1, Box 19C/file unnumbered.

Photograph of Rt. Hon. H.V. Evatt, Australian Minister of State for External Affairs, n.d. *HRHRC Photography Collection.*

end of his career Grattan made clear that "while it has become my second home, my real home remains the United States, where my roots are and which commands my primary loyalty."[52] This "outside" view of Australia probably is another secret of Grattan's success.

Although always something of an "outsider," Grattan never relinquished a desire to obtain what he saw as full recognition and status in the eyes of the Australians. While he was never offered a full-time academic post in Australia, his goal was at last accomplished in large measure in 1977 when he was awarded an honorary "Doctor of Laws" degree from the Australian National University. In his speech presenting the degree, Robin Gollan recalled that "Hartley Grattan introduced Australia to Americans and to many Australians. His books are still a very important part of the corpus of works which are essential to any student of Australian history and society."[53] In his acceptance speech, Grattan summed up many of his feelings:

> Long ago I lost all sense of strangeness at being in Australia. I early became as much at home in Australia as in the United States. Differently put, I acquired an identification with Australia so close as to be an integral part of my personality.[54]

This describes what is most likely the prescription for any person attempting to master a foreign subject.

THE GRATTAN PAPERS

Even before Grattan finally achieved his goal of receiving official recognition from the Australian academic community, Jack Crawford, Vice Chancellor of the Australian National University, approached him about obtaining his extensive collection of books and other materials. This query came in April 1963, about a year and a half before Grattan arrived in Austin. Replying favorably to Crawford's suggestion and anticipating what would be included in the sale, Grattan responded that just about everything could be sold with the exception of "the enormous accumulation of letters from Australians which I promised several years ago would go to the Mitchell [Library in Australia]."[55]

[52]From a draft of "Five Journeys to Australia," p. 1, Box 8-8A/file 2.

[53]Grattan's ANU degree and copies of Professor Gollan's speech of 9 September 1977 are contained in Gift Box 1513. Also present in this box are several copies of Grattan's acceptance speech and his honorary Doctor of Letters degree from Clark University, conferred on 7 June 1953.

[54]Ibid.

[55]Undated letter (circa April 1963) from Grattan to Jack Crawford, Box 31/file 4.

While the University of Texas acquired Grattan's collection of books and other materials, his manuscript and correspondence related to Australia remained in his personal possession. Previous to Crawford's query, other universities had asked for these private papers but had been turned down. Grattan refused the request of the University of Wyoming, which wanted his papers and writings because of the "revisionist" controversy, and Brooklyn College was likewise denied acquisition of his papers even though they wanted them because Grattan had been "a conspicuous New York intellectual."[56]

In June 1969, four years after he arrived at Texas, Grattan was again approached, this time by his alma mater, Clark University. On refusing to release his private papers, Grattan made his position quite clear to the curator at Clark: "I excluded my SwP papers from any proposed deposit in the USA. I long ago promised them to the Mitchell Library in Sydney, Australia. I stick to my promise."[57] Grattan placed special value on the Australian correspondence, calling it "infinitely more important and potentially useful" than the American material. He summed up his feelings when he wrote, in 1969, that "my identification with Australia is so close and enduring that I feel a strong obligation to the archivists of the country."[58] The opinion of the Australian archivists is not known. For whatever reason, the papers were formally transferred to the Harry Ransom Humanities Research Center by Hartley Grattan's widow in February 1982, more than a year after his death.

Physically, the papers of the Grattan Collection consist of 74 Hollinger boxes and 8 file drawers, which contain massive amounts of newspapers, clippings from newspapers and magazines, manuscripts, correspondence, a map collection, and miscellaneous notes and other materials used by Grattan for reference in his writings about Australia. To understand the present condition of the papers it is useful to recall Grattan's own description: "I have never been a conscientious paper-saver and my papers amounted to very little. . . . They were in terrible and daunting disorder and I did not have the inclination or time to sort and order them."[59] Although he tended to see little of value in much of his private papers, Grattan did believe that "there are some fairly choice letters among them."[60] His description of the papers being "in terrible and daunting disorder" was accurate during his lifetime and continues to be so today. Several boxes contain empty folders or blank notebooks of no known value. Scattered throughout are bundles of typed manuscripts of various published books and articles. Other boxes contain files of newspaper and magazine articles by Grattan, about Grattan, or in some

[56]Letter from Grattan to Paul S. Clarkson, curator at Clark University, 29 June 1969, Box 27J/ file 3.
[57]Ibid.
[58]Ibid.
[59]Ibid.
[60]Ibid.

cases not remotely related to Grattan. Others contain the expected correspondence with publishers and editors along with stacks of royalty accounts and book invoices. Grattan had a habit of making notes on books he read, and many of these are present in the collection. There are copies of student papers and lists of grade reports. One of the most valuable uses of the collection would be for anyone attempting to reconstruct Grattan's life, but it may be expected that relatively few researchers will migrate to Austin with this objective. In 1971 Grattan himself predicted that this "great mass of material which is gathering dust" would only be disturbed by "some pertinacious researcher, probably far less concerned with me than with a particular subject matter."[61]

The collection also includes numerous apparently unpublished articles, primarily on Australian matters. Among these are several articles sent to Grattan from other writers, who may not have published them, in which case it would be well worthwhile assembling them for publication. There is one paper written by Grattan about the Dies Committee, which accused him of disloyalty in 1942—a 28-page insight into one aspect of government life.[62] Also of particular interest is a file of numerous reports from high-level persons in Australia in response to the question "Explain Australia to Americans," which Grattan sent out in 1940.[63] Catherine Helen Spence, the Australian feminist reformer and novelist, is represented by her manuscript entitled "Democracy, Aristocracy and Plutocracy; Democratic Club 1901."[64] As Spence died in 1910, it is unclear just why this manuscript is in the Grattan Collection.

Grattan kept several notebooks, which are spiral books that include mostly his reminiscences about a particular subject. The most prominent notebook is the one of 83 pages about Dr. H.V. Evatt, which Grattan wrote while on holiday in Mexico in 1968 in response to a request from Kylie Tennant, the Australian novelist and "official" biographer of Evatt.[65] Although she was denied permission to copy the notebook, Tennant did use parts of it in her book. Together with numerous letters about Evatt and various speeches and articles on the man and his career, as well as many random notes, this material

[61]From a draft of Grattan's preface to the Healy bibliography, Box 12A/file unnumbered.

[62]"It Happened in Washington," originally written in 1942, with additional notes written at a later date, Box 26/file 45.

[63]Box 27/file 1. There is much of value in these replies, which form a large part of Grattan's *Introducing Australia*. Although quoted at length in the book, Grattan did not identify the sources; however, all are clearly identified in the originals.

[64]Box 23 (fourth box)/file 2.

[65]From an exchange of letters between Grattan and Kylie Tennant during 1968, Box 27A/file 1. In the Acknowledgments to her book, entitled *Evatt: Politics and Justice* (Sydney: Angus & Robertson, 1970), Tennant makes reference to the notebook and to Grattan's help. Grattan refused, however, to allow Tennant or the National Library of Australia to make a photocopy of the notebook.

on Evatt is of considerable value. Another notebook in the Grattan papers, consisting of 31 pages written sometime after 1964, concerns Louis Morton Hacker, the Columbia University economist and writer.[66] Still another notebook of 27 pages is labeled "On V.F. Calverton."[67]

Most of the photographs that were included among the Grattan papers have been transferred to the HRHRC Photography Collection, the one notable exception being a signed photographic portrait of Alice Henry.[68] Three boxes in the Photography Collection contain a total of 234 pictures, representing three separate groups of photographs. The first group of 164 derives mostly from newspaper photo services and the Victorian Railway Commission. These include photographs of well-known Australian political, military, and literary figures. There are also numerous views of Australian animals, the country-side, cities, industry, trains, and machinery. The second group of 14 photographs, mostly of Grattan, dates from between 1902 and the mid-1970s, many of which are small personal snapshots of family members and class-mates. The third group of 56 photographs includes mostly images of the Grattan and Campbell families. In addition, there are several duplicate portrait photographs of Grattan, as well as one of Harry Elmer Barnes and one of William Jennings Bryan.[69]

If Grattan was not a "conscientious paper-saver," he still managed to collect a very large number of letters. Fortunately, some of his own letters, surviving either in early drafts or through carbon copies, give valuable insights into his shifting moods and motivations. Study of Grattan's private correspondence in the HRHRC often reveals a side of the man and a view of his problems that are largely at odds with his more public statements and conversations. The impression is given that he was not an overly friendly man but one who could swing widely in mood and who was sensitive to negative criticism, which he often took as a sign of rejection. Among his incoming letters, which reflect a remarkably wide range of correspondents (see a partial listing on page 31), there is a 1929 letter from Clarence Darrow, asking to review Grattan's writings on the last days of W.J. Bryan, and a 1932 letter Upton Sinclair wrote in advance of Grattan's visit to California. There are also letters from Erskine Caldwell and James Thurber. In 1936, Beatrice (Mrs. Sydney) Webb wrote about sharing the diary of her 1898 visit to Australia. While interesting, these specific letters may not hold as much research value as the larger groups of

[66]Thirty-one-page handwritten, spiral notebook, entitled "Louis Morton Hacker, b. NYC, 17 Mar 1899," Box 31/file 1.

[67]Twenty-seven-page handwritten notebook, "On V.F. Calverton, written June 5-6-7, 1971, Canberra," Box 31/file 5.

[68]Box 32/file 2.

[69]The three boxes in the HRHRC Photography Collection are catalogued as follows: 957:017:001–090; 957:017:091–981:046:014; 986:030:001–056.

correspondence. In great quantities there are American letters from H.E. Barnes, Allan Nevins, and George H. Nadel. The considerable number of Australian letters includes significant correspondence with K.S. Prichard, Nettie Palmer, Miles Franklin, Alice Henry, Brian Fitzpatrick, Lloyd Ross, and Jack Crawford. Two "gift boxes" added to the collection more recently are of interest primarily because they include Grattan's actual ANU honorary degree and three of his early passports.

Photograph of prominent politicians of the day, taken at the Palmer House in Chicago, ca. 1913-1915. The center figure on the bottom row is William Jennings Bryan and the man to his right is possibly William McAdoo, Woodrow Wilson's son-in-law. The other figures remain unidentified. *HRHRC Photography Collection.*

The following is a partial listing of letters in the Grattan manuscript collection. Names were selected for inclusion either because there is a sizeable number of letters or because the specific names stood out as significant. Asterisks indicate the size and/or significance of the collection from each correspondent, with * indicating numerous letters that may be of some significance and ** for large, important groups of letters. Those names without an asterisk are represented in the collection by only one or at most a few letters that often are of limited interest. In a few cases where a prominent name appears but is represented by only one or two letters, the specific date of the correspondence is supplied.

Ball, W. Macmahon
Barnes, Henry Elmer**
Beard, Charles A.
Caldwell, Erskine (1932)
Casey, Richard G.
Clark, C.M.H.
Clark, Colin*
Cohen, Warren I.**
Crawford, John G.**
Crisp, L.F.*
Curtin, John
Darrow, Clarence (1929)
Eggleston, Frederick
Evatt, Herbert Vere**
Farrell, James T.*
Fitzpatrick, Brian**
Franklin, Miles**
Hancock, W.K.
Healy, Jack**

Henry, Alice**
Kerensky, Mrs. Alexander
McAuley, James
Maude, H.E.
Mencken, H.L.*
Menzies, Robert G.
Moore, T. Inglis*
Nadel, George H.**
Nevins, Allan**
Officer, F. Keith
Palmer, Nettie**
Prichard, K.S.**
Ross, Lloyd**
Rusk, Dean (1942)
Sinclair, Upton (1932)
Spender, Percy
Tennant, Kylie*
Thurber, James
Webb, Beatrice (1936)

The central part of the Grattan Collection is composed of over 20,000 books and pamphlets on the Southwest Pacific.[70] This total number includes over 700 serial titles, among which are numerous complete runs of Australian periodicals and public documents. Many of these publications are unusual and hard to locate items, making this one of the primary resources for research into Australian history. Any collection of this size, which was acquired by one person over a period of forty years and which measures some 1,100 feet of linear shelf space, can best be understood through a consideration of the collector himself. Along with the biographical information cited earlier,

[70]This number is based on a count of 9,439 separate titles in the HRHRC card catalog. Grattan himself considered the "Suggested Readings" section of his two-volume *Southwest Pacific* as the most complete inventory of his collection.

Grattan left numerous references to the collection that offer valuable insights into its meaning to him and to prospective researchers.

The collection now at the HRHRC originally grew out of Grattan's need and desire to gather material for his many and varied projects. Slowly Grattan used the collection in his lifetime search for professional and financial security. In serving to obtain this goal, the collection took on the characteristics of Grattan's immediate desperation rather than any quality derived from long-range planning. In this sense, the story of its creation helps to explain both the man and his archive.

The collection began, as did Grattan's interest in Australia, accidentally with his 1927 visit. In striving to learn more about the country, Grattan frequented the bookstores, fortunately at a time "when the volume of current publication was small and the opportunities for acquiring the older and rarer books were relatively rich."[71] In explaining his "method of operation," he stated that it "was to collect what I could find that would possibly help me to understand Australia."[72] It was during his 1936-38 visit that he became more systematic in building his collection "to the point where it is possible to say that few important books, other than expensive and scarce items dealing with the very early days which have never been reprinted, are absent from it. . . ."[73] In January 1943, in her review of one of Grattan's books, Nettie Palmer gave credit to the collection by saying that "today he has one of the finest collections in the world. . . ."[74]

In 1942 Grattan had been tentatively approached by Yale University about the ultimate disposition of his, by then, well-known collection on Australia. In reply, Grattan explained that he one day expected to "present it to the library of a university or some other learned institution."[75] He was a bit surprised at the Yale inquiry, since it was the first formal interest shown by an American institution. Grattan added, somewhat prophetically, "I say hopefully that I shall present it, but being a poor man I may in the ultimate have to sell it." For the following twenty years there appears to have been no further discussion of this matter.

The only way to understand why the collection is in the HRHRC today is to understand the pressures on Grattan leading to its sale in 1964. Although he quite often praised the flexibility of his life as a free-lance writer, Grattan always had private reservations. As early as 1939, when he proposed submitting his early books about Australia to a university in exchange for a

[71]Three-page, undated "Notes on C. Hartley Grattan's SwP Collection," Box 22A/file 2.

[72]An untitled draft of an article, written circa 1968, Box 24A/file unnumbered.

[73]Undated letter entitled "Plans for Work," Box 12E/file unnumbered.

[74]Nettie Palmer, "An American Introduces Australia," *ABC Weekly*, 9 January 1943, p. 17, Box 32/file 11.

[75]Letter from Grattan to Donald G. Wing, Head of Accessions Department, Yale University, 24 February 1942, Box 27F/file 4.

Doctor of Letters degree, he admitted privately, "I have long desired to obtain a university appointment."[76] When this did not work out he returned to writing articles and books independently. But of free-lance writers, he complained, "they may go along for months on top of the wave; but it is always eventually brought home to them that they are living precariously. When things go indifferently, it takes some fast footwork to survive."[77] By the early 1950s he was again searching for some type of steady employment, and in one letter he plainly states that he had "no wish to go on free-lancing" and wanted a teaching job of some type.[78] But by this time he perhaps felt that at his age and lacking an earned doctorate, he could not hope to find such a position. Although he enjoyed being a "generalist" with a wide range of expertise, he found that financial pressures caused him to long for the security of a teaching appointment. Allan Nevins, who became something of a mentor in Grattan's search for steady employment, wrote to him saying that "you are one of our most valuable intellectual assets in this country, and it is important that you get properly placed instead of being thrown back on free-lancing."[79] Grattan would have considered almost any job, but his preference was for teaching where he could be acknowledged as an expert in some specific field.

Increasingly finances became foremost among Grattan's concerns. In late 1951 he wrote to Harry Barnes, again in search either of employment or at least of some kind of institutional grant. At the time Grattan expressed his feelings by explaining that "my own inadequacies of personality may have contributed something to my downfall, but the general situation was powerfully against me."[80] In 1957 the situation seemed to improve when Allan Nevins hired Grattan to write the two-volume set on the Southwest Pacific, for which the University of Michigan Press was extremely generous, making five major advances against earnings from the book. But after almost six years of work, Grattan felt that he was not being treated fairly. In the end his income from the books barely covered the cash advances, and by the close of 1963 Grattan declared, "this is disgusting."[81] He saw no hope of paying off the debts that he felt had been incurred in the writing of the books and should have been repaid by the press. As 1964 began, he wrote that "you can imagine how frustrated and defeated I feel to be in this position at 61."[82]

Others were aware of Grattan's difficulties. In April 1963, Jack Crawford, at that time Director of the Research School of Pacific Studies at the Australian

[76]Undated letter entitled "Plans for Work," Box 12E/file unnumbered.

[77]Letter from Grattan to "Professor Williams," 12 January 1948, Box 27D/file 1.

[78]Draft of a letter from Grattan seeking employment, 1954, Box 27C/file 2.

[79]Letter from Allan Nevins to Grattan, 25 October 1955, Box 27G/file 2.

[80]Letter from Grattan to Harry Barnes, 3 December 1951, Box 27E/file 3.

[81]Letter from Grattan to the University of Michigan Press, 11 December 1963, Box 22A/file 3.

[82]Handwritten draft of an unaddressed letter (similar to others that were sent), undated but probably December 1963, Box 22A/file 3.

National University in Canberra, had a proposal that must have revived for Grattan his thoughts of twenty years before. Crawford asked Grattan, "Have you ever thought of your answer if you were asked to sell your Australian-New Zealand collection to a University like the Australian National University?"[83] Crawford added that "quite frankly I know of no better collection anywhere and would like to think that it was possible to acquire it one day as a collection named in your honour." Grattan quickly replied that, indeed, it might be a possibility.

Perhaps remembering the earlier inquiry from Yale, Grattan began a rapid series of negotiations with several American universities.[84] Realizing that a lump sum of money from the sale of the collection would solve his immediate needs, he also understood that without steady employment it would only be a temporary solution. Throughout his negotiations he attached the requirement that he be hired in an academic position along with the sale of the archive. The Universities of California at Los Angeles, Santa Barbara, and Santa Cruz were all actively involved in bidding for the collection. However, only Santa Cruz could offer employment, but for various reasons this bid was rejected by Grattan.[85] It may be that Grattan's reputation for having taken in the past a rather "non-interventionist" political stance contributed to his difficulty in finding academic employment. By July 1964, Grattan privately expressed his willingness to go ahead and sell the collection even if he were not offered a faculty appointment.

Allan Nevins not only supported Grattan through his many academic contacts, but he believed in the value of the collection itself. In May 1964 Nevins called the collection "the best library of books and pamphlets on Australia and New Zealand and the neighboring islands in the United States. It is one of the best libraries of such materials in the world."[86] Yet it was Robin W. Winks of Yale who was one of the first to suggest that, since Yale could not provide Grattan with a job, he should consider the University of Texas at

[83]Letter from Jack Crawford to Grattan, 2 April 1963, Box 38/file 3. By September 1963 Crawford wrote to Grattan asking for a catalogue of the collection and a specific sales price.

[84]These negotiations, which took place in 1964, are documented for the most part in Box 22A/file 2. Unfortunately, although Grattan mentions having sent complete inventories of the collection, no such list has been located either in his manuscript collection or among correspondence maintained in the HRHRC's administrative offices.

[85]On 21 August 1964, Dean E. McHenry of the University of California at Santa Cruz offered to purchase the collection and employ Grattan in the proposed "South Pacific Studies" program. There are early drafts of letters in which Grattan seems to be prepared to accept the offer. In the end he turned it down largely because the school was new and the program only a proposal, whereas the University of Texas represented a well-established institution. There seem to have been no other firm commitments. The other California schools had various reasons for rejecting Grattan. Yale did offer to purchase part of his collection, but only those items not already held by its library; no formal position was found for Grattan on Yale's staff.

[86]Letter from Allan Nevins to Professor T.A. Bailey at Stanford University, 8 May 1964, Box 27G/file 2. This is an information copy sent by Nevins to Grattan.

Austin. Winks felt that because Joseph Jones, a professor in the University's Department of English, "has built the best collection of Australian literature to be found, and his library wishes to build on its present strengths," Texas might be interested.[87] Within four days of receiving this suggestion from Winks, Grattan received a letter from Harry Barnes, who along with Allan Nevins was actively searching for a solution to Grattan's problem. Barnes was a realist; his advice was that Grattan should "try the University of Texas, which I understand is now lousy with money."[88] Barnes added that of almost equal importance was the fact that "Texas now has no horrors with air conditioning available." What more could one ask?

These suggestions by Winks and Barnes were being made at the end of May 1964, after Grattan only earlier in the month had written to Barnes that if something did not happen very soon "the collection goes back to Australia and it is as certain as such things can be that no U.S. university will EVER have a good collection on the Southwest Pacific."[89] Grattan threatened that "for American universities it is now or never."[90] Fortunately for those in this country with a keen interest in Australia and the Southwest Pacific, it was "now." Negotiations with the Humanities Research Center were carried on throughout the summer of 1964, and in October Grattan accepted an offer of the sale of his collection coupled with full employment and status at The University of Texas at Austin. In November Grattan received a letter from Angus & Robertson Ltd., in which this major publisher of Australian books expressed the knowledgeable Australian view that "the University of Texas [has] made an excellent buy," observing as well that "there would not be a better selected library of Australian books outside Australia."[91]

Grattan appears to have been completely satisfied with his arrangements at Texas. In October 1964 he wrote to the Chancellor at Santa Cruz to decline their offer and in doing so explained his understanding of his agreement with Texas. He said that he had been offered "(a) the rank of University Professor and (b) the Curatorship of . . . the Grattan Collection of Southwest Pacificana."[92] He went on to say that his job was to keep the collection up-to-date and "to expand it in any feasible way with regard to both old and new materials with the objective of constantly increasing its usefulness to students

[87]Letter from Robin W. Winks to Grattan, 22 May 1964, Box 22A/file 2. Winks became involved as the Yale professor most interested in Commonwealth history. He visited Grattan's home and later wrote that the collection was being undervalued by Grattan.

[88]Letter from Henry Elmer Barnes to Grattan, 26 May 1964, Box 22A/file 2.

[89]Letter from Grattan to Harry Barnes, 7 May 1964, Box 22A/file 2. This letter followed Grattan's refusal from the University of California at Santa Barbara and Yale's apparent reluctance to offer him a job.

[90]Letter from Grattan to Harry Barnes, 9 May 1964, Box 22A/file 2.

[91]Letter from E.H. Williams, General Manager (Retail), Angus & Robertson Ltd, Sydney, to Grattan, 17 November 1964, Box 27A/file 4.

[92]Letter from Grattan to Dean E. McHenry, 7 October 1964, Box 22A/file 1.

and researchers." It was this latter idea, or promise, that would cause some bad feelings for Grattan. But in 1964 he had a very positive view of Texas, seeing the University as an "impressive, thriving and stimulating place. Chancellor Ransom has the emphasis firmly on academic 'excellence.' The Library, with its several famous special collections, is distinguished."[93]

Grattan arrived in Texas optimistic that he could not only establish his collection but establish Austin as a center for Australian studies in the United States. He believed this was part of his role and an aim of the University, and even though he knew his collection was incomplete, he believed it was "quite the best in North America."[94] He did see a need for more than just spending money on the collection; he also wanted it to become the depository for American businesses involved in Australia, with donations of financial and other support to be gathered and publicized. He wrote that "it is necessary that [the collection] be brought vividly to the attention of all scholars in the United States and Canada."[95] In 1970, while asking for university funds for a trip to Australia, Grattan recalled that Chancellor Ransom had asked him to "look into the prospects for establishing and maintaining an exchange of personal [sic] with the Australian universities, with particular attention to visits from specialists in Southwest Pacific affairs to carry on my work at Texas into the future."[96]

Perhaps Grattan's ideas were a bit too grand for the University. Perhaps he misunderstood his role. Perhaps the economy brought about unavoidable changes. In any event, it was within a year of his arrival that problems began. At first the collection and Grattan himself were located in the Undergraduate Academic Center. Finding almost at once a shortage of space and supplies, he complained frequently about not being able to get proper support. The larger problem was obtaining what he considered adequate funds for purchases of new additions to the collection. As budget reductions continued through the late 1960s, Grattan saw his collection failing to keep up with his expectations. By 1969 he wrote to the Chancellor that "I run the risk of creating gaps in the collection which it will be tedious and costly to fill in future years."[97] He stressed that "what appears to be a temporary inconvenience thus turns into a permanent handicap" and would have the effect of lessening the value of Australian studies. He concluded, "time is running out on me and I want to leave [the collection] in first-class shape."

[93]Ibid.

[94]Letter from Grattan to William D. Blunk, Development Office, the University of Texas, 6 May 1965, Box 20B/file 4.

[95]Ibid.

[96]Request from Grattan for a University of Texas Research Grant, 15 November 1970, Box 27J/file 3.

[97]Letter from Grattan to Chancellor Harry Huntt Ransom, 11 May 1969, Box 27I/file 3.

As early as 1967 Grattan wrote to friends of his frustration at the University of Texas. He expressed the desire to leave, but seemed to have no specific alternative available. While he originally intended to stay for about five years, he discovered he would have to remain ten years in order to receive any retirement benefits. By 1974, when Grattan did retire from the University of Texas and the HRC, his interest in Australia continued, although in a relatively inactive manner.

On the departure of Hartley Grattan, the interest in Australia shown by the University essentially ended. The collection is still the finest available at any university outside Australia, but for the most part it remains frozen in time much as it was on its acquisition in 1964. In one way at least this is appropriate, since the Grattan Collection as it now exists is a reflection of the career of Hartley Grattan, representing most fully the period of his study of Australia and the Southwest Pacific from the 1920s through the 1960s. Thus, the Grattan Collection presents the story of one man's attraction to, and his relationship with, a part of the world whose history and literature he knew during forty years as an "outsider" but understood better perhaps than most "insiders" who have lived there all their lives.

Cover of *New Land New Language* (Oxford University Press, 1966), an anthology of Australian verse compiled by Judith Wright. Line decorations by Alison Forbes. *HRHRC Grattan Collection.*

Australian Literary Publications in the C. Hartley Grattan Collection

BY SUDHAKAR R. JAMKHANDI

C. Hartley Grattan's collection of Australiana in the Harry Ransom Humanities Research Center is perhaps the most comprehensive in the United States, with the books alone numbering over 20,000 volumes. Even though such a collection of Australiana of this magnitude is unavailable elsewhere outside Australia,[1] few scholars are aware of the Grattan archive, which was amassed over a span of six decades, from the 1920s to the 1970s.[2] As a result, these materials have only rarely been utilized by scholars and students of the Southwest Pacific, including both those in Texas and from around the world. Yet the possibilities for research among the published materials in the Grattan Collection are unlimited. My own special interest has been in the collection's literary publications, but this is merely one of many areas encompassed by the archive.[3]

Given the range of Hartley Grattan's own studies and publications in a wide variety of fields, it is not surprising that his collection includes biographies and autobiographies; narratives of exploration; travel and descriptive books; geography texts; publications on art, literature, Aborigines, labor, and culture; documentaries; and works on religion, education, government, and

---

[1]Begun modestly in 1940, an ongoing collection of Australiana exists in the Pattee Library at Penn State University and includes the Henry Ingram Moody Memorial Collection. The literary and cultural holdings of the Pattee Library now number around 6,000 titles. Present in the HRHRC collections are copies of Bruce Sutherland's *Australiana in the Pattee Library*, published in September 1957 as New Series Number 4 of *The Headlight on Books at Penn State*. Sutherland issued an updated bibliography in 1969, entitled *Australiana in the Pennsylvania State University Libraries* (University Park: Pennsylvania State University Libraries).

[2]C. Hartley Grattan first traveled to Australia in 1927, returning on a two-year grant in 1936-38. He visited the country again briefly in 1940, 1960, and 1971.

[3]I am presently preparing an annotated bibliography of the Australian literary publications in the Grattan Collection, which contains approximately 1,200 titles.

39

politics.[4] Grattan even collected a large number of books in French and Italian. In addition, he procured issues of out-of-print magazines, especially from the 1920s—the one period in Australian history that might be described as the Australian Renaissance. Grattan's collection of writings by Australians, and by students of Australia from around the world, includes views of the Australian scene from its wild frontier days in the eighteenth century to the time of its cultural sophistication in the twentieth; from the days of the great explorations to the troubled times of the settlement of the various colonies along the east coast; and from the period of Australia's umbilical ties to imperialistic England to the era of self-discovery and nationalism, in which Australia has participated as a leader in the Commonwealth and has held her own in the world's political, cultural, literary, and economic arenas.

As might be expected, Grattan's method of collecting was eclectic and even haphazard. However, during his many jaunts across the continent, he was aided in filling in gaps in his collection, when they were discovered, by friends he cultivated along the way. Especially on his trips to Australia in 1936-38 and 1940, a score of figures like Nettie Palmer gave him books and provided him with names of prominent writers, and budding writers presented him with limited editions of their collections of verse. Although Grattan was primarily a political scientist-historian-economist, he learned enough about Australian literature to write a literary history of his newly discovered land, which was published as a chapbook in 1929 by the University of Washington.[5] Later, in 1938, Grattan reexamined the literature in an essay for the *Australian Quarterly*,[6] and in 1957, the University of Oklahoma published his *Australia's Ten for UNESCO*, wherein he recommends ten Australian writers whose works should be translated.[7] The literary works in Grattan's collection are by renowned authors as well as by those whose books would never have seen print but for the numerous vanity presses active in Australia during the early part of the twentieth century. Grattan never looked upon these vanity publications with disdain but chose to include them in his collection, knowing full well that a young nation must rely upon such writers as happen to present themselves to the public. Some of the writers who resorted to vanity presses

[4]C. Hartley Grattan's principal publication was *The Southwest Pacific to 1900* and *Since 1900*, a study in two volumes published in 1963 by the University of Michigan Press. Other books, reviews, and introductions by Grattan are too numerous to list but are contained in a bibliography prepared by Jack Healy circa 1966 and available at the HRHRC.

[5]C. Hartley Grattan, *Australian Literature* (Seattle: University of Washington Bookstore, 1929).

[6]C. Hartley Grattan, "On Australian Literature, 1788-1938," *Australian Quarterly* 10, no. 2 (June 1938).

[7]C. Hartley Grattan, *Australia's Ten for UNESCO* (Norman: University of Oklahoma Press, 1957). The ten Australian writers recommended by Grattan for translation were: Henry Kendall, Rolf Bolderwood, Henry Lawson, A.B. Paterson, Joseph Furphy, Bernard O'Dowd, Katherine Susannah Prichard, Frank Dalby Davison, Kenneth Slessor, and Henry Handel Richardson.

for publication were later "discovered" by the respectable publishing houses, such as Angus and Robertson and F.W. Cheshire. Having discovered them first and having shared their works with a wider audience, Grattan can be credited with having nurtured their literary endeavors and the future of Australian literature.

The end result of Grattan's inclusive approach is a collection of publications from the eighteenth, nineteenth, and twentieth centuries which reflected and shaped the development of the Australian temperament, Australia's yearnings, and the country's recognition of its own worth, along with its evaluation of its relationship to the rest of the world. By the late nineteenth century, Australia already had a developing literature, enough at least for a literary history to be published in 1866 by G.B. Barton, entitled *Literature in New South Wales*.[8] Such literary histories were an obvious starting point for Grattan the bibliophile, and he collected the literature of Australia not because he was an aspiring writer but because his inquisitive mind would know no bounds.

The scope of Grattan's collection of Australian literary works is broad, yet the novels it contains outnumber the publications in other genres. Historical, epistolary, romantic, realistic, detective, science fiction, yarn, adventure, and children's novels are all among the types of novels in the Grattan Collection. The subjects treated in the novels are similar to those found in novels of other nations that have a long and rich literary history. They analyze universal concerns as well as those unique to Australia: the coming to grips with the bush, the emancipation of the convicts, and the unfathomable Aborigines. Prominent as well as lesser-known writers are featured: Frank Clune, Henry Lawson, John Keith Ewers, Miles Franklin (pseudonym, Brent of Bin Bin), Joseph Furphy, Xavier Herbert, Rex Ingamells, Thomas Keneally, Thea Astley, Eric Lambert, Will Lawson, Norman Lindsay, Eric Lowe, Leonard Mann, Nevil Shute, Vance Palmer, Katherine Susannah Prichard, Henry Handel Richardson, Tom Ronan, Christina Stead, Randolph Stow, Kylie Tennant, Edward Vivian Timms, Margaret Trist, and Patrick White. Students of narrative strategy are only partially informed if they have not read Australian novels, since one of the many contributions these works have made to the evolution of the genre is the yarn, an art form brought to its highest level of achievement by the Australian novelists. Historians too will undoubtedly substantiate their interpretations of world events through a reading of the sea fiction that recreates the sociology of seventeenth-century explorations of the South Seas and the "discovery" of Australia.

The "creative mind" of the general populace of most countries is primarily attracted to the writing and publication of poetry. In Australia, especially after the newly-arrived immigrants settled into middle-class ease, several self-

[8]G.B. Barton, *Literature in New South Wales* (Sydney: Thomas Richards, 1866). Barton believed that the groundwork had been laid for a "national literature."

taught poets began to publish their collections of verse. On commissions from such authors as Sandor Berger and Bertram Higgins, a number of presses issued limited editions of poetry collections, as well as books in other genres. For the greater part, Grattan met the established literati of Australia, so that most of the poetry volumes in his collection are by such leading poets as Bernard O'Dowd, Shaw Nielson, Vincent Buckley, C.J. Dennis, Dame Mary Cameron Gilmore, Adam Lindsay Gordon, James Brunton Stephens, Alec Hope, Judith Wright, James Phillip McAuley, Harley Matthews, Ian Mudie, William Henry Ogilvie, Andrew B. Paterson, Kenneth Slessor, and Frank Wilmot (pseudonym, Furnley Maurice). By adding anthologies of poetry published up to the seventies, Grattan made possible a reconstruction of the development of a genre that is still very popular in Australia.[9] In the light of Australian poetry written on the First and Second World Wars, scholars of world history and comparative literature will be able to review their assessments of the momentous events of those years and of Australia's role as an ally of England and the United States. Maurice Biggs's reflections on war and peace[10] and Gwen Bessell-Browne's portrayal of Australia's attitude toward her sons' leaving for participation in the Second World War[11] are just two examples of collections of war poetry whose sentiments may well change the complexion of scholarly interpretations as well as the emphases of literary criticism. Critics especially will be intrigued by Rex Ingamell's attempts to write an epic poem in which he traces the discovery of Australia by the Aborigines, its "discovery" by the great explorers, its settlement by the convicts and wardens, and finally the nation's entry into World War II.[12]

Like their counterparts elsewhere in the world, some Australian writers have practiced their craft in more than one genre. Novelist-poets such as Henry Lawson, Patrick White, and Furnley Maurice are outstanding examples. On the other hand, such writers as Brian James and Dallas Stivens exclusively practiced the craft of the short story. Like the novelists, Australian short story writers treat Australia's pioneer days, the emancipation of the convicts, the taming of the bush, tensions between the settlers and the Aborigines, the Gold Rush of the nineteenth century, sheep farming, and even the world of the fairy tale. As if to compete with Dickens, Benjamin

[9]Some of these anthologies include *Australian Poets, 1788–1899; Being a Selection of Poems Upon All Subjects, Written in Australia and New Zealand During the First Century of the British Colonization*, ed. Douglas Brooke Wheelton Sladen (London & Sydney: Griffith, Farran, Okedon & Welsh, 1888); *An Australian Anthology (Australian and New Zealand Poems)*, compiled by Percival Serle, possibly in 1929; *The Queensland Centenary Anthology*, ed. Robert S. Byrnes and Val Vallis (London: Longmans, 1959); and *Applestealers: A Collection of the New Poetry in Australia*, ed. Robert Kenny and C. Talbot (North Fitzroy, Victoria: Outback Press, 1974).

[10]Maurice Biggs, *Poems of War and Peace* (Sydney & London: Angus and Robertson, 1945).

[11]Gwen Bessell-Browne, *The Road to Kokoda and Other Verses* (Melbourne: Robertson and Mullens, 1943).

[12]Rex Ingamell, *The Great South Land; An Epic Poem* (Melbourne: Georgian House, [1951]).

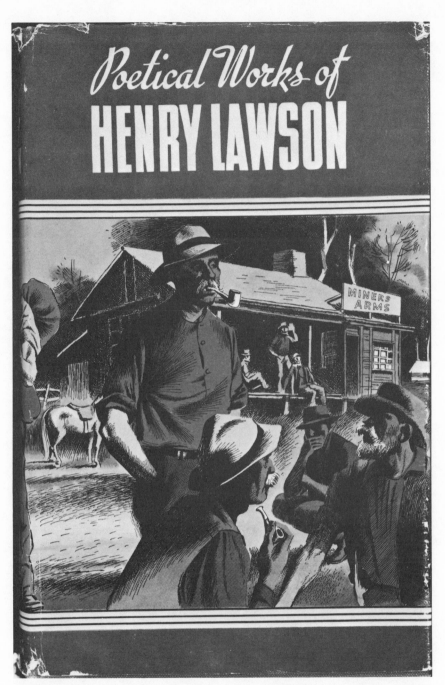

Dust jacket of Henry Lawson's *Poetical Works* (Angus & Robertson, 1951). Jacket design by Broadhurst. *HRHRC Grattan Collection*.

Dust jacket of Leslie Rees's *Towards An Australian Drama* (Angus & Robertson, 1953). *HRHRC Grattan Collection.*

Fryer wrote his "First Footing and Salute: Timely Footprint on the Sands," an "Australian-American Christmas Story," which he privately printed in 1938. Other short story writers include Barbara K. Baynton, whose *Bush Studies* feature the Australian pioneer woman, observations about bush life from a woman's perspective, and the appearance of Christianity in the bush.[13] A love for animals is revealed in the stories of James C. Bendrodt's *A Man, a Dog, Two Horses* and *Nine O'Clock*,[14] while Gavin Stodart Casey's *Birds of a Feather* depicts the Gold Rush days through a series of humorous portraits.[15] Like his collection of poetry anthologies, Grattan's collection of short stories published since the twenties reflects the historical development of this genre in the hands of Australian writers. Even as they deal with such familiar subjects as human relationships, Australian short stories will prove particularly significant to the student of Australian literature in that they allow the exotic to become familiar. Moreover, like the novel, the Australian short story is influenced by the art form made popular by Joseph Furphy, who wove many a good yarn in his classic novel *Such is Life*.[16] Grattan's collection of Australian short stories hence becomes invaluable to the scholar or student whose tastes are not confined to any one literary genre.

Grattan was no elitist, and his collection reflects this trait. Drama is well represented, including several radio plays. Youth plays—a possible carry-over from the mother country—as well as biographies of actors and theatre producers sit on the shelves alongside attempts at serious playwriting. Thus there are titles such as *Tiberius* (1894), by Francis Adams, as well as Max Afford's *Lady in Danger; A Comedy Thriller in Three Acts* (1944). Among the most interesting books on theatre are John Kardoss's *A Brief History of the Australian Theatre* (1955), Edward D.A. Bagot's *Coppin the Great, Father of the Australian Theatre* (1965), and Eric Irving's *Theatre Comes to Australia* (1971). In keeping with his desire to know everything he could about Australia, Grattan did not overlook women writers. Like his collection of the other genres, Grattan's archive of Australian dramatic works includes those by such women playwrights as Gwen Meredith (*Wives Have Their Uses, A Play*

[13]Barbara K. Baynton, *Bush Studies* (London: Duckworth, 1902).

[14]James C. Bendrodt, *A Man, A Dog, Two Horses* (Sydney: Angus and Robertson, n.d.); *Nine O'Clock* (Sydney and London: Angus and Robertson, 1949).

[15]Gavin Stodart Casey, *Birds of a Feather* (Sydney: Angus and Robertson, 1942).

[16]Joseph Furphy (pseudonym, Tom Collins), *Such is Life* (Melbourne: The Specialty Press pty., ltd, [1917]). Originally published in Sydney in 1903 by the Bulletin Newspaper Co. Ltd., Furphy's novel was reissued in a number of editions, many of which are included in the Grattan and especially in the HRHRC's R.G. Howarth Collection. The latter includes a copy of the 1948 edition published by the University of Chicago Press, with an essay on the author by C. Hartley Grattan, entitled "About Tom Collins." The Chicago edition reprints at the back the "Publisher's Note" from the 1917 printing, in which Furphy is quoted in response to the Bulletin's suggestion that he would be better off having his novel published in England: "Heaven forbid that I should think of treating with an English publisher. *Aut Australia aut nihil.*"

in Three Acts, 1944) and Jill Meillon (*The Jewel Casket. A Play for Eight Girls in Two Acts*, 1948). Feminist critics will find that throughout the Grattan Collection the Australian woman's perspective is fully represented, which would be expected given the collector's friendships with writers like Miles Franklin and Nettie Palmer.

Grattan's non-elitist stance also led him into the domain of children's literature. In this area, he acquired Australian editions of Aesop's fables, ballads of the bush (which even the adults enjoyed), adventure stories, novels, and plays. Several of Ion Llewellyn Idriess's titles are in the Grattan Collection, including *Drums of Mer* (1933), *The Great Trek* (1940), *The Wild White Man of the Coral Seas* (1950), and *Headhunters of the Coral Seas* (1951). Children's plays, such as Peter Batten's *The Kookaburra Who Couldn't Laugh* (1941), and short stories for children, such as Robert Henderson Croll's *Umph the Gargoyle* (193?) and Nuri Mass's *The Little Grammar People* (1947) and *Magic Australia* (1947), are also present. Another children's writer whose works are well represented in the collection is the detective novelist, Arthur William Upfield. Elementary school teachers and professors of reading education will benefit particularly from the Australian resources in the Grattan Collection.

Through his acquisition of critical assessments by scholars such as Zora Cross (*An Introduction to the Study of Australian Literature*, 1922), John Oscar Anchens (*The Australian Novel; a Critical Survey*, 1940), Geoffrey Dutton, John Keith Ewers, Henry Mackenzie Green, Cecil Hadgraft, Alan McLeod, Colin Arthur Roderick, Clement Semmter, Alfred George Stephens, and Reginald Percy Stephenson, Grattan's focus was sharpened as he went about collecting literary works by Australians. With the appearance of these critics, Australian literature reflected a newly gained respectability in a country where being "English" was still the norm. Also, with the emergence of native criticism of Australian literature, Australian scholarship entered a new era of self-worth and national identity. In 1946, one such scholar, Henry Seidel Canby, suggested the inevitability of the formation of an Australian literature whose story resembles, but is different from, that of American literature.[17] Grattan himself was part of Australia's growth into maturity by providing the outsider's perspective that helped indicate the peculiar insights and values of such a national literature.

That Australia accepted itself as an entity set apart from England can be seen when scholars began to recognize an Australian English. As early as 1898, Edward Ellis Morris's dictionary, *Austral English*, attests to the fact that Australia had in fact a national language.[18] This dictionary, which was soon

[17]This sentiment appears in Henry Seidel Canby's *A New Land Speaking; An Essay on the Importance of a National Literature* (Melbourne & London: Melbourne University Press, [1946]).

[18]Edward Ellis Morris, *Austral English* (London: Macmillan, 1898).

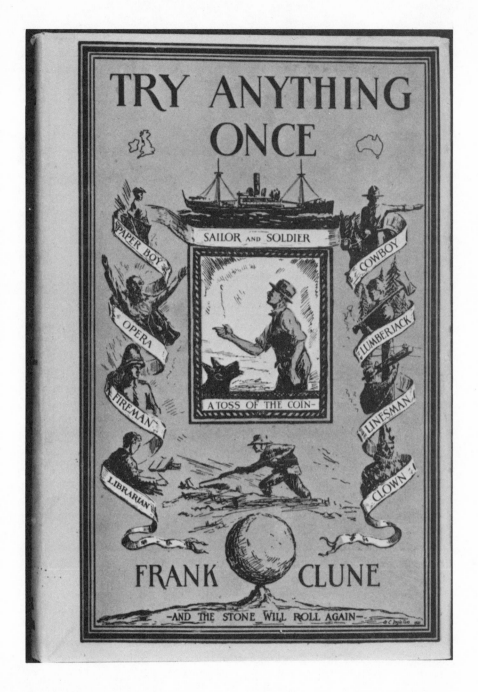

Dust jacket of Frank Clune's *Try Anything Once: The Autobiography of a Wanderer* (Angus & Robertson, 1947). Jacket design by G.C. Ingleton. *HRHRC Grattan Collection.*

followed by others, records "Australian words, phrases, and usages with those aboriginal-Australian and Maori words which have become incorporated in the language, and the commoner scientific words that have had their origin in Australia."[19] Given the Australian's sense of humor, it should come as no surprise that in *Aussie English* John Patrick O'Grady (pseudonym, Nino Culotta) introduces the non-Australian to the Australian idiom and provides humorous etymological explanations.[20] Perhaps more than any other works, dictionaries of idiomatic language signify that a language exists and an organic language not only draws upon people who contribute to its growth through slang and colloquialisms but also upon a body of literature. That Australian English has a vibrant literature to ensure its survival is well exemplified by the Grattan Collection.

If literary histories helped Grattan on his visits to bookstores across Australia, so too did the numerous checklists/bibliographies of poets, novelists, and playwrights. Scholars of Australian literature recognized the merit of some of their literary sons and produced reference materials that would be welcomed by fellow scholars as they set out to reconstruct and rewrite Australian history. In the Grattan Collection there are checklists of primary and secondary materials on Henry Lawson, Christopher Brennan, Shaw Nielson, Bernard O'Dowd, Hugh McCrae, and others. In some cases, Grattan also procured the updated versions of these checklists.

Magazines dating back to the 1920s help to recapture the Australian literary renaissance that produced some of the country's finest writers. That Australia was experiencing a new awakening is fully evidenced by the numerous publications that appeared during this period: *Angry Penguins, Austro-Verse, Austrovert, The Bulletin Reciter, The Edge, Jindyworobak Anthology, The Spinner, An Australian Magazine of Verse, Verse, Vision,* and *Voices.* While only a few issues of each of these magazines exist in the Grattan Collection, they were probably important to him as a means of learning of and then meeting many of the writers who later dominated the Australian literary scene in the thirties, forties, fifties, and sixties. Just as these magazines would have alerted Grattan to promising writers, such copies as are included in his collection will aid in recreating for scholars the publication ambience of the twenties and will recall those names that came to figure so prominently in the development of a distinctive national literature.

In his quest to know everything he wanted and felt he needed to know about Australia, and then some, Hartley Grattan has left to those interested in Australia an irreplaceable legacy. As a reflection of his renaissance mind, the literary publications in the Grattan Collection offer readers a wide-ranging and, in many cases, an in-depth source for the critical, cultural, and historical

[19]Ibid. This entire statement serves as the subtitle of Morris's dictionary.
[20]Nino Culotta, *Aussie English* (Sydney: U. Smith, [1965?]).

understanding of Australia's national language and literature. While the literary materials are only one aspect of the Grattan Collection of published works, they are representative of the collector's all-encompassing approach to an acquisition of written records for his own research and for that of future scholars and students who will share his curiosity and expertise in the fields of Australian studies.

Photograph of C. Hartley Grattan at work, n.d. *HRHRC Photography Collection*.

The C. Hartley Grattan Manuscript Collection:
A Critical Introduction

By Laurie Hergenhan

During a period of over 40 years, from the late 1920s to the 1970s, C. Hartley Grattan (1902-1980) built up a reputation as *the* American expert on Australia and the Southwest Pacific. This expertise, hard-won and all-embracing rather than narrowly specialized, was American both in its persistent energy and in its direction. The product of a "new world" reaching out to understand an even newer one, Grattan was challenged by this other "experiment" in democracy that was at once similar to and yet vitally different from the American experience. Unlike earlier observers such as De Tocqueville, who journeyed from the old world to America and viewed the latter with wariness and scepticism, Grattan approached this "new" continent as a shrewd, penetrating critic and a "social scientist" and yet as a believer in the quality of its future as a democratic society. In addition, Grattan saw his hopes—never unqualified—for the United States and the world bound up with his hopes for Australia.

In 1964, Grattan joined the faculty of The University of Texas at Austin as a lecturer in the Department of History and later as a professor, serving simultaneously as curator of the Grattan Collection of Southwest Pacificana, which would be housed in the Humanities Research Center beginning in 1969. The Center's Grattan Collection currently numbers over 20,000 volumes in the fields of Southwest Pacific literature, history, geography, government, economics, art (including Aboriginal art), education, journalism, and international and intra-Commonwealth relations. After Grattan's death the Center added a voluminous collection of his private papers, comprising 74 uncatalogued boxes of correspondence, research and miscellaneous materials, and publishing and other records relating to his varied writing career dating from 1929 to 1964. Apart from the practical limitations of sorting through such a massive collection of private papers, what one makes of it depends on what one is looking for, but this in turn can be modified by much that one does not expect to find in the documentation—uneven as it is—of the unfolding of a multifaceted career. Grattan's various roles as an Australianist influenced the creation of his manuscript collection, which itself provides evidence of how he saw, or constructed, his developing roles over many years, as well as the ways he was shaped by his changing times. In this last regard, the collection is especially useful, since Grattan kept redefining himself on paper, not only out of introspective curiosity but also out of practical necessity.

After graduating in 1923 from Clark College of Worcester, Massachusetts, Grattan broke into journalism by writing articles on early American literature for H.L. Mencken's *American Mercury*, on the recommendation of his favorite Clark teacher, historian Harry Elmer Barnes, a "learned crusader" for many radical political causes in the 1920s and '30s.[1] Barnes introduced Grattan to the field of revisionist history, and in particular the question of America's entry into World War I, which later led to Grattan's seminal study, *Why We Fought* (1929). At the same time that he was writing as a journalist, Grattan was teaching at Urbana University School in Ohio, and early letters from this period show him oscillating between youthful uncertainty and confidence.[2] Grattan found the Midwest confining and preferred a metropolitan lifestyle (even in the 1960s, on moving to Texas, he commented that he never expected to move west of the Hudson). But during this period in Ohio, Grattan believed that he had at least "one of Mencken's specifications for happiness: a comfortable feeling of superiority over my fellow men. I want to get something done."[3] It was a "puff" for Grattan to have the great Mencken, who was unaware of his youth, suggesting that he "write a history of American literature!"[4] As a contributor to a wide range of New York newspapers and magazines, including the leading ones, Grattan was later to remark that the three editors who influenced him most were Mencken, Alfred Dashiell of *Scribners*, and Frederick Allen of *Harper's*.[5] Grattan was proud of his association with such prestigious literary journals, yet he contributed to many publications, with his contributions "about equally divided between literature and politics."[6]

[1]See *Harry Elmer Barnes: Learned Crusader*, ed. Arthur Goddard (Colorado Springs: Ralph Myles Inc., 1968).

[2]Unless otherwise noted, all letters and unpublished writings quoted or referred to are from the Grattan Collection in the Harry Ransom Humanities Research Center. I am grateful to Mrs. Marjorie Grattan for permission to quote from these materials and also to Ms. Jay Cox for acting as my research assistant at the HRHRC.

[3]Letter from Grattan to Harry Elmer Barnes, 2 January 1924, Box 27G/file 2, item 35d.

[4]Letter from Grattan to Harry Elmer Barnes, 26 November 1923, Box 27G/file 2, item 35c.

[5]Grattan discusses his career in a self-styled "bio/chronology" (undated, 1938?, Box 27F/file 1, item 2) and includes a sample list of journals and newspapers in which his contributions appeared.

[6]Ibid. By the end of 1933, according to a bibliography compiled during the late 1960s by Jack Healy (the handwritten original of which is in the HRHRC), Grattan had published over 550 reviews of books on figures in American literature, from Cotton Mather through Emerson, Poe, and Dickinson to Faulkner and Lafcadio Hearne. While his later reviews emphasized sociology and political thought, Grattan reviewed widely in many fields from the 1920s through the 1960s.

When Grattan moved to New York in January 1926, he became a free-lance author-journalist, and even though he was successful in this profession, his economic existence was unpredictable and even at times precarious. This was partly the result of the journalistic trade but also was due to Grattan's own conception of himself as a free-lancer, as a self-styled "left liberal" progressive who placed high value on his independence. Besides writing widely on American topics, Grattan also covered British and British Commonwealth affairs, including Canada and Australia. A close study of his journal and newspaper publications would probably reveal that he reviewed all the notable books in the Australian field—literary, political, historical, and political economic—from the 1930s to the 1950s. Although his reviews of Australian works brought him "only a minor return in money over the quarter century," the review copies obviously made a considerable contribution to his book collection, and, as he also noted, the contribution his Australian studies made to his reputation and intellectual standing was "intense."[7] While he was willing, indeed compelled, to review in a wide variety of fields, Grattan did not identify himself "with any group, gang, or coterie but pursued an independent line."[8] Since he was constantly called upon to cite his skills and experience, his correspondence contains a changing series of *curriculum vitae*, official and otherwise, which formed part of his applications to editors, publishers, institutions, and funding bodies. These self-biographies, in conjunction with his writings and other manuscripts, chart some of the ways in which he presented himself to prospective employers, as well as providing a glimpse into the various activities that took place behind the scenes of his published works.

In addition to reviews and *Why We Fought*, Grattan's early publications included *Bitter Bierce* (1929), which showed his interest in a literary outsider;

---

[7]These remarks appear in another self-portrait, on microfilm, from 1966.

[8]Ibid. Grattan surveys his publishing career in these words: "For 38 years my public life was my published writings. Jobs were viewed as assists [*sic*] along my chosen way. I began my freelancing [in the later 1920s] as a literary critic, specializing in American literature, but unlike most of the fellows of my time I soon also began to write about politics—not however about contemporary politics particularly but historical politics—and in due course worked my way into economic journalism, and in the end became a 'social analyst' with strong cultural (ie literary, fine arts, education) interests. . . . I feel that the point of view that integrates what to many people is a surprising and puzzling miscellany of publications is the historical; and what saved me from degenerating into an utterly febrile scribbler was my deep and abiding respect for scholarship in the different fields I invaded. I also had, as appears in the perspective of 1966, the indispensable quality of *durability*: I had what it takes to stay the course . . . a rough one, particularly as I lacked the capacity to identify myself with any group, gang, or coterie but pursued an independent line. . . . The best summary of my career, I think, is that I contributed to Twentieth Century Authors [ed. Hayes and Kunitz]. 'It has not been my fate to suffer the burdens of popularity, nor have I ever courted that fate. I have hewn to my self-chosen life and the chips have fallen in strange places'."

The Peerless Leader (1929), a study of William Jennings Bryan completed from work begun by Paxton Hibben; *The Critique of Humanism: A Symposium* (1930, rptd 1968), a controversial collection of essays—aimed at contesting the views of Paul Elmer Moore and Irving Babbitt—edited by Grattan and including articles by such writers as Edmund Wilson, Malcolm Cowley, Kenneth Burke, R.P. Blackmur, Yvor Winters, and Lewis Mumford; *The Three Jameses: A Family of Minds* (1932, rptd 1962), written shortly before the Henry James revival; and *Preface to Chaos: War in the Making* (1936) and *The Deadly Parallel* (1939), two publicist, polemical works arguing against American involvement in World War II, which continued Grattan's anti-war stance. Though his early books on American literature and history are impressive, Grattan soon eame to see that while his journalism could interfere with his scholarly writing, the experience of metropolitan journalism offered him special advantages for being an historian and observer of other countries. Hence he found virtue in necessity and regarded his work as both journalist and historian in many fields as mutually reinforcing. In this way he was influenced by his own experience and by the "new history," which engaged the present in all the complexity of its "environing" forces and which saw the branches of knowledge and the past and present as indissolubly connected. In a sketch of his career dated 17 October 1961, Grattan commented that through Harry Barnes

> I became perforce one of the generation deeply influenced by James Harvey Robinson, Charles Beard and Veblen. . . . In short, my "intellectual history," and presumably the native caste of my mind, profoundly influenced by my Nova Scotia grandfather, conspired to make me a dissenter.[9]

Grattan's writings on Australia developed from his first and fortuitous visit to Australia in 1927, when he accompanied his first wife, singer Beatrice Kay, who performed in Sydney and Melbourne. The journalist-historian noted that this visit "planted a consuming interest in the country in all its aspects."[10] As a way of learning about Australia, Grattan began from this time his reading of its literature, which in turn resulted in the beginnings of his collection of Australian books. In February 1936 he prepared an application to the Carnegie Corporation for his principal Australian visit, which came about in 1936-38. Finding that Grattan had written so persuasively to him about his qualifications and aims, Harry Barnes forwarded the letter to Carnegie. In this letter to Barnes, Grattan suggests that his free-lance status handicapped earlier applications for grants, adding with characteristic irony that academic

---

[9]This four-page typescript sketch of Grattan's career is marked "Private and Confidential" and is attached to a letter from Warren I. Cohen, 17 October 1961, Box 27A/file 1.

[10]Letter from Grattan to Harry Elmer Barnes, 18 February 1936, Box 27D/file 2, item 45.

Dust jacket of C. Hartley Grattan's *Bitter Bierce: A Mystery of American Letters* (Doubleday, Doran & Company, 1929). *HRHRC Grattan Collection.*

symbolism is "not an absolute index of ability."[11] He remarks that his college training was chiefly in "sociology and history" and that after graduation he turned to American literature—although literature was always a primary interest—and to general reviewing. Later he moved into "politics and social questions," as did contemporary writers like Edmund Wilson and Malcolm Cowley, because of the interest of magazine readers in the Depression and its subsequent problems and because of its effects on writers themselves. From 1934 to 1935, Grattan also was involved in the government's social relief program as editor for research in the Federal Economic Relief Administration. He recalls in his letter to Barnes how he has "traversed a great deal of ground in the fields of literature, international and national politics, sociology and modern and historical thought," adding that he has made "contributions to the understanding of current problems, notably those surrounding our entrance into war, those growing out of the conflict of modern thought and Humanistic reaction, and the matter of relief."

In this same letter to Barnes, Grattan goes on to defend himself against Australian and American opinion that dismissed him as a "journalist," a prejudiced attitude he was to resent. As his lifelong friend, the late Sir John Crawford, pointed out, Australia did not have at that time, nor for that matter has it had since, any counterpart to the prestigious, "high-powered" kind of metropolitan journalist Grattan represented, nor the kind of wide intellectual circle of which he was thereby a member.[12] Some ten years later, in applying for a position as a "one-man research department," Grattan gave a clarified view of his career in journalism:

> As a journalist I have always been a writer of "think pieces." I have produced well-thought-out articles and books which depend a great deal on an analytical presentation of the facts. My most appreciative audience has been found amongst well-informed readers, specialists in the fields I have invaded, including economics. I have always taken pride in the durability of my work. . . .[13]

For Grattan, his interests as a journalist had strengthened rather than diluted his capacities as an historian:

> Necessity of earning a living. . .has made me "shop around". . .the total effect has been to provide me with a fairly comprehensive equipment for making a study of a nation as a whole. If I have had any guiding purpose at all, it has been to equip myself for just that task. . . . I have come to think of myself as being half a journalist and half a professor without a specialty except society as a whole.[14]

[11]Ibid.
[12]In a personal interview from 1984 conducted with Sir John Crawford in Canberra.
[13]Drafts of circular letter, 18 October 1948, Box 27F/file 2, item 5.
[14]Letter from Grattan to Harry Elmer Barnes, 18 February 1936, Box 27D/file 2, item 45.

Accordingly, Grattan felt he had built up a body of experience and knowledge relevant to the task of studying Australia in detail. And indeed his continuing experience, together with his ability in pursuing "historical and theoretical considerations," helps to explain why he still has claims to being Australia's most important as well as most persistent foreign observer.[15] Grattan also makes an important point to Barnes about his extensive reviewing for New York publications: ". . . My reviews [of Australian books] were, in effect, brief articles; that is, the reviews transcended the lesser task of 'reporting' the book." Grattan concludes in regard to his ambitious aims in wanting to visit and write about Australia by commenting:

> . . . my whole approach is one not generally cultivated by those Australians who have written about their own country or by foreigners who have. . . . Sometimes in an effort to state what I hope to do, I have said that I want to write a book analogous to Bryce's "American Commonwealth"—and after making all necessary reservations and qualifications that really sums up the matter!

Much later Barnes and Allan Nevins, accepting not only Grattan's model but his achievement of it, especially in his two-volume history of the Southwest Pacific, were to recommend him in the 1960s for academic posts as "the Lord Bryce of Australia."[16] Earlier, Barnes had written to Grattan: "I don't doubt you have the stuff to do for Australia, what Bryce, Laski and De Tocqueville did for the US."[17]

The Grattan manuscript collection also demonstrates how pluralism and the knowledge of current affairs were keystones of his approach to history. In a speech given to the American Historical Association on 30 December 1939, which he entitled with irony, even cheekiness, "Salute to the Professors," Grattan stresses the idea that journalists offset and even combat the deadening effects of specialized, academic approaches to history by reporting on a wide range of events and issues.[18] In this speech, he chose as his example a particular field of his own in which "journalists and professors collide," namely international affairs. What responsible journalists and historians should both deplore, he suggests, is the Hegelian view that people learn nothing from history. Journalists, he could see, are limited in their perspectives because they must necessarily concern themselves with current events and with polemics about public policies, writing for this reason "before all the facts are

[15]In his book, *From Deserts the Prophets Come* (Melbourne: Heinemann Australia, 1973), Geoffrey Serle comments that Grattan is "the only important modern foreign observer of Australia." See p. 238.

[16]Letter from Allan Nevins to Grattan, 11 January 1961, Box 27C/file 3, item 16. Grattan's two-volume "modern history," *The Southwest Pacific to 1900* and *Since 1900*, appeared in 1963 from the University of Michigan Press at Ann Arbor.

[17]Letter from Harry Elmer Barnes to Grattan, 12 March 1949, Box 27A/file 2, item 7.

[18]C. Hartley Grattan, "Salute to the Professors," Box 32/file 3.

in" and about only a part of the reality that William James described as "'that distributed and strung-along and flowing reality which we finite beings swim in.'" However, Grattan also felt that this was a strength, since, whether writing of the past or present, journalists bring to bear "an acute sense of the context in which men act. . . . In short, they bring to bear upon their work their total knowledge and experience." To create this context, and bearing in mind his own influential revisionist history, *Why We Fought*, Grattan declares that he has "sought to evolve a pluralistic, rather than a monistic, explanation of the event. . . . [I]f we are not to have a pluralistic history which reflects a pluralistic reality, then the prospects of having any rational history are poor."

In an untitled typescript in the Grattan manuscript collection, Grattan applies his pluralism to his approach to Australia, which includes his status as a foreign observer.[19] He comments that no single approach is sufficient, whether geographic, economic, cultural ("in the anthropological sense"), biographical or factual ("the historian is helpless without 'the facts'"). In his conclusion he links the difficulty of understanding in all its facets "a country not one's own" with the difficulty of understanding one's own, "if you inhabit a complex country like the United States." He implies that his knowledge as an Americanist fed his understanding as an Australianist and he goes on to state that in "this delicate and necessary—indeed, today, indispensable—business [of understanding Australia] the personal factors are all." Grattan does not have in mind any romantic ideas of individualism but rather the need to understand the historian as a person in the sense of understanding his individual experience of social life: "If as E. H. Carr has suggested one should study the historian before studying his history, then surely one should examine the purveyor of 'understanding' of a foreign land before one opens his book." This statement, which reads like advice to a biographer, suggests something about the way Grattan's personal papers may be used in conjunction with his writings. In the same paper he points to the need for good biographies of both "major" and "minor" Australian figures—a deficiency that is only currently being remedied. As the biographer of such figures as Ambrose Bierce, William Jennings Bryan (written with Paxton Hibben), and "the three Jameses," Grattan could speak with the experience of a producer as well as an eager consumer.

Having looked at Grattan's roles partly as he himself saw them, it is appropriate to turn now to more external views which hindsight makes possible and to which the Grattan manuscript collection can contribute. Of six ways of viewing Grattan's work, the first would be to consider it in relation to the American liberal/progressive movement of his day, especially of the 1930s and '40s, with its roots in the previous turn-of-the-century generation, and to

[19]This typescript is attached to Grattan's "lightly edited" xerox copy of his "Reflections on Australian History," published in *Quadrant* 1, no. 2 (Sydney, 1957). Box 27A/file 2, item 7.

this movement's counterparts in Australia. However, while the Australian scene was influenced by the American, and while the two had much in common, they cannot be equated. Nor is any parallel between the two meant to pigeonhole Grattan, whose particular kind of liberalism was always changing. Like the Progressive movement and its heirs, Grattan claimed the virtues of rationality while at heart he was emotive and idealistic.[20] A second view of Grattan's work would be to consider him as a "publicist." Not only did he immerse himself in current affairs and their polemics but he became involved in them in such a pragmatic, detached manner that he also performed the roles of authority, promoter, adviser, teacher, and reformer. He was often combative and controversial, a gadfly stimulating—sometimes stinging—people into examining their ideas and assumptions. A third view would take into consideration his mixed feelings about the emergence of American economic and military power in World War I. Grattan was both a sophisticated nationalist and an internationalist, and this was in large part his appeal to many Australians of the 1930s and '40s, a time when incipient nationalism and isolationism clashed with internationalist tendencies. A fourth view would consider Grattan as at once a regionalist and an internationalist by observing that his anti-British streak—which he himself denied—is connected with his espousal of the cause of Australia's independence as a Commonwealth and post-colonial country and of the recognition and development of the whole South Pacific region as an area in its own right. A fifth view would see him as an historian who was a synthesizer and generalist, and certainly his role as an expert must be considered with this in mind. Finally, a sixth view would place Grattan within an American and even a wider tradition of foreign observers.

These six categories and even more can be subsumed under Grattan's role as historian and evaluated within the framework of the history of American-Australian relations—cultural, economic, political, and strategic. As he realized, ideas about America, and American ideas, played an important part in the thinking of British "colonials" and post-colonials, including Australians, particularly in politics and cultural affairs. Grattan himself contributed both to that thinking process and to its understanding. With regard to his manuscript collection, the above categories can serve as underlying guidelines in surveying the three sections into which the collection may be roughly divided: 1) correspondence, including copies of many of Grattan's own letters; 2) voluminous materials relating to his written work, journalism, and books, as well as projects either not started or not completed, source notes, talks and lectures (some unpublished), publishing and other records, including correspondence with publishers and editors, and other miscellaneous materials; and 3) some manuscript copies of Grattan's published writings, as well as

[20]Michael Roe, *Nine Australian Progressives* (St. Lucia: University of Queensland Press, 1984), p. 13.

clippings of reviews and commentaries about his work.[21] Although Grattan did not select or organize the material according to any apparent principles, and despite the fact that it remains uncatalogued, which makes it difficult to separate what for any one reader may be the wheat from the chaff, there is no doubt that the collection is extremely important to the study of Australia and the Southwest Pacific.

The bulk of the Australian correspondence is post 1936 (the year of Grattan's principal visit to Australia), and generally, instead of being composed of large clumps of letters from particular persons (though there are exceptions), it tends to be widely dispersed, as befits Grattan's broad-ranging activities and interests. The correspondence is not only with a large number of persons but concerns the various fields of interest those persons represented. The range of Grattan's correspondence is suggested by his listing of Australian friends and contacts in his autobiographical essay, "A Garrulity About Australian Literature."[22] As a true metropolitan, Grattan thrived on exchanges and disagreements with a wide variety of persons, and thus his Australian experience and writings were shaped not only by observation and reading but by the people with whom he came in contact. His letters supply some idea of this interaction, as do his comments in a 1975 talk:

> A personal acquaintance with many, many of the actors on the Australian stage since 1927 . . . gives a dimension to my perspective on the Australian scene which I think should not be under-estimated. . . . The effect has been to intensify my sense of identification with Australia to the point that it is a very important constituent of my identity as a person, let alone a writer. . . .[23]

Unlike tourist views of Australia, especially those found in so many English accounts, Grattan's perspective was based on his encounter with Australian people, for he was, by his own admission, "probably the world's worst sight-seer."[24]

Part of the background to his 1930s visit was his correspondence with Nettie Palmer, a prolific critic, essayist, and wife of writer Vance Palmer. Both Palmers were prominent in Australian letters, Nettie through her journalism and through her cultivation by correspondence of an extraordinary range of

---

[21]The manuscript bibliography by Jack Healy includes many contributions by Grattan that are not represented by clippings present in the Grattan Collection. Unfortunately, an exhaustive search failed to unearth more than a few of the clippings. The possibilities are that they were somehow overlooked in the search, that they are not part of the Grattan Collection but exist elsewhere in the Center's collections, or that they did not find their way into the HRHRC.

[22]C. Hartley Grattan, "A Garrulity About Australian Literature Since 1927," *Meanjin Quarterly* 24, no. 103 (1965): 405-416.

[23]Because of the lack of opportunity to check my notes against original documents in the Grattan Collection, location details could not be supplied.

[24]Grattan, "A Garrulity," p. 411.

literary acquaintances. Along with Miles Franklin of Sydney, Nettie, who was based in Melbourne, helped Grattan plan his trip and kept in touch with him during his visit and afterwards. Much later Grattan would write: "If any Australian be credited with keeping me interested in Australia 1928-1936 it is Nettie Palmer, may she rest in eternal peace."[25] A number of her letters to Grattan were published with his permission before the HRHRC acquired his papers.[26] However, these do not include her very first letter to Grattan, dated 24 October 1928, which indicates some of the general links between Australia and the United States and typifies a receptive attitude toward Grattan.[27] Nettie, who at the time was living about 60 miles north of Brisbane at Landsborough, tells him that his article on Australian literature in the August *Bookman* (later published as *Australian Literature*, [1929]) has attracted much "astonished" attention in Australia and hot on its heels has come a piece of his on "Colonial Writing" in the *New York Herald Tribune*.[28] Nettie's response is typical of those sympathetic to Grattan: While she finds he is wrong about some details, she believes that basically he shows a remarkable understanding of Australian literature. She comments that even many Australians do not know as much as Grattan because they are divided by distance and because the few books published are brought out by obscure presses, or else by English publishers who do not distribute them properly in Australia. Behind Nettie's remarks lies a sense of surprised pleasure, almost of being flattered, as an Australian, by such metropolitan and informed notice as Grattan's. Nettie also shows a shrewd sense that the two writers could be of use to one another in exchanging information and opinions, as proved to be the case. She ends on a note that again typifies many 1930s responses to Grattan: his "comprehending words" eased the isolation of Australian writers, like a window being opened, even when he mixed criticism with praise. This letter led shortly to Nettie Palmer's volunteering to write the introduction to Grattan's *Australian Literature* (1929), after Louis Esson, a pioneer of Australian nationalist drama, had written to say he felt unable to do the job.

Like other Australians, Nettie Palmer welcomed American interest in Australian culture, in part out of a reaction against British lack of interest. In writing to Grattan in 1945 about the chapter on "Culture" that he had commissioned Vance and herself to write for his collection of essays entitled *Australia*, Nettie comments with characteristic Australian ambivalence that she is glad of this opportunity to prove the existence of Australia on the international scene, even though "history" is doing that, for she is increasingly convinced of the importance of Australia's reciprocal contact with America,

[25]Ibid., p. 409.

[26]*Letters of Vance and Nettie Palmer*, ed. Vivian Smith (Canberra: National Library of Australia, 1977).

[27]Letter from Nettie Palmer to Grattan, 24 October 1928, Box 35/file 4.

[28]C. Hartley Grattan, "Colonial Writers," *New York Herald Tribune*, 17 June 1928, sec. XII.

particularly through books.[29] By way of contrast with British attitudes, she mentions a visiting English publisher (from Heinemann), whom she had met earlier in London through Henry Handel Richardson, and quotes him as stating blandly: "'Of course we don't know *anything* about your writers in England.'"

Another woman writer who corresponded with Grattan was the notable Australian novelist, Katharine Susannah Prichard, whom the American visited in Perth on his 1930s and 1940 trips. Just as Grattan's first contact with Nettie Palmer predated their actual meeting, his visits with Prichard were preceded by knowledge of and praise for her work. In his 1929 monograph on Australian literature, Grattan had described Prichard as "the hope of the Australian novel," and at this time he served as a reader for W.W. Norton's American editions of two of her novels. In 1938 Prichard discussed her writing in letters to Grattan preserved in the HRHRC collection, and thereafter she remained appreciative of his longstanding admiration of her efforts, though Grattan was not uncritical in his appraisal.[30] As he did with Nettie Palmer, Grattan introduced Prichard to American writers, in particular Granville Hicks, whose leftist ideas Prichard found sympathetic to her own, which gave the Australian renewed confidence in seeking acceptance for her work, despite what she called her "communisticness." Prichard contemplated sending Hicks a copy of her misunderstood novel, *Intimate Strangers* (1937), for she believed that he might appreciate that the "only hope for its characters, Greg & Elodie, was to join the communist party."[31]

Like Palmer and Franklin, Prichard took up the Australian theme of isolation, showing unwittingly that she too was torn in two directions. She repudiated a tendency to overvalue the estimation of "strangers" and "foreigners"—or what a later critic would call "the cultural cringe"—and she included in a letter to Grattan a paean of praise to her native Western Australian outback, which she said would "bore" an outsider like Grattan.[32] But she ended by thanking him for reinvigorating her creative talent and for all he had generously done to arouse and "energise" the people of Australia to an awareness of the country's "economic and cultural potentialities."

Eleanor Dark, another novelist-friend of Grattan's, was not convinced that isolation could only be a drawback. In questioning Grattan's claim in his article in *Australian Quarterly* for December 1938 that "isolated cultures . . . have always first stagnated and then died," Dark cited the Incas and South Sea Islanders as examples of civilizations that had thrived in isolation but had eventually been destroyed by intruders from outside.[33] In thus

[29]Letter from Nettie Palmer to Grattan, 9 March 1945, Box 35/file 3, item 26.

[30]Letters from Katharine Susannah Prichard to Grattan, Box 35/file 4, items 12, 13, 16, 31.

[31]Letter from Katharine Susannah Prichard to Grattan, 27 June 1938, Box 35/file 4, item 13.

[32]Letter from Katharine Susannah Prichard to Grattan, 14 August 1938, Box 35/file 4, item 12.

[33]Letter from Eleanor Dark to Grattan, 28 August 1938, Box 37/file 2, item 43. Dark refers to Grattan's "The Future in Australia," *Australian Quarterly* 10, no. 4 (December 1938): 7-29.

rebutting Grattan's views she may have had in mind the dangers of American imperialist penetration of the South Pacific.

While on his 1930s visit, Grattan not only came to know many of the major Australian writers, most of whom were concentrated in Sydney, Melbourne, and to a lesser extent in Perth, but he also spent a good deal of time with academics, politicians of different colors, businessmen, industrialists, and professional people, including senior public servants, all of whom are represented by correspondence in the Grattan manuscript collection. From this diverse group, I have selected as representative Grattan's correspondence with Brian Fitzpatrick, Geoffrey Remington (a lifelong correspondent), Dr. H.V. Evatt, and Herbert Gepp. With an engaging openmindedness characteristic of the man, Grattan commented that "after a long experience of meeting people I suppose I should be clear about the significance of knowing individuals to understanding a country, but I am not."[34] He made it clear, nevertheless, that the two are closely linked, hence the importance of his correspondence.

Brian Fitzpatrick, a Melbourne historian writing from the late 1930s, helped to pioneer the modern writing or rewriting of Australian history in the radical-nationalist vein, especially in the economic and social areas. At Dr. H.V. Evatt's suggestion, Grattan read Fitzpatrick's manuscript of what would become the latter's *British Imperialism in Australia* (1939) and made welcome suggestions. The Grattan papers contain a copy of a letter from Fitzpatrick to Evatt thanking him for his introduction to the book and also for submitting the manuscript to Grattan, whose opinion he (Fitzpatrick) respected.[35] Fitzpatrick added that he would naturally incorporate Grattan's suggestions and that this would be a help in getting his manuscript a reading. Fitzpatrick in turn offered Grattan advice about the latter's projected study of Australia, including names of people he could consult, the need for primary research, and the backwardness of universities in this respect. In subsequent correspondence, Fitzpatrick sought Grattan's help with his second book, *The British Empire: An Economic History 1834-1939* (1941). For example, he asked Grattan for information about Canadian and American farming developments between 1866 and 1888, submitted draft chapters for Grattan's comments, and acknowledged the justice of the American's criticism of his (Fitzpatrick's) treatment of the unlocking of the land.[36] In the correspondence, Fitzpatrick warns Grattan of "insistent calls" on his "cooperation."[37]

[34]Grattan, "A Garrulity," p. 411.

[35]Letter from Brian Fitzpatrick to Dr. H.V. Evatt, 1 September 1937, Box 37/file 2, item 36.

[36]Letter from Brian Fitzpatrick to Grattan, 1 March 1938, Box 37/file 2, item 29.

[37]Letters from Brian Fitzpatrick to Grattan, 10 March, 24 March, and 16 May 1938, Box 37/ items 30-32. Permission to quote from her father's (Brian Fitzpatrick's) letters was given by Dr. Sheila Fitzpatrick.

Photograph of Katharine Susannah Prichard, n.d. *HRHRC Photography Collection*.

It is likely that Fitzpatrick valued Grattan not only because of his knowledge of Australian history but more because of the knowledge and techniques that he, Grattan, as an historian of American and world problems could bring to bear on Australian affairs. For many Australian writers, association with Grattan also could be valued because of the American's prestige as a metropolitan, "outsider" intellectual and because he was sympathetic to, and yet could detach himself from, the radical-nationalist stance. In fact, in a letter dated 28 September 1938, Fitzpatrick refers to an "Evatt-Grattan-Fitzpatrick solidarity"; interestingly, Grattan is the center of the trinity.[38] Behind the jocular reference lies an awareness of a left, "against-the-government" affinity that included an anti-British streak, though Grattan was less likely to be carried away by it than the other two.

Evatt, also a revisionist Australian historian, must have valued Grattan for reasons similar to those of Fitzpatrick, but in the case of Evatt, who aimed at a world stage, there also was the importance of Grattan's knowledge of international affairs and his strategic location in New York. Grattan's association with Evatt, the brilliant Sydney lawyer who became Attorney General, Minister for External Affairs, Deputy Prime Minister, and first president of the United Nations Assembly, is a story in itself. The HRHRC collection contains a few Evatt letters but more importantly a notebook of Grattan's that records their long relationship. According to the notebook, Grattan first met Evatt in 1937, probably through Miles Franklin, and saw much of him in Australia and later during Evatt's visits to Washington and New York. Evatt spoke of Grattan's "magnificent" Foreword to the former's *The Rum Rebellion* (1938)[39] and of his "exciting introduction" (which, however, did not appear with the book) to Evatt's *Australian Labor Leader* (1940).[40] At the end of Grattan's 1930s visit, Evatt wrote a reference letter, stating that in his writings on Australian literature, history, and economics, Grattan had "equaled if not surpassed" the best work done in Australia and was the one non-Australian able to speak with authority in these areas.[41]

There are a number of letters in the Grattan manuscript collection to Geoffrey Remington, whose lifelong correspondence is representative of a different type of correspondent from Fitzpatrick and Evatt. Remington was a Sydney solicitor and an active public figure in many fields, serving, among other capacities, as director of the Free Library Movement in New South Wales; as president of the Trustees of the New South Wales Public Library; as executive chairman of the Royal Institute of Public Administration (New South Wales branch); as a member of the Board of Directors of the Australian

[38]Letter from Brian Fitzpatrick to Grattan, 28 September 1938, Box 37/file 2.
[39]Letter from Dr. H.V. Evatt to Grattan, 24 December [1937?], Box 30/file 1.
[40]Letter from Dr. H.V. Evatt to Grattan, 28 August 1937, Box 30.
[41]Reference letter from Dr. H.V. Evatt for Grattan, 12 October 1939, Box 30/file 1.

Institute of Political Science; and as chairman of Directors of Rolls Royce in Australia. Although Grattan himself preferred to work out of his own collection, he was always a supporter of public libraries and wrote *Libraries: A Necessity for Democracy* (1938) for the New South Wales Free Library Movement. According to Remington's letters, this pamphlet enjoyed an extraordinarily wide distribution throughout the provincial towns of New South Wales, where it received considerable notice in newspapers. Copies of Grattan's pamphlet were sent to every Town and Shire Clerk and were circulated statewide by the Apex Club, a kind of junior Rotary. Likewise, Remington reported that Grattan's article, "Australian Arms," published in *Asia* (1938), was widely read and favorably commented on by Australian intellectuals, public figures, and influential people like Remington and Sir Herbert Gepp.[42] Remington regularly reported Australian news to Grattan, who reciprocated by sending news of American political and social issues, such as attitudes on the war and on the possibility of its spread to the Pacific region.

As someone whom Grattan called the most pro-American man in Australia, Remington felt free to comment to him on Australian anti-American feeling. Grattan could be critical of his own country, but he tended to be touchy if Australians were too censorious. As a close friend and notable public figure, Remington could let Grattan know firsthand about current Australian feeling without offending him. For example, Remington reported a widespread and justified resentment at flamboyant United States advertising of her wealth.[43] Such information was grist for Grattan's mill as a writer/commentator and served to keep the American up-to-date on Australian views.

Sir Herbert Gepp, a member of Remington's circle, also knew and admired Grattan. As a mining metallurgist and manager, public servant, industrialist, and publicist who served on a number of Royal Commissions, Gepp was an important figure in the postwar reconstruction in the 1940s and was "an influential transmitter of advanced British and American ideas to an Australian public."[44] The Grattan Collection contains several of Gepp's letters, and Remington's letters also report on Gepp's reactions to Grattan. In one of his letters, Gepp wrote to Grattan to congratulate him on his *Harper's* article for May 1940, entitled "An Australian-American Axis," calling it the clearest and most accurate analysis of Australian and American policies in the Pacific Basin.[45]

[42]Letter from Geoffrey Remington to Grattan, 10 November 1938, Box 35/file 3, item 1.

[43]Letter from Geoffrey Remington to Grattan, 5 November 1945. Location details could not be supplied.

[44]"Sir Herbert Gepp," in the *Australian Dictionary of Biography, 1891-1939*, vol. 8 (Melbourne: Melbourne University Press, 1981), pp. 640-642.

[45]Letter from Sir Herbert Gepp to Grattan, 2 September 1940, Box 37/file 4, item 11.

Photograph of Sir Herbert Gepp, Chairman of Development and Migration Commission of the Commonwealth of Australia and President of Australasian Institute of Mining and Metallurgy, n.d. *HRHRC Photography Collection.*

Another area of the Grattan manuscript collection covers the various kinds of publishing records and correspondence associated with books he published. Apart from his work on adult education, *In Quest of Knowledge* (1955), Grattan's only book to sell well was *Introducing Australia* (1942), which was the result of the fortunate timing of its appearance almost simultaneously with America's entrance in the Pacific war. Dal Stivens, a Sydney author, mentioned to Grattan that he had used his book in teaching Army Education courses.[46] After the war, *Introducing Australia* was one of the few Australian histories appropriate as a textbook for the earliest university courses on Australia. In his obituary on Grattan, Manning Clark recalled that in 1946 when he was teaching Australian history at Melbourne University before the Pacific Southwest became "a boom industry," Grattan was one of the few authors, and the only non-Australian author, "to whom one turned for ideas."[47]

Correspondence in the Grattan manuscript collection that concerns *Introducing Australia* came both from American and Australian readers, the former including many "general" readers, such as wives of servicemen whose husbands were stationed in Australia. One of these American wives wrote to Grattan to ask his advice about places in outback Queensland that her husband might visit while on leave; perhaps she was hoping to get him away from the fleshpots of Sydney.[48] Among the more interesting comments found in letters are those from author Graham McInnes, who, as the son of Angela Thirkell and her Australian husband, had grown up in Australia. Also present are letters from C. E. W. Bean, historian of Australia's involvement in World War I and the principal founder of the associated Anzac myth to the effect that the heroic involvement of Australian forces in war action in 1915 in Gallipoli marked a "baptism" of blood whereby Australia at last proved itself to the world as an independent nation.[49] Bean praised Grattan's book but was concerned that the American should appreciate the fact that although Australians could be scathing critics of the English, there were still strong "idealistic" bonds on the Australian side.[50] In America, Selden Rodman, one of the editors of *Common Sense*, wrote to praise Grattan's book and to ask where he could acquire certain volumes of Australian poetry, some of which he later included in an anthology.[51]

[46]Letter from Dal Stivens to Grattan, 1 June 1943, Box 37/file 1, item 15.

[47]Obituary on Grattan by Manning Clark in the Melbourne *Age* for 20 September 1980.

[48]Letter from (Mrs.) Alma Hemphill to Grattan, Box 38/file 1.

[49]Anzac, an abbreviation for the Australian and New Zealand Army Corps, supposedly demonstrated specific Australian virtues of male egalitarianism and "mateship" and was applied beyond Gallipoli to Australia's total involvement in World War I, especially in France where losses were greatest. Anzac Day, which observes the Gallipoli landing on 25 April 1915, continues as an annual commemoration of Australia's involvement in the First World War and other wars as well.

[50]Letter from C. E. W. Bean to Grattan, dated 22 March 1943, Box 37/file 2, item 16.

[51]Letter from Selden Rodman to Grattan, 2 April 1942. Location details could not be supplied.

The Grattan manuscript collection also provides valuable information about the genesis of parts of *Introducing Australia*. Chapter 1 is entitled "As I See Australia" and Chapter 2 "As Australians See It." In the book, Grattan states that for the second chapter he solicited representative views by questionnaire, and as the chapter unfolds he is specific about the kinds of people he approached: a judge, an economist, an historian, a librarian, a woman novelist, a distinguished scientist, a leading industrialist, a "woman leader," a banker, among others. A copy of the questionnaire is present in the Grattan manuscript collection, along with a list of the people to whom it was sent, so that many of the above types he refers to in the book as sources are identifiable.[52] A copy of Miles Franklin's reply contains comments by Australians on what they saw as among the most important issues of the time, including pessimistic and acerbic points about the dangers of Australian subordination to either England or the United States.

> 13 Australians today are filled with terror of Japan and Germany. Germany would be accepted in preference to Japan without any division of opinion. America would be welcomed.

> 14 Only the older generation of English garrisoners would suffer in being torn from English forms and placed under American. Very few exceptional people would long for their own individuality: 99 haven't any, and while young can be moulded to anything (*vide* German youth and its worship of Hitler). The young generation would be happy under USA and would be a fertile accretion to be speeded-up possibly to its (U.S.A.'s) worst characteristics, because young Australia is without thought, and already Americanised by the (to them) pleasant anaesthetic of American films.

In a cover letter, Franklin wrote, somewhat disgruntled: "I could give you a hundred such points but probably they are not what you want or will be covered more orthodoxly by business men & professors & politicians."[53]

For Grattan's *Australia* (1947), the manuscript collection traces the book's evolution from the first rough draft of contents, through emended outlines (which specify chapters and contributors) and general editorial guidelines for contributors, to the detailed editorial briefs for each chapter, contributors' reactions to these, and reports on writing progress.[54] As one of the earliest collections of essays by authorities in various fields, this was an important and pioneering volume, the scope of which was ambitiously wide and the

[52]Box 32/file 1, item 25.
[53]Letter from Miles Franklin to Grattan, 7 October 1940, Box 32/file 1, item 25.
[54]These materials are found throughout the Collection, with a number of items contained in Box 32.

contributors to which now read like a roll call of many of Australia's distinguished intellectuals of the day.

Grattan's *Australia*, part of a United Nations series, expressed both his own view as an historian and that of the series in its emphasis on the importance of current events and developments. In soliciting work for this publication, Grattan advised all contributors to devote a substantial portion of their chapters to contemporary incidents and issues. As a result, Grattan avoided the tendency in Australian studies of the time to dwell on the distant past. For instance, he encouraged H.M. Green in his chapter on "Literature" to devote about one third to a contemporary survey (the last twenty years).[55] Similarly, "a quarter" of Elkin's chapter on "Native Peoples" was to be concerned with the situation at the outbreak of the war.[56]

Since Grattan's editorial briefs were in general gratefully accepted as guidelines, the assumptions which the briefs embody and the way in which they measure up against the achieved results are a useful source of study. Some of the chapters—for instance, the Palmers on "Culture" and the one by Clive Turnbull on "Journalism"—were pioneering studies. For the chapter on "Culture," Grattan advised concentration on institutions and the process of cultural transmission, hoping thereby to elicit some comment on American influences. Grattan's brief for the chapter on "Literature" by H.M. Green was unconventional in suggesting that "About two thirds of the essay should be history, the balance a contemporary survey (ie the last twenty-odd years)."[57] Although Green was a little uneasy that contemporary writers would receive more space than they deserved, he did abide by Grattan's advice.[58] Previous to Grattan's book, such contemporaneity had not been offered in Australian histories.

A third area of the manuscript collection concerns documents that are related in various ways to Grattan's role as publicist, particularly for those activities which accompanied and drew on his own writing but which went on "behind the scenes." This role often involved him as adviser, publicizer, and sometimes publicizer-teacher, though not in any simplistic or pejorative sense. As an important area of Australian-American cultural relations, Grattan's work as publicist sheds light on what people of the one country found of interest in the other, on what images each built up, and on how these interests and images were cultivated and exploited. In Grattan's case, he could cater to specialized intellectual interests, to "the educated reader" (as in his *Harper's* articles), and to popular taste. With *Introducing Australia* he appealed to all three. In relation to Grattan's role as publicist-teacher, the manuscript collection contains records of his lectures at educational and other

[55]Box 32/file 8, item 5.
[56]Ibid.
[57]Letter from H.M. Green to Grattan, 8 August 1945, Box 35/file 3, item 29.
[58]Box 32/file 8, item 5.

institutions, his public lectures, and his numerous radio talks. Included as well is correspondence from a number of Australians who wrote to him shortly before his departure from Australia in August 1938 to thank him for his broadcasts. Also related to this aspect of his role as publicist-teacher are his many contributions to mass circulation American-"world"-encyclopedias (for example, *Encyclopedia Americana* from 1945 and its subsequent editions), either as a writer of principal entries or as a publisher's reader for contributions by others.

Yet another value of the collection lies in the information it provides about the use of Grattan's Australiana library by his fellow scholars. Generous in extending invitations for queries and in answering inquiries by letter, Grattan also made his library available for use at his home at Katonah, an hour's commuting distance from New York. Thus the Grattan library became a clearinghouse of information and a mecca for many Australian visitors. Queries came to Grattan from students writing theses, authors working on books, teachers, and the general public. For example, he aided Professor Bruce Sutherland of Pennsylvania State University, a pioneer in the teaching of Australian literature in the United States, in obtaining Australian books, lending him as well his personal copy of Joseph Furphy's *Such is Life* (1903), a novel considered *the* originating "classic" in the Australian literary tradition. Although it was not until 1948 that Grattan's edition of Furphy's novel appeared from the University of Chicago Press, the American's part in promoting the reputation of Furphy began as early as 1929. Grattan's role as a promoter of the Australian author, which is a story in itself, is also revealed by holdings in the HRHRC collection.

The Furphy case represents still another area of Grattan's activities: his advisory work as reader of Australian books for American publishers and as literary agent—probably honorary for the most part—for Australian authors seeking American publication. On 2 November 1929 Grattan wrote that there had been an outburst of Australian books in America and that "apparently it is still to go on, for I have read some of the books the publishers have had submitted to them . . . [and] they have read my booklet [*Australian Literature* (1929)] to get leads on what to look for."[59] P.R. Stephensen, an Australian "wild man of letters" who had been manager of the Mandrake Press, which published D.H. Lawrence's paintings in a banned edition, and who was an ardent nationalist—so ardent that he was interned in Australia for his "Australia First" activities during World War II—wrote to Grattan asking him to be American representative of his newly founded Endeavour Press in Sydney, which aimed at promoting Australian publishing and Australian books.[60] Like Grattan's early promotion of Furphy, this exchange with

[59]Letter from Grattan to Glen Hughes, 2 November 1929, Hughes Collection, HRHRC.
[60]Letter from P.R. Stephensen to Grattan, 27 May 1933, Box 35/file IA, item 3.

Stephensen took place even before the two met on Grattan's 1936-38 visit to Australia.

Among the authors in the literary field for whom Grattan acted as publisher's reader and/or agent were Xavier Herbert (author of *Capricornia* [1938]), K.S. Prichard, Miles Franklin, Dal Stivens, George Turner (author of *Scobie* [1959]), Mollie Skinner (collaborator with D.H. Lawrence on *The Boy in the Bush* [1924]), J.K. Ewers, William Baylebridge, David Martin, and Alan Moorhead (author of *Cooper's Creek* [1963]). Other authors, whose important works were on history or on general topics, included George Nadel (*Australia's Colonial Culture* [1957]), Sir Frederick Eggleston, T. Inglis Moore (*Social Patterns in Australian Literature* [1971]), and Manning Clark. Publisher W.W. Norton, who had been to Australia and maintained an interest in such writers as Henry Handel Richardson, was advised by Grattan on the American publication of Prichard's *Coonardoo* (1930) and Herbert's *Capricornia*—the first two influential novels to take up the cause of the Aborigines—and on Prichard's *Haxby's Circus*, which was published in America in 1931 as *Fay's Circus*.

The American branch of Cambridge University Press asked Grattan to serve as a reader of the first volume of Manning Clark's *A History of Australia* (1962), and Grattan provided, in typical style, a judicious report dealing with the work in some detail. He concluded with a judgment which time has confirmed: that it was a remarkable piece of historical writing (Grattan said "the most remarkable ever," and many would agree), indeed "'somehow great'."[61] But he added perceptively: "The terrible risk is that it will be received as simply eccentric." In a letter some years later, Clark wrote to Grattan to say that his debt to him was "greater than he might realize" and that Grattan's work "helped me to think about those 'qui trans mare currunt'." (The Latin phrase is a condensation of Horace's "coelum, non animum, mutant, qui trans mare currunt" as cited in full by H.H. Richardson in her 1930 novel *The Fortunes of Richard Mahony*. The full quotation translates as: "Those who cross the seas change their skies but not their hearts.")[62] According to a letter from Grattan to Victor Weybright, Clark had inscribed a copy of his *History of Australia*: "For Hartley Grattan who taught me many things."[63]

In 1955 B.W. Huebsch of Viking Press sent to Grattan, for his comments, an advance copy of Patrick White's *The Tree of Man*. Huebsch confessed that he had had a soft spot for Australia after having read K.S. Prichard's *Working Bullocks* (Viking, 1927).[64] Grattan sent an appreciative response to the White novel and part of his response was used on the dustwrapper of the published

[61]Report from Grattan to the American branch of Cambridge University Press, 4 March 1962, Box 27C/file 2, item 8.

[62]Letter from Manning Clark to Grattan, 21 March 1967, Box 27A/file 2, item 4.

[63]Letter from Grattan to Victor Weybright, 24 January 1964, Box 27C/file 1, item 36.

[64]Letter from B.W. Huebsch to Grattan, 11 May 1955. Location details could not be supplied.

book. Grattan's full statement foreshadowed the later wording of the Nobel judges' report for 1973.

> You may, if you want to, quote me as saying
> "The Tree of Life" [*sic*] by Patrick White is the most remarkable novel to come out of Australia in years. *It declares the maturity of a striking talent.* Here we have fiction founded in a deeply-rooted philosophy of life, accompanied by technical mastery of the means of rendering it vividly. White presents, in an Australian setting of striking authenticity, ordinary, useful, constructive lives lived as basically emotional experiences with gropings for a larger comprehension of it. Stylistically its concrete imagery is masterly. *Reading the book is a memorable experience. It asserts once again Australia's right to a place in world literature.*" [The underlined portions were printed by Viking.]

The American edition of *The Tree of Man* (1955) was the first of White's novels to be widely read anywhere. Grattan later would review White's *Voss* (1957) in the *New York Times Book Review* for 18 August 1957.

It is impossible to cover adequately the range of Grattan's activities as a publicist, but before concluding, I would add a few examples of his work on an official level. For a short time he was employed in the Washington Bureau of Economic Warfare, which was formed to combat Nazi economic aggression and to make the blockade of Germany more effective. Grattan was hired to give advice about the Pacific area but was forced to resign on 3 April 1942 after he was charged with being a communist, which was a foretaste of McCarthyism that was also to affect Grattan. However, the U.S. Office of War Information (OWI) later asked Grattan, as an Australian specialist, to write a weekly feature on the Pacific warfront, with emphasis on Australia's role, to be sent to OWI "outposts" in Sydney and Wellington. Grattan's activities often involved consulting for the Australian government's efforts to establish an Australian presence in New York. In 1948 he was quoted at length as saying that "the opening up of a channel for distribution of Australian books in this country is a most important event," since Australian literature was thriving and more Americans were aware of it.[65]

Given Grattan's substantial and varied contribution as Australia's main foreign observer, the HRHRC holdings are of value to anyone studying the history of Australia, of the South Pacific, and of the relations of both of these areas to the United States from the 1930s through the 1950s. These holdings provide essential information about the contexts in which Grattan wrote, his aims, and his network of Australian and American friends and activities, all of which fed into his writings. As he himself said, "one should examine the

[65]Quoted in a press release from the Australian Government Trade Commission, 17 November 1948, Box 33/item 1.

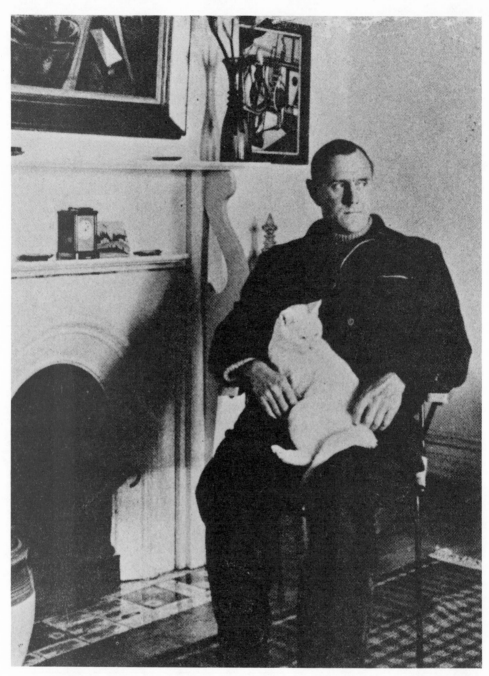

Photograph of Patrick White by Hugh Clunies Ross, on back of dust jacket of White's novel, *Voss* (Viking, 1957). *HRHRC Grattan Collection.*

purveyor of 'understanding,'" not simply the history itself, if one is to understand what the historian has written.[66] Grattan described himself as "a fellow who has made a desperate effort to understand the world in which we live,"[67] and it is this unremitting direction of an exceptional intelligence which gives impetus and significance to his contribution. But the Grattan Collection is notable not only for the information it contains about him but for the correspondence concerning the views of many important Australians in various fields. Also, the Grattan Collection is directly relevant to the study of some of the central issues of the time, especially the changing nature of Australian nationalism and liberalism and of their connections with what may be seen as the growth of American imperialism, which replaced British influence in the South Pacific Basin and in the adjacent Southeast Asian area. Although Grattan would have stressed as well the need for reciprocity, he would have endorsed Christina Stead's comment in 1972 that "with the Americans having so much influence now in Australia and using our men for their wars it would not be a bad idea for Australia to know something about this fierce, turbulent, gifted and dangerous country."[68]

[66]Box 27A/file 2, item 7.
[67]Two-page typescript entitled "What am I?," n.d. (unpublished), Box 27F/file 2.
[68]Quoted by Michael Wilding in "Christina Stead," *Australian Literary Studies* 11 (October 1983): 151.

Photograph of Miles Franklin (ca. 1904) in *Joseph Furphy: The Legend of a Man and His Book* (Angus & Robertson, 1944). *HRHRC Grattan Collection.*

"Tremenjus Good For What Ails Us": The Correspondence of Miles Franklin and C. Hartley Grattan

BY JILL ROE

"One of my most charming and enthusiastic reviewers says you must have a copy of *Up the Country*, because you collect Australian books and because she thinks you will be interested in this one," wrote "Brent of Bin Bin" to "Mr Hartley C. Grattan" in a letter dated, with characteristic obscurity, "February (some date or other)," probably 1930, possibly 1931.[1] "Brent of Bin Bin" gave Blackwood and Sons, Edinburgh, as his address and referred to himself as an ancient squatter—in Australian parlance, a rich and influential rural land-owner. The typewritten letter, signed simply "B of BB," explained that *Up the Country* was the first of four historical novels portraying pastoral life in Australia to 1928, adding a polite request for an opinion on its possible appeal to American readers. The mysterious Brent wanted to know why Grattan collected Australian books. "Is it simply that you are an inveterate collector. . . . Or do you find Australia interesting per se?" Outsiders found Australia extremely difficult to understand, since it was hard to see beyond the banality of Australian society and politics and because it was "so English" there seemed to be no differences; but, Brent averred, the differences were there to distill. Knowing that Grattan had recently published articles on Australian literature, Brent then posed a test question for the promising young American, asking if he possessed a copy of *Such is Life* by "Tom Collins." If Grattan could appreciate this then little-known Australian classic, he would be able to "grasp some of the differences to which I refer." Grattan recalled in 1937 that he passed Brent's test with flying colors; in his *Australian Literature* (1929), he had already discovered and praised *Such is Life* as a superb book, analogous to

---

[1]Letter from "Brent of Bin Bin" to "Hartley C. Grattan," February (n.y.), Grattan Collection, Harry Ransom Humanities Research Center, The University of Texas at Austin. All correspondence from Miles Franklin to C. Hartley Grattan in the HRHRC's Grattan Collection is located in Box 32/folder 1. Permission to quote from the Miles Franklin correspondence has been granted by the Permanent Trustee Company Ltd., Sydney, for the Estate of Stella M.S.M. Franklin.

Moby Dick.[2] Likewise, Grattan would later commend wholeheartedly the work of "Brent of Bin Bin."[3]

With this response Miles Franklin—for she it was who wrote under the pseudonym "Brent of Bin Bin," though this was not definitely established until well after her death in 1954—was greatly pleased. "[B]less the boy," she wrote in April 1931 to Alice Henry, her compatriot and comrade from Chicago days.[4] Even so, perhaps because Franklin was then on an extended world trip in pursuit of publishers, it seems that quite a time elapsed before she first wrote to Grattan in her own name, from London, about Australian literature. "I am so vitally interested in the subject and your treatment of it," she wrote in March 1932, something of an understatement coming from the author of *My Brilliant Career* (1901), not to mention *Up the Country* and two more Brent books since 1928.[5]

So begins a substantial and vigorous correspondence between legendary Australian writer Miles Franklin (1879-1954) and the American publicist C. Hartley Grattan (1902-1980). The correspondence spans over twenty years, from the early 1930s to the early 1950s, and was sustained virtually until Miles Franklin's death. Starting with the letter more or less out of the blue from "Brent of Bin Bin" (undoubtedly inspired by Melbourne critic Nettie Palmer and apparently the only surviving letter between Brent and Grattan), the exchange ends with a lively, mainly literary, and vintage Miles letter to the Grattan family on 17 May 1953, from 26 Grey St., Carlton, Sydney— Franklin's address from late 1932, when she had returned to Australia after nearly three decades of expatriatism.

[2]C. Hartley Grattan, "Tom Collins's *Such is Life,*" *Australian Quarterly* 10, no. 3 (September 1937): 67. In "Australian Literature" (*The Bookman* 68, no. 6 [August 1928]: 629), which was reissued as *Australian Literature* (Seattle: University of Washington Bookstore, 1929), with a foreword by Nettie Palmer, Grattan wrote: "Humor and hardship, denunciation and love, mingle in Tom Collins's *Such is Life* (1903), a trite title for a superb book. . . . Tom Collins (Joseph Furphy) is the nearest approach to a Herman Melville that Australia has produced, and the curious thing is that he actually does bring Melville to mind. He has the same capacity for mingling the most abstruse speculation—discursive essays in history, sociology, morals, anthropology, and Shakespearean criticism—with veridic glimpses of actuality. . . . Collins lacked fluidity, but he had vigor, originality and independence, which are vastly more important. He was an adventurer of the mind as well as an adventurer of the body. He was a speculative materialist and he was a great writer."

[3]Letter from Miles Franklin to Mrs. F.E. Hobson, London, 30 April 1933, Miles Franklin Papers, Mitchell Library, Sydney, vol. 23. Franklin thanks Mrs. Hobson for a review by C. Hartley Grattan in the New York *Nation,* "in which I was mentioned and Brent of Bin Bin tremendously commended." See also C. Hartley Grattan, "On Australian Literature, 1788-1938," *Australian Quarterly* 10, no. 2 (June 1938): 28.

[4]Letter from Miles Franklin to Alice Henry, 29 April [1931], Franklin Papers, vol. 16.

[5]Letter from Miles Franklin to C. Hartley Grattan, 18 March 1932, Grattan Collection, HRHRC.

Publisher's ad for Brent of Bin Bin's *Ten Creeks Run* (William Blackwood & Sons, 1930). *HRHRC Grattan Collection.*

These first and last letters from Franklin to Grattan are among the highlights of thirty-nine items of Franklin/Grattan correspondence preserved in the Grattan Collection at the Harry Ransom Humanities Research Center. The HRHRC collection contains thirty items of correspondence from Franklin to Grattan, plus nine third-party items from after 1938, *viz.*, eight letters from Miles Franklin to Grattan's mother and to his second wife Marjorie, and a notification in 1955 of Franklin's death the previous year from Magdalen Dalloz of Jacksonville, Florida, another Franklin friend from Chicago days. The Franklin/Grattan letters in the HRHRC collection appear to be the only original letters from Franklin to Grattan now extant, although copies of many are preserved in the Miles Franklin Papers in the Mitchell Library, Sydney, which also include copies of seventeen other letters to Grattan. In addition, the Miles Franklin Papers contain an estimated forty-nine letters from Grattan to Franklin, which illustrates what Franklin scholars well know, that Miles was always the better hoarder!

What Miles Franklin's letters to Grattan at the HRHRC show—and in this they are buttressed by the Franklin Papers, and for that matter by the Palmer Papers at the National Library of Australia, Canberra—is Grattan's continuing involvement with Australia after his first visit in 1927, especially in the early 1930s before he finally wangled a return as Carnegie fellow (1936-38), and the importance of Miles Franklin's support and encouragement throughout. The HRHRC letters also cast light on Franklin's own commitment to cultural nationalism in Australia, which she believed could be strengthened by closer links with America. It is obvious from Franklin's letters that despite a considerable age difference—Grattan was not yet thirty when he first heard from "Brent of Bin Bin" and Franklin was over fifty by then—a firm and mutually respecting friendship was early established. This friendship, which developed around Grattan's need for Australian support and Franklin's enthusiasm for radical America, had a dynamic bearing on the development of Australian culture.

Miles Franklin and Hartley Grattan first met in person in New York, in late 1932. Miles was returning to Australia from London via America, where she saw many old friends and tried (unsuccessfully) to interest American publishers in her work. She had previously sent *Old Blastus of Bandicoot* to Grattan, in March 1932, when she first wrote with a response to his open letter to Nettie Palmer on Australian literature, published in the Brisbane *Telegraph* for 19 December 1931. This book, she pointed out, was "written from the inside instead of the outside, as is the case with many novels with the Australian setting."[6] Never one to miss an opportunity, she added that she would have called it "Old Barry of Bin Bin" but had been beaten by Brent:

[6]Ibid. The full title of Franklin's book is *Old Blastus of Bandicoot: Opuscule on a Pioneer Tufted with Ragged Rhymes* (London: Palmer, 1931).

"The name is a great favorite of mine. . . . It occurs frequently among aboriginal names, in various versions, as ban ban, ben ben, boon boon and so on." When after two months Grattan had not replied, she wrote again, suggesting that America was not interested in Australian fiction, unlike Germany, and hoping they could meet when she passed through New York.[7] Grattan replied apologetically, noting that he had in fact reviewed *Old Blastus*, in the *New York Herald-Tribune* for 15 May 1932. He pointed out that the American reading public was not utterly indifferent to Australian fiction, taking an interest, for example, in Henry Handel Richardson. He did acknowledge that not enough had been done to promote Katharine Susannah Prichard. Grattan also replied with "Call me up immediately you land."[8]

All this delighted Miles, whose spirits were high, due to a bold new venture in Australian publishing by P.R. Stephensen, whom she had encountered in London.[9] As she believed that Australia was the coming field of fiction, likely to be "as absorbing as the Russian to that larger audience which must first be initiated by the omnivorous articulate people whose interest includes the world," Franklin found Grattan's remarks about the American market quite encouraging.[10] In a feisty note thanking him for "kind mention of my latest little book; and particular whoops for your observation that my first was neurotic," which she vigorously denied, she acclaimed him "a non-Australian authority on Australian books."[11] This was not simply a self-interested judgment. As she later recounted to Kate Baker, the self-appointed custodian of the reputation of Joseph Furphy ("Tom Collins") and his novel *Such is Life*, "I know Mr. Grattan's estimate of [Furphy's book] and consider it his charter to speak on Australian literature."[12]

For his part, Hartley Grattan was as welcoming in person as in print. In 1965 he recalled "going to somebody's apartment to meet Miles Franklin";[13] earlier, in 1934, Grattan had told Nettie Palmer that he liked Miles Franklin immensely.[14] Considering that many Australians were later to find the forthright freelancer rude, his perception and tact is notable: "When I met

[7]Letter from Miles Franklin to C. Hartley Grattan, 28 May 1932, Franklin Papers, vol. 23.

[8]Letter from C. Hartley Grattan to Miles Franklin, 12 June 1932, Franklin Papers, vol. 23.

[9]Craig Munro, *Wild Man of Letters: The Story of P.R. Stephensen* (Melbourne: Melbourne University Press, 1984), pp. 108-111.

[10]Letter from Miles Franklin to C. Hartley Grattan, 21 July 1932, Franklin Papers, vol. 23.

[11]Letter from Miles Franklin to C. Hartley Grattan, 1 September 1932, Franklin Papers, vol. 23.

[12]Letter from Miles Franklin to Kate Baker, 7 May 1933, Kennedy Papers, La Trobe Library, Melbourne.

[13]C. Hartley Grattan, "A Garrulity About Australian Literature Since 1927," *Meanjin* 24, no. 103 (December 1965): 409.

[14]Letter from Nettie Palmer to Frank Dalby Davison, 12 March 1934, *Letters of Vance and Nettie Palmer 1915-1963*, selected and edited by Vivian Smith (Canberra: National Library of Australia, 1977), p. 96.

Miles I *sensed* but was not told I was meeting Brent of Bin Bin. And as well as I got to know Miles in Sydney later on I never tried to find out if that was the case. I scrupulously respected her privacy—or mystification."[15] He inscribed for her his recently published study *The Three Jameses: A Family of Minds* (1932): "[To Miles Franklin] whose characters have a culture quite different from the Jameses but just as real and important."[16] (Perhaps he was thinking also of his grandfather, the "Novia Scotia laborer and farmer whose Remembered Sayings are Humorous and Luminous Truths," to whom *The Three Jameses* is dedicated.)[17]

In his version of their New York conversations, Grattan summarized several literary projects, notably a book on D.H. Lawrence in Australia, and canvassed the possibility of being able to arrange a return trip. He expressed himself candidly: "We are pretty low and Australia looms up as an escape if only I could find the money for a year there while this country straightens out or collapses altogether."[18] Could a sponsor be found? Nine hundred pounds, some of which he might earn himself from lectures, would enable him to do the job he had in mind, "i.e., to write a large book on the country after the manner of James Bryce's *American Commonwealth*."[19]

Reflecting on his survival as literary man during the Great Depression, Hartley Grattan described how his priorities were slowly reordered by bad times, from literature, politics, and economics to economics, politics, and literature. Australia, he recalled, faded to the periphery of his concerns, a recollection supported by his publications in the early 1930s and his appointment as editor of research for the New Deal organization, Harry Hopkins's Federal Emergency Relief Agency, 1934-35.[20] The Franklin/Grattan correspondence shows that up to August 1933 Grattan harbored hopes that another

[15]Grattan, "A Garrulity," p. 409.

[16]Letter from Miles Franklin to C. Hartley Grattan, 18 August 1936, Grattan Collection, HRHRC.

[17]The dedication is cited in *C. Hartley Grattan, One Man's Writing Over Fifty Years (1924-1974). A Checklist of an Exhibition Featuring Writings on American Literature, Education, Public Affairs, as Well as on the Southwest Pacific* (Austin: University of Texas at Austin, 1974), item 74 (no pagination), hereafter *Checklist*.

[18]Letter from C. Hartley Grattan to Miles Franklin, 6 December 1932, Franklin Papers, vol. 23.

[19]James Bryce, *The American Commonwealth*, 2 vols. (New York: Macmillan, 1927-28), first published in 1888, afterwards in numerous editions, and recently reissued in America. As stated in the introduction, this work aimed at presenting "a general view of the United States both as a Government and as a Nation" and its main theme was "the character, temper, and tendencies of the American nation." Bryce's plan of approach would have appealed to Grattan, *viz.*, "first to write down what struck me as the salient and dominant facts, and then to test, by consulting American friends and by a further study of American books, the views which I had reached" (p.8). Bryce's approach was positive: "America excites an admiration which must be felt upon the spot to be understood" (p. 10).

[20]Grattan, "A Garrulity," p. 409; *Checklist*.

Australian trip might be financed by a foundation. As her first biographer Marjorie Barnard noted, Miles Franklin worked to bring Grattan back to Australia.[21] She pursued likely avenues in Sydney while Nettie Palmer worked the more promising and plutocratic, but ultimately even more frustrating, boulevards of Melbourne.[22] But by June 1933 Nettie despaired, as well she might, given the hot-cold response of Herbert Brookes, a leading wealthy citizen and erstwhile first Australian trade commissioner to the United States.[23] (She opined, plausibly, that Grattan's radicalism alarmed people like Brookes; in an article in *Current History*, Grattan referred to representatives of the conservative side of politics in Australia as "disciplinarians.")[24] Miles, relieved to think that her failures with lesser lights in Sydney were not necessarily due to her own insignificance/ineptitude, wrote scathingly to Grattan about the literature professor who snaffled her copy of *Current History* and specifically queried Grattan's academic qualifications, and of a leading newspaper editor "embalmed in caution and fear of the present crisis."[25] Their efforts came to nothing, mainly because of what Miles called (reasonably enough, considering the times and her own small income) the "opulence" of Grattan's requirements.[26] No sponsor was forthcoming; and unlike Americans, Australians were not used to paying substantial sums for public lectures and other cultural services.

Nettie Palmer was probably right in thinking that, after her own efforts in Melbourne came to nothing, Grattan dealt mainly with Miles Franklin.[27] (On one occasion, in a letter preserved in the Franklin Papers and headed "Carlton, Wednesday," apparently written in mid-1933, Miles wrote to her reassuringly, "We'll hatch little Grattan out presently.") In writing to Grattan, Miles kept up the flow of commentary on Australian books—"I can read

---

[21]Marjorie Barnard, *Miles Franklin* (Melbourne: Hill of Content, 1967; New York: Twayne, 1967), p. 143.

[22]Letter from Nettie Palmer to Miles Franklin, 28 February 1933, and Miles Franklin to Nettie Palmer, 31 March 1933, Franklin Papers, vol 24. (Grattan had written to Nettie Palmer that Miles Franklin had full details of his "hare-brained schemes," PPS to letter, 6 December 1932, note 18 above).

[23]Letter from Nettie Palmer to Miles Franklin, 10 June 1933, *Letters of Vance and Nettie Palmer*, pp. 90-91. For Herbert Brookes, see *Australian Dictionary of Biography* (Melbourne: Melbourne University Press, 1979), vol. 7.

[24]C. Hartley Grattan, "The Australian Political Seesaw," *Current History* 37 (January 1933): 437.

[25]Letter from Miles Franklin to C. Hartley Grattan, 5 May 1933, Grattan Collection, HRHRC. Regarding his academic qualifications, Grattan replied "precisely none. And if I did . . . I should certainly feel somewhat disgraced"; Franklin responded sympathetically that she shared his opinion "but it wd not be gracious of a person like I—whose ignorance is totally unimpaired—to say so." Franklin Papers, 27 April and 21 June 1933, vol. 23.

[26]Letter from Miles Franklin to Nettie Palmer, 14 June [1933], Franklin Papers, vol. 24.

[27]Letter from Nettie Palmer to Frank Dalby Davison, 12 March 1933, *Letters of Vance and Nettie Palmer*, p. 95.

anything about Australia"—accompanied by off-the-cuff judgments. Confident of common ground, she noted in the case of Frank Dalby Davison's *Manshy* (1931) that it was "instinctively Australian in its fibre."[28] Franklin believed Grattan's radicalism would be "tremenjus good for what ails us";[29] and she never lost sight of the "big book" she hoped to see him write. On 14 March 1935, in a letter praising *The Three Jameses* as a work "in keeping with the estimate I formed of your courage and honesty," she wrote:

> Well, I still hope you may come again to us. No one of your standing has since visited us. We had Dr Wood (Cobbers), another angle, and there have been half a dozen people on small scholarships, making small investigations . . .[but] not in your class.[30]

It was a bad time for Australian literature, she reported. There had been visiting German professors, who might commend the musicality of Brent's *Back to Bool Bool* (1931) but were probably Nazis, and "a veritable blight" of "small grade Britons" in the universities. Reporting that one Professor Cowling ("Yowling") of the University of Melbourne had even declared that not much could be expected of literature in Australia, Franklin lashed out, "No one with any self-respect wd put up with such a driveller," adding that

> Yes, you must come again; this unique field remains your own, and it wd be a pity to give it away to lesser men. There are plenty of men, no doubt, who cd go through Australian literature and appraise it as ably as you did, but wherein you remain unrivalled was in your understanding of Australia as the possible source of a new literature, as evidenced by your feeling about *Such is Life*.[31]

The mature Miles Franklin deplored Australian cultural dependence and frequently satirized what she called "the garrison," meaning the anglophile cultural establishment. It may seem strange that she should court another overlord, American, in the person of Hartley Grattan. Her enthusiasm for Grattan's country might strike the modern ear as overdone, perhaps even slightly craven. However, Franklin's correspondence shows that she was never at a loss for a salient comment on America; for example, that it had not solved the problem of unemployment. At the time, Franklin was probably better placed than anyone else in Australia to appreciate what Grattan had to offer—better placed even than the patrician Nettie Palmer who usually, and

[28]Letter from Miles Franklin to C. Hartley Grattan, 5 May 1933. One-third of a sheet from this letter is in the HRHRC and contains the return address, the date, the salutation, and three paragraphs. The phrase quoted here appears in a copy located in the Franklin Papers, vol. 23.

[29]Letter from Miles Franklin to Nettie Palmer, 14 June [1933], Franklin Papers, vol. 24.

[30]Letter from Miles Franklin to C. Hartley Grattan, 14 March 1935, Grattan Collection, HRHRC.

[31]Ibid., p. 2.

with justification, is credited with Grattan's return as Carnegie fellow in late 1936.[32]

Biographical and cultural perspectives are relevant here. Miles Franklin grew up in the era when Americans were "radical cousins," spending her salad days in America, and retaining a special affection for the country for the rest of her life. In 1906, aged twenty-six, Franklin had left Australia to further her by then less than brilliant literary career. Thanks to the international feminist network, she found herself in Chicago in 1907 and for nine heady years, from 1908 to 1915, was employed by the National Women's Trade Union League on Dearborn Street. Late in 1915, unnerved by American attitudes toward the outbreak of World War I, she went to London, where in 1917 she joined the Scottish Women's Hospitals for Foreign Service and served for six months in Macedonia; and, despite mixed feelings about the imperial capital, stayed on for a decade, working and writing as she had done in Chicago. (No one knew about her writings in Chicago, partly because of her use of various imaginative *noms de plume*, such as "Mr & Mrs Ogniblat L'Artsau," which she used more than once, most notably for *The Net of Circumstance*, published by Mills and Boon, London, in 1915; read in reverse as "Austral, Talbingo," this pseudonym refers to Franklin's birthplace.) When she finally returned to Sydney in November 1932, after two trips there in the 1920s for family and literary reasons, she was welcomed by the literary fraternity, burgeoning but beleaguered, and committed herself to the cause of Australian literature. But her rich expatriate perspectives, combined with an eager loyalty to the spirit of the 1890s, especially to Joseph Furphy's legacy, made her impatient. "I am sicker and sicker of the colonialness of Australians. . . . Haven't a thought that isn't dictated from London," she once complained to expatriate poet and dear friend Mary Fullerton in London; and to an American friend she wrote, "We are way back in the stage USA was in before Sinclair Lewis came along and indulged in adult criticism."[33] Like many Australians before and since, Miles Franklin hoped to apply her experiences to a culture which still seemed hidebound, in the 1930s even retrogressive. Grattan, trained in the new frontier history, fostered by the stars of radical New York journalism, and honed by the great drama of the New Deal, seemed just the thing, a fast-forward no less.

[32]Grattan, "A Garrulity," p. 409; letter from Nettie Palmer to Frank Dalby Davison, 10 August 1936, *Letters of Vance and Nettie Palmer*, p. 139.

[33]Letter from Miles Franklin to Mary Fullerton, 13 April 1936, Franklin Papers, vol. 17. For biographical information, see *Australian Dictionary of Biography*, vol. 8; Verna Coleman, *Miles Franklin in America, Her Unknown (Brilliant) Career* (Sydney: Angus & Robertson, 1981); and Drusilla Modjeska, *Exiles at Home. Australian Women Writers, 1925-1945* (Sydney: Angus & Robertson, 1981). Letter from Miles Franklin to C.A.W. [Carrie Whelan], 22 July 1937, Franklin Papers, vol. 20. (It is interesting to note that Vernon L. Parrington published a paper on Sinclair Lewis in 1927 as No. 5 of the University of Washington chapbooks, and Grattan's *Australian Literature*, with an introduction by Nettie Palmer, appeared in the same series in 1929.)

Miles Franklin as a young woman, from her autobiography, *My Childhood at Brindabella: My First Ten Years* (Angus & Robertson, 1963). *HRHRC Grattan Collection.*

A trickle of publications through to the mid-thirties indicates Grattan's continuing commitment to Australia. No Australian correspondence seems to have survived for 1934, but if he abandoned hope of another visit at that time, it was but briefly. On the day of his divorce, 13 April 1935, he wrote Miles Franklin a forward-looking letter about "if and when I get a chance to revisit Australia," and then more confidently, "when I come." FERA work had widened his grip:

> When I come to Australia I shall be well primed with the investigatory spirit and technique and I very much fear that not only will the literary circles fall foul of me but the social critics as well. Nevertheless I shall continue to sharpen my understanding of what makes the wheels go round in capitalistic society in the hope that I can explain Australia more adequately.[34]

He reported that the troglodytes of the once proud Sydney weekly, the *Bulletin*, had been attacking him over a recent review of Australian books. But he was unperturbed, for he had never seen eye to eye with the *Bulletin* writers. They would have to look to their laurels, a prospect which no doubt pleased Miles Franklin, who lamented the decline of the *Bulletin* from its radical nationalist stance in the 1890s. "I like [the young] to be rebellious and if that is beyond them they cd at least be rowdy."[35]

Grattan's personal and professional support meant much to Miles Franklin as a writer. His sympathy for her domestic circumstances, which she said approximated those of a telephone girl in a busy office, marked him as an unusually sympathetic male. "I hope your remarks about domesticity do not mean that you are neglecting your proper work. It is only by production that the battles can be won," he wrote.[36] Grattan was an observer of, rather than a competitor in, the literary stakes; but it is hard to imagine an Australian male writing thus. Miles's appreciation is evident in her letter of 18 August 1936, the last written before hearing of Grattan's return as a Carnegie fellow. Grattan's inscription to Miles in *The Three Jameses*, previously mentioned, relieved her empty depression after a struggle with "a long thing," what turned out to be her prizewinning *All That Swagger* (1936), which she assured him was also written "from the inside, on Australia's own terms, in defiance of European postwar literary convention."[37] Grattan's critical standing with

[34]Letter from C. Hartley Grattan to Miles Franklin, 13 April 1935, Franklin Papers, vol. 23.

[35]Letter from Miles Franklin to C. Hartley Grattan, 25 June 1935, Franklin Papers, vol. 23. On the *Bulletin* (weekly, Sydney, 1880 to date) as a "great print circus" of the 1890s, see Sylvia Lawson, *The Archibald Paradox. A Strange Case of Authorship* (Ringwood, Victoria: Allen Lane, 1983).

[36]Letter from C. Hartley Grattan to Miles Franklin, 13 April 1935, Franklin Papers, vol. 23.

[37]Letter from Miles Franklin to C. Hartley Grattan, 18 August 1936, Grattan Collection, HRHRC.

Miles, who shared his sociological interests to a much greater extent than Nettie Palmer, is evident in her interest in the American's estimate of her writing: "You never answered my question as to the relative merits of *Red Heifer, Manshy*, and *Back to Bool Bool*."[38] She also wanted to know what he thought of Sydney poets Baylebridge and Brennan. She signed off with a characteristic flash of independence, rating the neglected nineteenth-century South Australian novelist Catherine Helen Spence above the generally commended Henry Kingsley.

Suddenly Grattan was coming. Cables flew back and forth and letters were *en route*. Miles was astonished to learn that he would have ten pounds a week for the "gorgeous work." (The average wage for Australian males in December 1937 was less than half that amount.)[39] She approved all his plans, to come via England where he could meet "all the emigres," to come the whole way by steamer, and to live in Sydney. She reassured him that the marital circumstances of his previous visit would not attract the gutter press, and she issued press releases. "Australia awaits you," she wrote him, at the same time alerting expatriates in London to this "very serious man who will be a great acquisition to the Vast Open Spaces of our culture."[40] (More restrained was her chortle to the Goldstein sisters in Melbourne: Grattan "takes himself so seriously.")[41] Nearly there, Grattan cabled from Adelaide praising *All That Swagger*: "Danny Delacy triumphant creation. Yarn with you first."[42]

C. Hartley Grattan arrived in Sydney 23 December 1936 on the "Narkundah." He was welcomed by what he later remembered as a curious delegation,[43] led according to the *Sydney Morning Herald* by Miss Stella Miles Franklin and Mr. P.R. Stephensen.[44] Grattan told the press that big business was opposed to Roosevelt to the point of viciousness and that thinkers in America were keenly interested in Australia. He mentioned among others his most recent book, *Preface to Chaos* (1935), an anti-war publication. It was the event of the week for Miles Franklin, but that was more or less the last she knew of him until sometime in January.[45] Apparently Grattan was whisked off

[38]Ibid.

[39]*Commonwealth Year Book* (1938), p. 560: average male wage 90 shillings 2 pence, December 1937.

[40]Letters from Miles Franklin to C. Hartley Grattan, 23 September and 23 October 1936, Franklin Papers, vol. 23; Miles Franklin to Guy Innes, 23 October 1936, Franklin Papers, vol. 24.

[41]Letter from Miles Franklin to "Dear Girls," 4 November 1936, Franklin Papers, vol. 10.

[42]Letter from C. Hartley Grattan to Miles Franklin, date stamp 19 December 1936, Franklin Papers, vol. 23.

[43]Grattan, "A Garrulity," p. 410.

[44]"Roosevelt's Victory. Visiting Author's Impressions," *Sydney Morning Herald*, 24 December 1936, p. 8.

[45]Letter from Miles Franklin to Kathleen Moneypenny, 30 December 1936, Franklin Papers, vol. 22; letter from Miles Franklin to Nettie Palmer, 31 December [1936], Franklin Papers, vol. 24; letter from Miles Franklin to Alice Henry, 9 March [1938], Franklin Papers, vol. 115.

by bohemian journalists, and when he apologized she wrote back staunchly:

> No, . . . neglect if any wd have been on my side and there was none. I deliberately left you to get certain bearings without interpolation which wd be lost in the first confusion. Babel is inevitable amid a nest of individualists. You are making splendid progress. I judge from the symptoms. With your equipment you cannot fail.[46]

Miles Franklin proved a great help with "bearings." She smoothed things over with the importunate widow of Louis Stone, whose Sydney larrikin novel *Jonah* Grattan had edited when it was reissued in New York in 1933, a disastrous timing; she sympathized with his disappointment in Australia and Australians and his horror of public meetings, praising his performances; and she told him homesickness was inevitable, that suffering brought knowledge and fellowship without which he might as well be an arid professor, and that it was a comfort to find him "as human and sensitive and vulnerable as myself."[47] When Grattan said he regretted ten years of preparation and doubted he could stay even twelve months, she wrote soothingly of his high purpose:

> No my dear, you will be here every minute of your two years and find them not enough for the big thing that you will make, and which will make you. Nowhere in human history is there record of such a phenomenon as this capricious and extensive continent staffed by a skeleton crew of ordinary beings stone blind and deaf to their extraordinary situation.[48]

Her response to his complaint that people regarded him as a mere thinking machine and never thought to introduce him to young ladies was to reflect that "the Australian scene is unnecessarily cluttered with men."[49] There were nice girls galore; but he should not mind to be a monk: "stick to your lessons, so that you wont be grizzling about waste of time [later]."[50]

In many ways Franklin was behaving like the sympathetic supervisor of a very promising young postgraduate student. "It is the combination of artist

[46]Letter from Miles Franklin to C. Hartley Grattan, 7 January 1937, Grattan Collection, HRHRC. Nevertheless, she had been irritated. See letter from Miles Franklin to Mary Fullerton, "[1936]," Franklin Papers, vol. 119.

[47]Letter from Miles Franklin to C. Hartley Grattan, 9 February 1937, Franklin Papers, vol. 23. See *Checklist*, item 100, and letter from C. Hartley Grattan to Miles Franklin, 17 August [1933], Franklin Papers, vol. 23. Letters from C. Hartley Grattan to Miles Franklin, Wednesday [10 February 1937], Franklin Papers, vol. 23, and from Miles Franklin to C. Hartley Grattan, 11 February [1937], Grattan Collection, HRHRC.

[48]Ibid.

[49]Letters from C. Hartley Grattan to Miles Franklin, [14 February 1937], Franklin Papers, vol. 23, and from Miles Franklin to C. Hartley Grattan, Monday [February 1937], Grattan Collection, HRHRC.

[50]Ibid., Franklin to Grattan.

and student that makes you so special," she wrote.[51] Grattan obviously regarded her as special, too, a close friend "who can 'take' anything."[52] In his blackest moments he thought of her as the only decent thing about Australia. Some people, offended by his criticisms, for example of agriculture, behaved as if Grattan was a sort of illegitimate son whom Franklin should discipline.[53] But Miles agreed with what Grattan had to say, and she continued with her discreet morale boosting. She even told him after a lecture in May 1937 "you looked very nice yesterday."[54] (About this time Grattan reported that his mother loved *All That Swagger*, adding cryptically "So you see!," and it was not long before a friendly correspondence was established between the two women.)[55]

Cultural and intellectual affinity carried the two through this unexpected early jumble. Miles might jibe that Grattan was "a touchy petted little beggar," make envious remarks about his happy position as a writer, and announce that she had a crow as big as a vulture to pluck with him; but his presence in Australia did her reputation no harm, and they had never agreed on everything, as shown by differences over the White Australia Policy as far back as 1933.[56] Grattan would react angrily to some unsatisfactory responses to his jaunty question from Townsville in July 1937: "Am I seeing Australia?," or perhaps to the view he had developed that "the future of this continent as far as population goes is not to be found in the outback"; but it was true that "only madmen like Stephensen" could possibly differ, and he sought Miles's opinion on his powers of observation. (He also offered "a private lecture.")[57] By September 1937 Grattan was in full swing, "raising bristles on all sides," to

[51]Letter from Miles Franklin to C. Hartley Grattan, 11 February [1937], Grattan Collection, HRHRC.

[52]Letter from C. Hartley Grattan to Miles Franklin, [14 February 1936], Franklin Papers, vol. 23.

[53]Letter from Miles Franklin to C.A.W. [Carrie Whelan], 22 July 1937, Franklin Papers, vol. 20.

[54]Letter from Miles Franklin to C. Hartley Grattan, 5 May 1937, Grattan Collection, HRHRC.

[55]Letter from C. Hartley Grattan to Miles Franklin, Friday [21 May 1937], Franklin Papers, vol. 23.

[56]Letter from Miles Franklin to C. Hartley Grattan, Tuesday night, Grattan Collection, HRHRC. On the White Australia Policy, in force from 1901 to the mid-1960s, see letter from Grattan to Franklin, 6 December 1932 ("I don't, as you guessed, sympathize much with the policy, think it mistaken economically and socially"), and her reply to Grattan, 29 March 1933 ("Perhaps neither of us has expressed all we mean on the White Australia policy. . . . Perhaps the mingling of Asiatic and European types would make a splendid race eventually. My mind is open on the question. But for the present, what are we to do, after striving for conditions above starvation level? Would you let the swarming Asiatics sans birth control devour U.S.A.?"), Franklin Papers, vol. 23.

[57]Letters from C. Hartley Grattan to Miles Franklin, 5 July and 11 July 1937, Franklin Papers, vol. 23.

Photograph of C. Hartley Grattan by Allied News Service, New York, late 1930s. On the back of the print, Grattan has written: "Marjorie sweetheart This may not be your idea of me. Pictures rarely are satisfactory in meeting the idea of those who know us best. But it is how the camera sees me! Hartley." *HRHRC Photography Collection.*

good effect according to Miles.[58] Her own hackles were up, too, on a matter pertaining to "Tom Collins." In this regard, as well, Grattan proved very useful.

Whether or not Grattan was getting on with "the big book"—"collate fearlessly and think deeply," urged supervisor Miles[59]—by late 1937 he had seen a good bit of Australia and he was making a mark in cultural affairs, with articles and introductions to significant Australian books, such as H.V. Evatt's *Rum Rebellion* and Tom Inglis Moore's *Six Australian Poets* (1938, unpublished until 1942), which advanced the important notion of the need for "a canon."[60] To Miles Franklin, Grattan's "Tom Collins's *Such is Life*," which appeared in the *Australian Quarterly* (September 1937), mattered most. In 1936 Jonathan Cape had published an abridgement of *Such is Life*, by Vance Palmer,[61] and while not objecting in principle to abridgement (this may be doubted), Miles thought what had been done "a heinous offence" and said so.[62] But she felt exposed to "the clique" and she wanted support, yet Grattan was unwilling to join local disputes, a highmindedness, however, that with P.R. Stephensen's wild ways would soon be eroded. (In the *New York Times* for 15 August 1937, Grattan did write critically of a case brought by Stephensen against the *Bulletin*.) However, Grattan was perfectly happy to have his unpublished preface to *Such is Life*, which had been languishing in the Mitchell Library, appear in the *Australian Quarterly* "at this strategic moment."[63] It was an oblique comment, not exactly what Miles wanted, but it served.

Grattan's participation in Australian intellectual life benefited Miles Franklin in another way. P.R. ("Inky") Stephensen had raised and then dashed her hope of a breakthrough in native publishing in the early thirties, and she quickly distanced herself from his erratic business activities. It was not a complete break, however; at least Stephensen was "rowdy," and Miles was fond of his long-suffering wife Winifred, whom she first met in America. "Yowling's" pronouncements, which prompted Stephensen's most significant

[58]Letter from Miles Franklin to C.A.W. [Carrie Whelan], 22 July 1937, Franklin Papers, vol. 20.

[59]Letter from Miles Franklin to C. Hartley Grattan, 14 July 1937, Grattan Collection, HRHRC.

[60]*Checklist*, items 107 and 128; Grattan, "A Garrulity," p. 415.

[61]See Robert Darby, "The Penguin and the Man-o'-War Hawk: Joseph Furphy's Critical Reputation, 1903-1947," *Australian Literary Studies* 8, no. 2 (October 1987): 213.

[62]Letter from Miles Franklin to C. Hartley Grattan, 5 June 1937, Franklin Papers, vol. 23. For Franklin's review of the abridgement, see *Bulletin*, 26 May 1937, p. 8, where she wrote *inter alia* "This is not abridgement; this is alteration of the text."

[63]Letters from Miles Franklin to C. Hartley Grattan, 14 July 1937, Grattan Collection, HRHRC, and from C. Hartley Grattan to Miles Franklin, 10 July 1937, Franklin Papers, vol. 23. Miles earlier judged the preface "magnificent," and arranged for its safekeeping in the Mitchell Library (Miles Franklin to Kate Baker, 12 February, 25 February, and 24 March 1937, Kate Baker Papers, National Library of Australia).

cultural statement, the swingeing *Foundations of Culture in Australia* (1936), refreshed the bonds between the two cultural nationalists; and Miles subscribed to his next venture, *The Publicist*, a periodical backed by wealthy Sydney businessman W.J. Miles. The first issue of *The Publicist* appeared in July 1936, the month the Spanish Civil War began. Its slogan was "Australia First," and its original aim was to keep Australia out of the next war; but it headed in a fascist direction. (Stephensen, a "hired pen," at first claimed the magazine was a preliminary to a true Australian publishing house.)[64] Miles was among the "puzzled patriots" in Sydney attracted by "Australia First," writing to a friend in London that an Australia First Party was "very much needed."[65] "Australia First" eventually led to the internment of Stephensen and some of his associates during World War II for supposed fifth column activities, a trumped up intelligence charge from which Stephensen's reputation never recovered. Franklin was fortunate to maintain sufficient intellectual distance to be untouched by the scandal.

From the outset Franklin had kept Grattan informed of "Inky's" literary enterprises, and Grattan did his best to support them in New York. He arrived in Sydney brimful of advice. (It will be recalled that Stephensen met the "Narkundah" when Grattan returned to Australia in 1936.) But Grattan soon rejected Stephensen's larrikin chauvinism and was outraged to find that Stephensen responded to criticism by dubbing him an "'enemy' of Australianness":

> What rubbish. He's his own enemy, what with making long lists of dubiously significant books, vaunting one value that it would take a metaphysician to define, and ignoring quality almost altogether.[66]

"And now," he added, "*The Publicist* adds the anti-Semitic note. Half a jump from Australian fascism!"

Franklin was then in some disagreement with Stephensen regarding Aborigines (thus, though Australians did not learn to capitalize the word until the 1960s), and she loathed his partner W.J. Miles as sexist. She agreed, "yes, there is always fascism in chauvinism." She knew that fascism was reactionary and anti-working class. Still, she responded coolly:

> I have evidently missed the anti-semitism to which you refer and have sent my copies of the magazine away. All who write to me of the

[64]Munro, *Wild Man of Letters*, pp. 170-171.

[65]Letter from Miles Franklin to Kathleen Moneypenny, 30 December 1936, Franklin Papers, vol. 22; Bruce Muirden, *The Puzzled Patriots. The Story of the Australia First Movement* (Melbourne: Melbourne University Press, 1968), p. 45.

[66]Letter from C. Hartley Grattan to Miles Franklin, 9 November 1937, Franklin Papers, vol. 23. When Grattan first saw Stephensen's list, he supposed Stephensen must be a good businessman (letter from C. Hartley Grattan to Miles Franklin, 5 May 1933, Franklin Papers, vol. 23).

Photograph of "Reso" (Resources) Tour Party railway car, by the Victorian Government Railways, Australia, n.d. *HRHRC Photography Collection*. By permission of the State Transport Authority, Melbourne, Victoria, Australia.

magarine are aggrieved but say they do not want to miss a copy, so I dunno; abeyance claims me.[67]

Grattan's hope that Miles Franklin might moderate Stephensen was an overestimate of her influence. Soon there would be a considerable spat between Grattan and the opportunistic Stephensen in *The Publicist*, more substantial than the "romp" Franklin mentioned to Alice Henry.[68]

On 30 January 1938 Grattan delivered a paper before the annual summer school of the Australian Institute of Political Science, Canberra, entitled "Could Australia Remain Neutral in a World War?" He argued that it might be able to do so in theory, but in practice would not act independently of Britain: "It is one of the characteristics of Australian life today, that all is confusion in the matter of how to formulate distinctively Australian policies in public affairs."[69] He was right in every respect, but Stephensen made merry in *The Publicist* for months (and it has been suggested had the better of the argument).[70] Grattan suffered "a dishonest portrayal of my position" and having put his case again in *The Publicist* for 1 April 1938, to no avail, finally wrote Stephensen off as a madman.[71]

Hartley Grattan's interpretation of political trends was of deep interest to Miles Franklin. At this time she may well have experienced a conflict of loyalties, being "agin" all wars; and she certainly was confused politically, caught by the contradictions of liberalism, maybe also by disastrous division in the New South Wales Labor Party. Writing to Grattan's mother in January 1938, Miles reported that she had heard "his Nibs" on the neutrality question, broadcast that day from Canberra, and "he was up to the subject."[72] She expressed disappointment that she did not see more of him, hastening to add that it was her loss entirely; he no longer needed the association, having found many congenial friends among forward-looking people "who thought as much of his visit of study to us as I did myself." She also expressed confidence in his work: "I am sure he will be famous in America following his report." Maybe, she speculated, he would do something to stimulate Australia to salvation,

[67]Letter from Miles Franklin to C. Hartley Grattan, 11 November 1937, Grattan Collection, HRHRC.

[68]Letter from Miles Franklin to Alice Henry, 9 March [1938], Franklin Papers, vol. 115.

[69]C. Hartley Grattan, "Could Australia Remain Neutral in a World War?," in *Australia's Foreign Policy*, ed. W.G.K. Duncan (Sydney: Angus & Robertson, in conjunction with the Australian Institute of Political Science, 1938), p. 148.

[70]See, for example, P.R. Stephensen, "Could Australia be Neutral? C. Hartley Grattan Asks and Answers a Question," *Publicist* (Sydney), 1 March 1938, pp. 3-7, and subsequent issues; Munro, *Wild Man of Letters*, p. 189.

[71]C. Hartley Grattan, "'Could Australia Be Neutral?' A Foreigner on 'The Bunyip'," *The Publicist* (Sydney), 1 April 1938, p. 10. (This article outlines disagreements with Stephensen). C. Hartley Grattan to Miles Franklin, "Friday" [postmark 29 April 1938], Franklin Papers, vol. 23.

[72]Letter from Miles Franklin to Mrs. Grattan (C.H. Grattan's mother), 30 January 1938, Grattan Collection, HRHRC.

though basically Australians must do it themselves: "peoples, like people, have in the final analysis to save themselves from within. Dynamics cannot be applied like a poultice." She was eager to discuss matters with Grattan, as when she invited him to accompany her on her annual Easter outing to the amphitheatre at the northern Sydney suburb of Castlecrag built by the Chicago architect-planners Walter Burley Griffin and his wife Marion Mahony Griffin:

> I do so want to discuss with you your closing address and especially the spoken end concerning politics—most arterial and thoughtful. . . . Congratulating you on that foretaste of your final premises.[73]

Of ensuing conversations, no evidence survives, but Franklin continued to note Grattan's commentaries, particularly the theme "Australia awaits a cue."[74] One thing is clear: Grattan's prescriptions were a world away from those offered by Stephensen.

In her second letter to Grattan's mother, a "flippant screed" of April 1938, Franklin said blandly that she had seen Hartley several times lately and that his work was going well; they had had a pleasant lunch at a friend's beach house recently "to settle the affairs of Australia in relation to the universe."[75] At that turbulent period in Grattan's affairs, it is conceivable that he and Miles Franklin might have sometimes found themselves at cross-purposes, but during his time in Sydney she always sympathized when ill-conceived attacks were made on his integrity. Like Grattan, Franklin deplored mere bad manners. The way she later recalled to him their lunch together suggests that he was a good influence politically.

> You may remember one Sunday at Palm Beach I was asked as to my political orientation and you helped me out of my nebulosity. That awakened me from drifting, and, though the war increased and for a time caused a relapse into confusion, I now have my mind clear . . . .[76]

[73]Letter from Miles Franklin to C. Hartley Grattan, 12 April 1938, Grattan Collection, HRHRC. For the Griffins, see *Australian Dictionary of Biography*, vol. 9.

[74]Letter from Miles Franklin to C. Hartley Grattan, 19 July 1938, Grattan Collection, HRHRC. The theme "Australia awaits a cue" appears in Grattan's "Could Australia Remain Neutral in a World War?," p. 148, with a reference to *Current History* (December 1937). See also his "The Future of Australia," *Australian Quarterly* 10, no. 4 (December 1938).

[75]Letter from Miles Franklin to Mrs. Grattan, 28 April 1938, Grattan Collection, HRHRC.

[76]Letter from Miles Franklin to C. Hartley Grattan, 18 September 1940, Grattan Collection, HRHRC. For an early defense of Grattan, see a letter from Miles Franklin to Mary Fullerton, 23 February 1937, Franklin Papers, vol. 17: "I have to admit that he is rude but oh so penetrating and true. He finds conditions appalling and says so just like a cross child." See also a letter from Miles Franklin to Guy Innes, 17 August 1937, Franklin Papers, vol. 24: "Grattan has been childishly and vulgarly and ignorantly attacked by the *Bulletin* and affronted by the University [of Sydney] which wd not make known his course of lectures because he said [our farmers] were 15 years behind the times."

The gratitude was mutual. On one occasion Grattan observed "Whenever I see you in print I always read the piece with confidence that I am really learning something," and on 29 April 1938 he wrote that her presence in Australia was one of the very few things that reconciled him to her country.[77]

The Carnegie fellow's time was running out. Grattan, tearing about the country and publishing numerous articles, turned to Miles for help with last minute research. Could volunteer notetakers be found? Miles hailed this "grand plan" with heavy irony and nothing more seems to have been said of it.[78] Anticipating his departure, she wrote, "I shall miss his presence in Australia keenly but so long as he is in the world & healthy & strong all is well," an overwrought but understandable way of putting it as she was then grieving over her mother's death a month earlier, on 15 June 1938.[79] "Dreadful that we are so soon to lose your understanding and sympathetic presence" was how she put it to Grattan.[80]

He sailed on 5 September 1938, having accumulated "an incredible mass of material" according to an undated letter from him in the Franklin Papers written, according to an annotation in Miles's hand, on 29 April 1938. Miles saw him off. Very likely, as he once predicted, she was one of the last to whom he talked in Australia, "as you were one of the first."[81] Miles said she felt his going "like a bereavement—snapping a paper ribbon with my beloved America," and to write a farewell letter, presumably to catch him in New Zealand, was like a reprieve.[82] Brooding on the futility of mere technology, still boosting his spirits, she offered some final advice: "Everything has to be brewed out of yourself. . . . I have understood your coming to us and hope you will come again."

Grattan must have received the letter. Eight days later, on 14 September 1938, Franklin was writing again to protest he had misunderstood her comment on technology. It wasn't a case of deracinated idealism; but there would be no happy outcome without goodwill and that was not created by pure intelligence. It seemed as if their conversations would continue *ad infinitum*, especially from the following:

> You'd like to shake Australia or give her a kick in the pants: you have
> earned the right to feel like that by going deeply into our strange
> malaise of inaction—our lack of any action off a mainspring of our
> own. You will take it out in controversy. Being in a different kind of

[77]Letters from C. Hartley Grattan to Miles Franklin, Sunday [November 1937?] and 29 April 1938 [postmark], Franklin Papers, vol. 23.

[78]Letter from Miles Franklin to C. Hartley Grattan, 27 April 1938, Franklin Papers, vol. 23.

[79]Letter from Miles Franklin to Mrs. Grattan, 21 July 1938, Grattan Collection, HRHRC.

[80]Letter from Miles Franklin to C. Hartley Grattan, "Saturday," Grattan Collection, HRHRC.

[81]Letter from C. Hartley Grattan to Miles Franklin, 17 April 1938, Franklin Papers, vol. 23.

[82]Letter from Miles Franklin to C. Hartley Grattan, 6 September 1938, Grattan Collection, HRHRC.

confinement (for life is so complex and so are we that there are none free but the animal primitives) I use the only weapon to my hand, and if you'll think again you'll see that the end of my novel [*All That Swagger*] garners the Australian political and mental miasmata in a way to make it a work of realism. . . . I left my Australians in the same great eroding desert that baffles you and me awaiting leadership, or dictatorship or another depth of colonial mental subjugation. . . . You'll come again and be welcomed astonishingly. . . .[83]

So it turned out, for Grattan returned briefly in September 1940, commissioned by the American Institute of Current World Affairs.[84] The news pleased Miles Franklin; but she was upset by the onset of war, which she saw in the light of 1914 as a "relapse of that collapse." She was also distracted by a difficult collaboration with Kate Barker on a biography of Furphy: "I am sure that you are more *au courant* with Australian affairs than I am at present. I must keep to my burrow with this biography. How I should like to discuss it with you!"[85] The old spark was alive, but war censorship made her grumpy and she harped on old themes:

> Something more than a rabbit birthrate and men applied to lethal weapons is called for. We get no outside nourishment here now in articles by thinkers, which leaves me free to think my own thoughts, though censorship does not leave me free to express them to you.[86]

She perked up when he arrived and asked her to lunch at the Hotel Australia.[87] "What a delight it is to have you here again. . . ."[88] He found time to read and commend the Furphy manuscript, and he also circularized a number of prominent Australians for assistance with a talk intended to explain Australia to Americans, asking for eight to ten points from each. Miles easily managed ten points—"I cd give you a hundred such points but probably they are not what you want or will be covered more orthodoxly by business men and professors"—beginning with the White Australia Policy ("Desirable, provided it could also be a right Australia," but "How enforceable except as a

[83]Letter from Miles Franklin to C. Hartley Grattan, 14 September 1938, Grattan Collection, HRHRC.

[84]"Hartley Grattan and Australian Backbones," *Smith's Weekly*, 24 August 1940, p. 8.

[85]Letter from Miles Franklin to C. Hartley Grattan, 18 March 1940, Grattan Collection, HRHRC.

[86]Letter from Miles Franklin to C. Hartley Grattan, 25 July 1940, Grattan Collection, HRHRC.

[87]Telegram from Miles Franklin to C. Hartley Grattan, 11 September 1940, Grattan Collection, HRHRC.

[88]Letter from Miles Franklin to C. Hartley Grattan, 18 September 1940, Grattan Collection, HRHRC.

colony of Great Britain or a protectorate of USA?") and ending with some grim thoughts about mental vassalage to London, not improved if replaced by native exploiters or American bag men.[89] Departing New Zealand, Grattan confessed that Australian politics still baffled him, yet he saw the coming American-Australian alliance clearly, the first to do so.[90]

"I have seen Hartley and found as always great pleasure and congeniality in an exchange of ideas," Miles wrote to Grattan's mother (who from this letter was now apparently a friend of Miles's federal member, the redoubtable Dr. H.V. Evatt).[91] By way of explaining to Mrs. Grattan her son's attraction to Australia, Miles drew on her own experiences, as she had so often in 1937 to cheer Grattan:

> If we take a big journey to any place when young that place is part of the enchantment of youth—we always want to go back. If we leave the returning too long it is heavy with poignant sadness. Hartley didn't. He came back soon enough to pick up threads . . . and to gain a thorough hard-won knowledge of the people: and, he has returned now, again, soon before his information and interest have had time to slump. . . . [Australia] has become his country, his subject; he is in a fair way to be *the* expert on Australia.[92]

Australia she said was unique, sufficiently complex to engage an intelligent mind, but presenting no language barrier. In another wartime letter, to Grattan's second wife Marjorie, with whom she was now corresponding, Franklin wrote that "Hartley knows ever so much more about Australian literature than I do," which is perhaps the flattering beginning to a telling attempt at analysis of personal affinity:

> He is representative of a new synthesis in human intellectuals—both literary and sociological. They—the litterateur and the sociologist— have been separate and the reformer has been a great menace to the artist in the past. I have of old said wrathfully that a reformer would sacrifice a Bernard Shaw to lick postage stamps on his (the reformer's)

[89]Letter from Miles Franklin to C. Hartley Grattan, 7 October [1940], and enclosure, Grattan Collection, HRHRC.

[90]Letter from C. Hartley Grattan to Miles Franklin, 14 November 1940, Franklin Papers, vol. 23; "Hartley Grattan and Australian Backbones," *Smith's Weekly*; *Checklist*, item 74; and "An Australian-American Axis?," *Harper's Magazine* 180 (May 1940).

[91]Letter from Miles Franklin to Mrs. Grattan, 1 October 1940, Grattan Collection, HRHRC. Dr. Herbert Vere Evatt (1894-1965) entered federal politics in 1940 as member for Barton, Miles Franklin's electorate, and was Attorney General and Minister for External Affairs of the Commonwealth of Australia during the Labor administration, 1941-1949. He was president of the General Assembly of the United Nations Organization, 1948-49. For a portrait by C. Hartley Grattan, see "Evatt of Australia," *Asia and the Americas* 55, no. 10 (October 1945): 474-477.

[92]Letter from Miles Franklin to Mrs. Grattan, 28 October 1940, Grattan Collection, HRHRC.

pesky dull circulars about some social ill. The two minds or con-
sciences welded will make a doubly powerfully-functioning being in
any new order; and C.H.G. is a forerunner. . . .[93]

Miles Franklin and C. Hartley Grattan never met again, though they kept
in touch. There was a flurry of letters in 1942-43, with books exchanged and
Miles wanting Grattan to find a publisher for all *six* Brent books.[94] Grattan,
who was keeping busy "these insane days" preparing a "large anthology" on
Australian social and literary development, was unable to help, but he
remained encouraging: maybe things would improve after the war.[95] These
were hardly times for gossip; all Miles dared say about Stephensen's
internment was that "Inky was caught up in a raid. . . ."[96] (Grattan had been
attacked in Washington just then also, simultaneously as a Communist and a
Nazi sympathizer.)[97] Although to hear from Grattan was always a treat, the
thought of America comforted Miles Franklin only somewhat, as during the
collapse of Singapore, February 1942, a turning point in Australian history:

> . . . Japan has decided to gamble on Asiatic conquest. If America does
> not decide to forgive her for her treble and double talk she will get
> that lesson which she nor the world will not forget, but ah, what it will
> cost us.[98]

It is no surprise to read in Franklin's letter to Hartley Grattan of 19 December
1946 that she "went mute" after 1943: "I dislike being broken into by
censors."[99] However, there was a great expansion in Miles Franklin's always
vast correspondence after World War II, which was due to the sentiment she
expressed at that time, when renewing contact with the Grattans: "It is time
we took up the thread of our conversation again, if it is not permanently
broken."[100] The thread was not broken; but it now ran very thin. Grattan's 1943
letter is, apparently, his last extant missive to Miles Franklin, with only
Christmas cards from the Grattans preserved thereafter. Only one letter, and
a fragment of a letter, from Miles Franklin to the Grattans survive after 1946.

---

[93]Letter from Miles Franklin to Mrs. Marjorie Grattan, [probably 1940], Grattan Collection,
HRHRC.

[94]Letter from Miles Franklin to C. Hartley Grattan, 11 August 1942, Grattan Collection,
HRHRC.

[95]Letter from C. Hartley Grattan to Miles Franklin, 17 August 1943, Franklin Papers, vol. 23.

[96]Letter from Miles Franklin to C. Hartley Grattan, 8 June 1942, Grattan Collection, HRHRC.

[97]Letter from C. Hartley Grattan to Miles Franklin, 1 October 1942, Franklin Papers, vol. 23.

[98]Letter from Miles Franklin to Hartley, Marjorie, and Rosalind Grattan, 10 February 1942,
Grattan Collection, HRHRC.

[99]Letter from Miles Franklin to C. Hartley Grattan, 19 December 1946, Grattan Collection,
HRHRC.

[100]Ibid.

What Franklin thought of Grattan's book *Introducing Australia* (1942), which contains one of her ten points of 1940, is unknown. It arrived in 1943, but she was too busy to read it; she had had a hint that if she completed the Furphy manuscript it might "get into the paper quota."[101] There is no letter reacting to his edited work, *Australia* (1947), presumably the anthology mentioned in 1943, nor to the American edition of *Such is Life*, which finally appeared in 1948 after some twenty-five years' endeavor by Baker, Franklin, and Grattan. (Maybe Miles had given up at last on Furphy: "Poor old Furphy is now really dead as evidenced by the dominies beginning to rummage in his dust," she wrote in 1946.)[102] Grattan's major work, a two-volume history of the southwest Pacific in 1963, came too late for Miles Franklin. Nor was it really the "big book" on Australia she envisaged in the 1930s.

In what seems to have been a penultimate letter sometime in the early 1950s, Franklin was again urging Grattan to visit Australia to keep him "tops," and proffered the highest praise: he had shown "an interest and understanding equalling that of a native son."[103] "Well, Hartley me jool" begins her last report on the Australian literary scene, dated 17 May 1953.[104]

Hartley Grattan always spoke up for Franklin/Brent, and for Furphy. He livened things up in Australia in the late 1930s, and from the 1940s he served extensively as interpreter of Australia to the American people, and as American friend of Australian intellectuals. Even though Grattan remained a generalist and the Cold War negated Franklin's hope that he would be a forerunner of a new type of intellectual, when, in later years, he conceptualized his long-maturing view of the development of Australian culture and turned his remarkable archive of Australiana into a research collection at the Humanities Research Center, the opportunities for critical exchange between Australia and America, which the two correspondents had in mind, were achieved at last.[105]

[101]Letter from Miles Franklin to C. Hartley Grattan, 3 March 1943, Grattan Collection, HRHRC.

[102]Letter from Miles Franklin to C. Hartley Grattan, 19 December 1946, Grattan Collection, HRHRC. See Darby, "The Penguin and the Man-o'-War Hawk," p. 222.

[103]Letter from Miles Franklin to C. Hartley Grattan, incomplete letter, undated [early 1950s], Franklin Papers, vol. 23, p. 305.

[104]Letter from Miles Franklin to C. Hartley Grattan, 17 May 1953, Grattan Collection, HRHRC.

[105]C. Hartley Grattan, Introduction to George Nadel's *Australia's Colonial Culture* (Cambridge, Mass.: Harvard University Press, 1957); *The Southwest Pacific to 1900* and *The Southwest Pacific Since 1900* (Ann Arbor: University of Michigan Press, 1963), passim; and "Notes on Australian Cultural History," *Meanjin* 33, no. 3 (1974).

Joseph Furphy, from *Joseph Furphy: The Legend of a Man and His Book* (Angus & Robertson, 1944), by Miles Franklin in association with Kate Baker. The caption reads: "Joseph Furphy (1889). Before he became 'Tom Collins'." *HRHRC Grattan Collection.*

"I Hope Here Be Truths": R.G. Howarth as Editor of Joseph Furphy

By Robert Zeller

In 1945, the Australian literary journal *Southerly*, edited by R.G. Howarth, published a special number paying tribute to Joseph Furphy. In the "Preamble" to the issue, Howarth notes that a revived interest in Furphy's work seemed to have taken place with the centenary of the author's birth (in 1843): Furphy's major work, *Such is Life*, had been reissued in 1944;[1] also in that year there appeared a Furphy biography by Miles Franklin in collaboration with Kate Baker;[2] and 1946 would see the publication of *Rigby's Romance*, an excised portion of *Such is Life*.[3] Howarth comments that "The outstanding remaining necessity is a collection of Furphy's short stories, essays and letters."[4] The R.G. Howarth Collection at the Harry Ransom Humanities Research Center contains materials that shed light on the publication history of Furphy's writings, including Howarth's editorial work on *Rigby's Romance* and *The Buln-buln and the Brolga* (the latter also cut from *Such is Life*, and published separately in 1948), and on his unsuccessful attempts to bring Furphy's short stories into print.[5] The two most prominent features of the Furphy material in the Howarth Collection are the letters, which are mostly to Howarth and concern matters relating to Furphy, and Howarth's typescripts of Furphy's stories, some of which remain unpublished. In addition, the Howarth Collection includes a manuscript of what appears to be part of an unpublished, previously unnoted Furphy short story.

Joseph Furphy's *Such is Life* (first published in 1903) has long been considered a classic of the national literature. Purporting to be "annotations" by Tom Collins of randomly selected entries from his diary for 1883-4, the

---

[1] Joseph Furphy, *Such is Life* (Sydney: Angus and Robertson, 1944).

[2] Miles Franklin and Kate Baker, *Joseph Furphy: The Legend of a Man and His Book* (Sydney: Angus and Robertson, 1944).

[3] Joseph Furphy, *Rigby's Romance: A "Made in Australia" Novel* (Sydney: Angus and Robertson, 1946).

[4] R.G. Howarth, "Preamble," *Southerly* 6, no. 3 (1945): 3.

[5] For an overview of the Howarth Collection, see Joseph Jones, "From Sydney to Cape Town to Austin: The R.G. Howarth Collection," *The Library Chronicle* 13 (1980): 65-69. Boxes 14 and 15 in the Howarth Collection contain the materials relating to Furphy.

novel is instead an intricately interconnected series of yarns—or rather one long, convoluted yarn—with characters reappearing and incidents recounted in one chapter or reflecting on those in another. As "Deputy-Assistant-Sub-Inspector" for the New South Wales government, Collins has traveled through the Riverina region in the southwestern part of that colony, and as a result, he can present the reader with a panorama of Riverina life, with all classes of society represented, from the lowly swagman to the lordly station owner. The most notable characterizations are of the bullock-drivers: Furphy's novel gives the reader an intimate depiction of life on the track with those engaged in the hauling trade.

Such is Life also marks the first and most complete use of the Australian yarn as a structural device in an extended work of fiction, proceeding at a leisurely pace, with long digressions repeatedly leading away from the main story line. Throughout the novel, the reader must stay alert to the connections among the various yarns—connections of which even the narrator Collins is seemingly unaware. For example, Collins does not know the true identity of Nosey Alf, and the latter's long scene with the boundary rider in chapter 6 takes on a great deal of irony because Collins fails to identify Alf Jones as Molly Cooper. The reader, however, can make the identification easily because Molly's brother has told the story in chapter 1 of her accidental disfigurement and subsequent disappearance and because Furphy supplies abundant clues throughout the scene. Collins also does not realize, as does the reader, that Warrigal Alf (Alf Morris) is the suitor who deserted Molly after the accident. In a sense, then, Furphy has the reader collaborate with him in judging Collins as an imperfect narrator. At the same time, by implication the reader comes to see that he or she is also living in a world where it is not always apparent to the participants how events connect to or reflect upon one another.

Because of its immersion in the local scene and its use of the yarn structure, Such is Life can be difficult to follow; indeed, it can be almost impenetrable to the non-Australian reader. In a letter to J. F. Archibald of the Sydney Bulletin, which eventually published the novel, Furphy characterized his work in the now-famous phrase, "temper, democratic; bias, offensively Australian,"[6] and in a sense the novel is a test of one's Australianness as a reader.

Such is Life was never a commercial success, and even with the novel's and its author's reputations secure, it still did not enjoy a wide readership. Because of this, Such is Life was the only work by Furphy to be published in book form during his lifetime. Although a number of his short stories appeared in various magazines, and he hoped to publish Rigby's Romance and The Buln-buln, no publisher was willing to take a further risk on a commercially

[6]John Barnes, Foreword, Such is Life by Joseph Furphy (Sydney: Angus and Robertson, 1986), p.v. Collins announces his intention on p. 2, to "undertake the annotation of a week's record," but he later changes his plan when he deems it prudent.

unsuccessful author.[7] After Furphy's death in 1912, it was up to his friends and admirers to continue efforts for publication of his writings. Chief among these was Kate Baker, who had first met Furphy in 1886 in Shepparton, Victoria, where she had gone to teach school. Baker devoted most of her life (she lived until 1953) to promoting Furphy's work and to trying to arrange for its publication, and in 1916 she did manage to publish a volume of Furphy's poems.[8] Thirty-six of the letters in the HRHRC's Howarth Collection are from Baker to Howarth, spanning the period from 1945 to 1953, during which time Howarth edited *Rigby's Romance* and *The Buln-buln and the Brolga*. The letters reveal Howarth's efforts to put together a collection of Furphy's stories, an enterprise in which Baker also was obviously interested. In 1926 Baker had sent a collection of fourteen Furphy stories to a London publisher, only to have them rejected.[9] Except for the first reissue of *Such is Life* in 1917 and abridgements of *Rigby's Romance* in 1921 and of *Such is Life* in 1937,[10] the efforts of Furphy's admirers to bring his work into print met with little success until the 1940s.

The first of the "new" Furphy material to be published was the unabridged version of *Rigby's Romance*, which appeared in 1946 and was edited by Howarth. *Rigby's Romance*, part of the original manuscript of *Such is Life*, was removed at the suggestion of editor A.G. Stephens, after which Furphy reworked it into a separate novel, which was published in 1905-6 as a serial in *The Barrier Truth* of Broken Hill, New South Wales. In the novel, a group of men gather at the Murray River to fish for a thirty-pound cod reputed to be in the area, telling in the meantime a series of tales of failed love affairs. As the book progresses, the conversation becomes dominated by the American, Jefferson Rigby, who holds forth on the virtues of state socialism. Since *The Barrier Truth* was sympathetic to the cause of labor, this philosophical aspect of the novel made the newspaper a natural place for publication. The reader coming to *Rigby's Romance* from *Such is Life* is on familiar ground, for several characters reappear, including narrator Tom Collins, and the novel develops themes present in the longer work, such as egalitarianism, the need to help one's fellow man, the delusions of romance, and the clash between philosophy and its practical application.

A number of letters in the Howarth Collection relate to the publication history of *Rigby's Romance*. In March 1945, Kate Baker wrote to Howarth,

[7]"Joseph Furphy," *The Oxford Companion to Australian Literature*, eds. William H. Wilde, Joy Hooton, and Barry Andrews (Melbourne: Oxford University Press, 1985).

[8]*The Poems of Joseph Furphy*, ed. K[ate] B[aker] (Melbourne: Lothian, 1916). A few poems not in this collection are in the Howarth papers: a copy of "The Wayfarer," which Howarth later published in *Biblionews*, and "My Birthday. An Ollapodrida," in typescript.

[9]Franklin and Baker, *Joseph Furphy*, p. 170.

[10]Joseph Furphy, *Rigby's Romance* (Melbourne: De Garis, 1921); *Such is Life* (London: Jonathan Cape, 1937).

approving of his suggestion to the Commonwealth Literary Fund that it assist in the novel's publication, and informing Howarth that she had the typed manuscript of the unabridged work.[11] The project evidently got under way soon thereafter, since in May she writes asking whether the first five chapters have arrived and offering to send the next six.[12] In November of that year comes word that the firm of Angus and Robertson has agreed to publish the novel.[13]

In March 1946, replying to questions from Howarth, Baker says that she does not believe that Furphy's original manuscript is still in existence or that Furphy read the proofs for the serial version of the novel.[14] She explains that Furphy's niece cut out and saved the work as it came out in *The Barrier Truth* and sent the exercise book containing the clippings to her. Baker then had the novel typed. However, a letter from Lloyd Ross, whose father published the work, tells a somewhat different tale: "I have been told by old associates of my father that when he provided the volume of Barrier Truth for Miss Baker he expected her to type out the novel, instead, to his consternation, she cut the bound volume."[15] In any case, Howarth was able to work with a complete version of the text, and in 1945 he published chapter 6—one of those omitted from the 1921 edition of the novel—in the Furphy issue of *Southerly*, a copy of which, containing a few notes by Howarth, is in the HRHRC collection. In a letter of January 1947, Baker reports that she received her copy of the *Southerly* chapter, commenting that "The next thing are the short stories."[16]

The Howarth Collection contains other materials relating to Howarth's editorial work on *Rigby's Romance*, including his notes for, and manuscript of, the Foreword he wrote for the new edition of 1946. Also, there are manuscript and typescript lists of Furphy's chapter epigraphs, corrected and in some cases identified. In addition, the collection includes the manuscript and typescript of a textual note by Howarth that was not published, in which he complains about the publisher's treatment of Furphy's novel. In the manuscript version, he writes, "The whole was presented as ready for the press, but was not seen again by me, having passed through Angus and Robertson's editorial treatment, which, except where I stressed Furphy's individual spellings and word forms, would reduce it to 'house style' uniformity (a stupid process for a literary work, even the rhythm of a date being spoilt thereby)." Howarth later says that "the words 'edited by' me were not allowed to appear on the title page, as they should have done." Evidently this note was written after the fact for publication elsewhere, since Howarth also mentions the

[11]Letter from Kate Baker to R.G. Howarth, 20 March 1945.
[12]Letter from Kate Baker to R.G. Howarth, 18 May 1945.
[13]Letter from Kate Baker to R.G. Howarth, 20 November 1945.
[14]Letter from Kate Baker to R.G. Howarth, 4 March 1946.
[15]Letter from Lloyd Ross to R.G. Howarth, 28 May 1946.
[16]Letter from Kate Baker to R.G. Howarth, 4 January 1947.

Kate Baker, O.B.E. (1937), from *Joseph Furphy: The Legend of a Man and His Book* (Angus & Robertson, 1944). *HRHRC Grattan Collection.*

Photograph of Professor R.G. (Guy) and Lilian Howarth, from *The Argus* (Cape Town, South Africa), n.d. *HRHRC Photography Collection*. Used by permission of *The Argus*.

publisher's treatment of *The Buln-buln and the Brolga*, which he edited in 1948 for Angus and Robertson.

One interesting related piece in the Howarth Collection is a typescript review of *Rigby's Romance* by L. Shephard, which appeared in the *Sydney Morning Herald* of 14 June 1947. The reviewer praises Howarth's role in preparing the work for publication: "The text of this book was restored by Mr. R.G. Howarth, who not only edited it but also provides an admirable foreword to the edition."[17] Above "Shephard" on the typescript is printed "HOWARTH." L. Shephard was Howarth's wife Lilian.

Although the 1944 reissue of *Such is Life* enjoyed some success, *Rigby's Romance* did not sell well. A letter from Kate Baker in 1952 notes that Angus and Robertson remaindered the book and sent her fifty copies, which she sent off "to each of the principal universities of the world."[18] This lack of commercial success hindered Howarth from seeing through another of his projects, an edition of Furphy's collected stories.

The bulk of the material in the Howarth Collection relates to Furphy's stories, with typescripts of twenty-three of these, two of which are revised versions of others in the collection: "Dad's Artillery" (a later, shortened version of "A Boy of the Old Brigade") and "The Unburied Past" (a revision of "The Man Rodgers"). Also included are a one-page manuscript of "The Passing of a Pioneer," scattered fragments of typescripts (presumably typed by Furphy) of a few of the other stories, and a copy of "A Vignette of Port Phillip" clipped from the Melbourne *Age* of 25 September 1937, which is not present in typescript, Howarth having noted on the clipping "only copy." In addition, there are typescripts of two Furphy articles, "*Re* Burns" and "Black Australia." Also, much of the correspondence in the HRHRC collection concerns Howarth's efforts to put together a collection of Furphy's stories.

Apparently Howarth began collecting the Furphy stories as early as 1945, since a letter from Kate Baker in April of that year seems to be her response to an inquiry by Howarth about gathering copies of the stories. Baker replies that she had given all her Furphy material to the National Library on the occasion of his centenary year.[19] A list of Furphiana that accompanies an August 1946 letter from a librarian at the National Library includes "typescript copies (mostly by Furphy himself) of unpublished short stories and sketches."[20] Seventeen stories are listed, and pencil markings indicate that Howarth made use of the list, for next to each of the stories and poems he penciled in a small "x," placing as well a check mark above each story and a "+" above and after "The Discovery of Christmas Reef" and "A Vignette of Port Phillip," which

[17]L. Shephard, typescript review of *Rigby's Romance*, p. 3.
[18]Letter from Kate Baker to R.G. Howarth, n.d., marked "received London Jan. 22 1952."
[19]Letter from Kate Baker to R.G. Howarth, 11 April 1945.
[20]Letter from Kenneth Binns to R.G. Howarth, 26 August 1946.

may have been stories he needed to add to his collection. Howarth also penciled "A Point of Honour*" into the margin, perhaps indicating that this was a story he possessed which was not in the National Library. Since there are twenty-four stories in the HRHRC collection, Howarth obviously was able to find several others elsewhere. Two stories, "An Idyll of the Wimmera" and "A Box of Pandora," are mentioned several times in the correspondence, but no one was ever able to locate these.[21]

It seems that Howarth also contacted Miles Franklin in search of material, for there is a note from her dated March 1945. "I shall," she says, "willingly give you what help I can about the Furphy papers. We'd better have another walk and talk in the Gardens like Adam and Eve as I don't feel like the fag of letters." Just what role Franklin played in Howarth's collecting is not clear, but she did send him at least one manuscript, which I will discuss at some length below. The second paragraph of her 1945 note is intriguing: "Surely you would not be so recklessly unacademic as to commit yourself to an *appreciation* of my unacademically reckless challenge about Furphy?"[22] The Franklin/Baker biography of Furphy had appeared the previous year, but I find nothing in it by way of a challenge. Perhaps it came during an earlier walk in the Gardens (presumably the Botanic Gardens in Sydney).

In June 1946 Kate Baker wrote to Howarth concerning Furphy's stories, saying that she would like friends to "approach A & R asking for the short stories in book form. If requests come in from all parts of the Commonwealth, I think they would be interested."[23] Later that month, Baker reported that she had spoken to Walter Cousins, the head of Angus and Robertson, about publishing the stories. "I am wondering," she writes, "whether Sam Furphy has a copy of 'Here Be Truths.' I suggested to Mr Cousins that he might ask if Sam Furphy had a copy? Joseph Furphy himself thought that some of his best work was in 'Here Be Truths'."[24] This letter is of interest for two reasons. First, it involves Joseph Furphy's son Sam in the publishing project; he would later donate Furphy material to the University of Western Australia, and he would give his house in Perth, built by Joseph Furphy after he moved to Western Australia in 1905, to the Fellowship of Australian Writers. Second, Baker here mentions the title "Here Be Truths," which Furphy took from Shakespeare's *Measure for Measure*. This phrase, which Howarth would adopt for the projected short story collection, appears on Howarth's manuscript and typescript title pages, which are also included in the HRHRC collection.[25]

[21]Mention is made in Franklin and Baker, *Joseph Furphy*, p. 173, and in a letter from Clive Hamer to R.G. Howarth, 4 December 1950.

[22]Letter from Miles Franklin to R.G. Howarth, 9 March 1945.

[23]Letter from Kate Baker to R.G. Howarth, 2 June 1946.

[24]Letter from Kate Baker to R.G. Howarth, 21 June 1946.

[25]The phrase "I hope here be truths" appears in Act II, scene i. Furphy also uses it in *The Bulnbuln and the Brolga* (Sydney: Angus and Robertson, 1948), p. 116.

These title pages also give Angus and Robertson as the publisher, so Howarth must have reached some sort of agreement with the firm. An arrangement with Angus and Robertson would have been natural, given the fact that the firm was at that time involved with the publication of *Southerly*.[26] Also suggesting an agreement is a letter from Howarth to Beatrice Davis of Angus and Robertson in which he discusses the copyrights of the Furphy writings: "The stories were mostly printed in periodicals, but I took it that the collected and edited text prepared by me for Angus and Robertson was their property. I think A & R would have the copyright in the whole and any parts of this book, *Here Be Truths* (Furphy's own title)."[27] In addition, the typescripts of some of the stories have contiguous pagination, as though Howarth had assembled them into a completed typescript for the publisher. Early on, the prospects for getting the stories into print must have seemed promising. In a July 1946 letter to Howarth, Sam Furphy writes, "I had a letter from Mr. Cousins at A & R suggesting they may be able to publish the short stories in book form."[28]

But publication of the stories was delayed, for reasons that the letters do not make clear. As mentioned above, the limited market for a collection of Furphy's stories would probably have been the main reason. Throughout the next two decades, Howarth's correspondents repeatedly ask when the stories will appear. For instance, author Henrietta Drake-Brockman complains in a 1949 letter describing the Furphy bequest in Perth that "I suppose we shall see the collection in 'due' course. This is a word that I feel requires, in modern times, a more precise definition."[29] As late as 1969, Nina Knight, a graduate student working on Furphy, could write, "I agree with you completely about publication of the stories and am only sorry to hear that A & R do not. . . . I am so sorry that there is no 'collected short stories' of Furphy's easily available."[30] There is an obvious implication here that Howarth had clashed with the publisher on the merits of issuing the stories.

Since the manuscript title page bears the date 1951, Howarth must have had reason to believe that the stories would appear in that year. By this time, of course, the long story (or short novel) *The Buln-buln and the Brolga* had been published separately (Howarth having suggested this be done in 1946, with the result that the book came out in 1948). Since *The Buln-buln* was the most interesting of the unpublished writings (representing another reworked version of material Furphy cut from *Such is Life*), issuing this book may have reduced the publisher's inclination to print the collection of short stories,

[26]See "*Southerly*," in *Oxford Companion*.

[27]Letter from R.G. Howarth to Beatrice Davis, 8 December 1969. Permission requested from the Syfrets Trust, Cape Town, South Africa, for citations from the unpublished writings of R.G. Howarth.

[28]Letter from Sam Furphy to R.G. Howarth, 15 July 1946.

[29]Letter from Henrietta Drake-Brockman to R.G. Howarth, 25 October [1949].

[30]Letter from Nina Knight to R.G. Howarth, 11 February 1969.

most of which are in fact of lesser quality. A good deal of material in the Howarth Collection relates to *The Buln-buln*: In addition to a complete typescript of the book and a copy, both with Howarth's corrections, the archive contains manuscript and typescript versions of Howarth's foreword. *The Buln-buln* is of particular interest because, first, it gives the reader a glimpse of Tom Collins's youth (which is further depicted in the stories "Dad's Artillery" and "High Art"), and second, in it Furphy explores the nature of truth in storytelling, contrasting the romantic lies of Fred Falkland-Pritchard with the bush yarns of Barefooted Bob.[31]

The publication of the stories was put on hold in the early fifties, and so the matter stayed for a while. Howarth left Australia in 1955 to take a position at the University of Cape Town, where he would remain until 1971. The only correspondence relating to the stories during the sixties regards the use of Howarth's typescripts by graduate students in Australia. Howarth must have been resigned to the fact that Angus and Robertson was not going to publish the collection, since the few letters of his at the HRHRC answer questions about the stories rather perfunctorily. But apparently he felt tied to whatever he had agreed to earlier with the publisher, since there is never any suggestion that he would try to find someone else to publish the stories.

Three letters from January 1971 end the account of the projected collection. A note from Kevin R. Gilding of the Bedford Park Teachers College to literary scholar and former Howarth colleague H.J. Oliver asks about typescripts of the stories; Gilding says he is editing a collection of Furphy stories and has copies of those in the Kate Baker collection in the National Library.[32] Oliver replies to Gilding, "I do know that an edition of them has been in preparation for some time and indeed I suspect that your work may be cutting across somebody else's."[33] Oliver then refers Gilding to Howarth. In his reply to Gilding, Howarth informs him that he has returned all the original typescripts he possesses, and Howarth advises Gilding to contact Nina Knight for photostats of the other typescripts. "No doubt," continues Howarth, "your publishers have looked into the question of copywright [*sic*]. The present holding will expire next year."[34] Later in 1971 *The Buln-buln and the Brolga and Other Stories*, published in Adelaide by Rigby, appeared with Gilding's introduction to the collection, which, in addition to *The Buln-buln*, contains twelve of Furphy's stories. Gilding makes no mention of Howarth or his efforts to have the stories published. It may be that Gilding was simply not aware that such a project had been proposed twenty-five years earlier as a logical culmination to the Furphy publications of the 1940s.

[31]I develop this idea further in "Yarning about Yarning: *The Buln-buln and the Brolga* and the Rhetoric of *Such is Life*," *Antipodes* 2 (1988): 44-48.

[32]Letter from Kevin R. Gilding to H.J. Oliver, 13 January 1971.

[33]Letter from H.J. Oliver to Kevin R. Gilding, 18 January 1971.

[34]Letter from R.G. Howarth to Kevin R. Gilding, 28 January 1971.

Even with Gilding's collection, though, a fair amount of Furphy material has never been published or was published only in now-obscure periodicals. Included in this unpublished material are twelve of the typescript stories in the HRHRC's Howarth Collection, several of which might bear further study for a variety of reasons, including Furphy's technique in revising. A study, for instance, of Furphy's revision of "A Boy of the Old Brigade" into "Dad's Artillery" would provide insight into how he tried to adapt his technique and his material to the literary marketplace of the time.

Another story of interest is "Under the Tarpaulin," where Dixon gives Tom Collins his interpretation of the biblical story of Moses. The phrase "Not to be used" appears at the top of the first pages of the typescript and one of the copies. Presumably Howarth decided against using the story in his collection because it had already appeared in virtually identical form as the last part of chapter 8 and all of chapter 9 of *Rigby's Romance*. Furphy altered the story very little when he incorporated it into the novel, with the only major change a revision of the opening in order to make the episode fit more smoothly into the larger story: Instead of taking shelter from a rainstorm under Dixon's wagon, Collins stops at his camp in response to an earlier invitation.

As an illustration of the bushman's practical turn of mind, "Under the Tarpaulin" presents Dixon interpreting events in terms of his own experience. Moses, says Dixon, "was the foolishest (person) ever lived. Bible cracks him up, mind you, because he was a decent feller in his own sort o' soft-headed way. But he didn't know his road roun'. Cripes, if I got slants like him I'd shift things a bit!"[35] Dixon thinks Moses should have taken advantage of the "slants" he was provided with for his own personal aggrandizement rather than intervening with the Lord on behalf of a people Dixon presents as unappreciative and undeserving. When he comes to the story of the golden calf, Dixon asserts that Moses should have taken it for himself; instead,

> He seized it, like a case o' tobacker at Customs, an' ground it into powder, an' mixed it with water, an' made the delinquints drink the water—an' so good-bye to as much as would have kep' him independent for life. Fair chased with every (adj.) description o' slants, an' never froze on one o' them. Got worse as he got older an' died at last on top of a mountain, like some poor swaggie—a man that might have been at the very top o' the tree if he'd collared half the slants that come his road. I got no pity for a feller like that.[36]

Furphy is poking fun at Dixon's method of biblical exegesis, in which he ignores the religious or philosophical import of the stories he recounts. Ironically, Dixon is practicing a reading that is just the opposite of what

[35]Furphy, *Rigby's Romance*, p. 39.
[36]Ibid., pp. 44-45.

Furphy would have expected from his reader. In addition to representing the author's typical use of irony, "Under the Tarpaulin" demonstrates how in assembling his longer works from a series of disconnected shorter episodes Furphy could fit this story smoothly into *Rigby's Romance*.

Another story, "O'Flaherty's Troubles," was, as Gilding notes, originally part of chapter 6 of *Such is Life*, with Collins contrasting the singing abilities of O'Flaherty and Nosey Alf, much to the detriment of the former.[37] Otherwise the story is without interest except for a typical Collins digression on the tenuousness of the property rights of the poor.

Not all of the stories are narrated by Tom Collins, but in several of them Furphy did use Collins, and, taken with the longer works, they help to round out the narrator's "life story." A number of the stories find Collins in the gold fields, with Gilding's collection containing two of these, "The Jeweller's Shop" and "The Haunted Tunnel." Three others—"The Law's Delay," "The Whir-ligig of Time," and "The Unburied Past"—remain unpublished, and the last of these is the best. The HRHRC collection includes typescripts of "The Unburied Past" in its final version and in its original version as "The Man Rodgers." The two versions are virtually identical, except that the character of Sandy in the original becomes Abraham Spoker in the revision. The story is typical Collins narration, opening with the reflection that he once knew the now-respectable "Abraham Spoker, Esp., Deacon of the Church, Worshipful Master of the L.O.L., and president of the local Reform League" when he had been with him on the gold diggings. Collins continues: "Nor can his ostentatious rectitude of walk and conversation ever annul the fact that I have seen him edge around a tree like a goanna, or vanish down a hole like a wombat, when his apprehensive eye caught sight of the more practically apprehensive local zarp."[38] Collins goes on to tell how Abe was picked up by Constable M'Bride in that officer's fortnightly effort to fill his quota of offenders before the warden would arrive to hold court. Abe escapes from the cell, leaving an opening through which the constable's later guests can also flee. Abe is able to avoid M'Bride thereafter, but the strain of constantly being on his guard drives him from the diggings:

> His face began to wear a haunted look, and the general breaking-up of
> his constitutional nonchalance seemed to be poorly balanced by that
> abnormal improvement in sight and hearing which resulted from the

[37]Kevin Gilding, Introduction, *The Buln-buln and the Brolga and Other Stories* by Joseph Furphy (Adelaide: Rigby, 1971), p. xviii. The section of *Such is Life* (Sydney: Angus and Robertson, 1986) dealing with the singing of Alf Jones, known as Nosey Alf, is on pp. 318-22. Copies of the relevant pages of the original manuscript of *Such is Life* are in the papers of Bruce Sutherland in the Pattee Library of Pennsylvania State University.

[38]Joseph Furphy, "The Unburied Past," p. 1. Permission to quote from the unpublished writings of Joseph Furphy has been granted by Duncan K. Furphy of Adelaide, Australia.

necessities of his situation. It became more and more evident that nothing but a change of scenery would meet his case.[39]

The appeal of this story lies not just in the simple tale of the digger outwitting the constable but more in the contrast between Collins's erudite and punctilious manner of presentation, replete with Shakespearean and biblical allusions, and the behavior of the other characters in the story. Here, for instance, is Collins's account of how M'Bride discovered Abe's escape:

> On Sunday, Mac, filled with the desire of being his brothers' keeper, had gone out into the highways and hedges and compelled them to come in; little anticipating the wholesale backsliding which would reward his propaganda. Altogether, during the day, he had secured and warehoused five fairly presentable respondents to the charges of "insultin' behavor", "drunk an' disorderly", and "tarin' me uniform"—but what was the good? Each captive, in rotation, as his eyes became accustomed to the darkness, had simply gone out the back way and crept off under the cover of the ferns, thinking, no doubt, with Sir Lucio, that he had as lief have the foppery of freedom as the morality of imprisonment. In fact, they had their exits and their entrances, and that was the full scope of their experience for the time being. It was like catching leeches, and keeping your bottle corked with a tuft of grass. And the sting of the loss lay in the fact that Mac knew nothing of his own insolvency till he looked in on Monday morning, with a bucket of water and a couple of mildewed loaves, and found all his pretty ones gone at one fell scoot. Then his trained faculties put that and that together, and he started in search of Abe.[40]

As in *Such is Life*, the reader can identify with Collins and laugh at the actions of the other characters, in part because Furphy has placed Collins physically among but intellectually above the others.

In the short run, both Spoker and M'Bride seem to be defeated—Abe returns home broke, and M'Bride has no prisoners for the warden (as well as a hole in his jail cell). Collins notes, "Such, be it observed, is the meed of those who thus profanely undermine any of the glorious institutions wrung by our gallant forefathers from—from—well, from themselves, I presume, seeing that we all boast the same species of ancestral honour."[41] However, the story takes on added irony in that both Spoker and M'Bride eventually come out ahead; though defeated in the short run, Spoker eventually gains the prosperity noted at the outset of the story, and M'Bride is promoted to sergeant. Thus, as he often does in the Tom Collins episodes, Furphy

[39]Ibid., pp. 7-8.
[40]Ibid., pp. 6-7.
[41]Ibid., p. 8.

undercuts Collins's self-assurance and the reader's too-easy identification with Collins's superior attitude toward the other characters.

Probably the most intriguing, if not the best, of the remaining stories is "The Bullock Hunter," primarily because it is the longest, running to 74 typescript pages. Although it does not hold the reader's interest for long, it does have its moments, especially early in the tale, when the bullock hunter Willie Primrose arrives on the scene to help the bullockies keep the carrying business going. Later, the narrative bogs down in a long court trial, but the story has interesting possibilities, and the enterprising scholar should find plenty of connections to other Furphy works.

The two articles, "*Re* Burns" and "Black Australia," are both listed as being by Tom Collins. The former consists of some observations on Robert Burns as a radical rather than as a popular sentimental poet; the latter gives Furphy's recollections concerning the Aboriginal inhabitants of the district where he grew up.

Of special interest is a Furphy manuscript story which is not referred to in any of the letters or in any of the lists of Furphy's stories. About 2600 words long, it is written in pencil on ledger paper bearing the Furphy Brothers letterhead. (Joseph Furphy began working at the Furphy Bros. foundry in Shepparton in 1883 after spending several years bullock driving.) An accompanying envelope marked "University of Cape Town" in the lower left is inscribed, "Presumably a Furphy ms sent to Miles Franklin and thence to RGH." The story apparently was written some time between 1900 and 1905, for the letterhead on the ledger paper reads "19—," and Furphy left for Western Australia in 1905. It is obviously in rough draft form: A few sections have been crossed out and rewritten, and there is no ending. The words "Nejd Arab," possibly the title, appear at the end of the text. Because Nejd is a region of Saudi Arabia, Furphy may have meant to associate the nomadic existence of the Nejd Arabs with that of the bushmen. (Since the phrase appears on the last page, another possibility is that Furphy intended to use this as a pseudonym when submitting the story.) It is hard to tell whether the beginning is missing, whether the story begins *in medias res*, or whether the story has been taken out of a longer work (the first of these is the most likely, with the second a strong possibility).

In some ways the story is unique among Furphy's writings, and in others it is typical. One of the unusual features of "Nejd Arab" is its structure, which is that of a tale of flight and pursuit. Charley has stolen Cecil's horse Sard, and Cecil (referred to several times in the story as a "poet") pursues him across the Riverina. Rather than the usual Furphy technique of leisurely narration, the action is driven forward by the chase; the story covers a lot of ground in a few pages. This could be because Furphy had in mind sending the story to the *Bulletin*, which published a few of his stories during the 1900–1905 period and which demanded a more concise style than Furphy generally employed. The desire to "boil it down" may also account for the story's abrupt opening. The typical Furphian features of the story include the locale, the characters, and the use of dialogue. Indeed, the story takes the reader through the heart of the Riverina region, which is Furphy country, for he was intimately familiar with the area through his travels, and he used it as the setting for a good deal of his fiction. In his pursuit of Charley, Cecil follows his trail to Hay, across the Murrumbidgee and north to Booligal, across the Lachlan and north past Mossgiel. After Cecil has tracked Charley along the Willandra Billabong, the story breaks off.

In having Cecil pursue Charley and Sard through the Riverina, Furphy is able to draw on his usual cast of characters, including station hands in the story's opening pages and the bullockies whom Cecil encounters later on. Since the story is really about a horse—or the bushman's relation to his horse—the best characterizations are given to the horses Cecil has to borrow or buy or swap for in order to reclaim his incomparable Sard. At one point, he has to purchase Moses, a worthless piebald, in order to continue his pursuit, but the horse proves too lazy. Cecil then buys a long whip to spur the horse to action:

> Cecil, though morbidly humane by nature, eagerly purchased this unholy weapon, judging it to be about the correct thing for Moses; &, thus furnished, he crossed the bridge at a slow, pile-driving canter, while the mighty sjambok cracked like a pistol each time it curled round the fur-clad form of the piebald. And the poet ground his teeth as he thought of Charley sailing ahead on the easy and tireless Sard— probably increasing his distance hour by hour & minute by minute.

Later Cecil is able to swap Moses for Brian Boree (or Boru? there could be an Irish/Australian play on words here, since *boree* is the Aboriginal name for a kind of tree) from the bullocky O'Dwyer, who has been unable to ride him. This transaction calls to mind Tom Collins's deal to acquire Cleopatra in *Such is Life*: Early in that novel, Collins devotes several pages to an account of how he was able to get the better of a swap for this horse.[42]

In the dialogue with the bullock drivers, Furphy makes use of heavy Irish dialect for O'Dwyer, something he does many times elsewhere with various sorts of accents. Also in this section—the most lively part of the story—the terse dialogue conveys, as it does at its best in all of Furphy's fiction, the atmosphere around the campfire on the track. As O'Dwyer goes off to fetch his horse for Cecil to inspect,

> his companion turned to Cecil and asked significantly,
> "Can you ride?"
> "Middling."

[42]Furphy, *Such is Life*, pp. 9-13.

"Well, this O'Dwyer—he's a Vic. cockie trying to make a cheque— he got the horse in a swap with a drover, a week ago. Well, O'Dwyer he got onto the horse 3 mornin's runnin' to fetch in his frames, but the horse slung him punctual every time; so he give it best at that; an' I have to do all the bullick huntin'. Same time, he ain't a bad style of a horse, an' he don't look no ways vicious."

"I'll chance him," replied the poet, "This horse of mine is a bit lazy, but,"—

The iron-grey man raised his hand deprecatingly—

"Steady," he murmured. "I know him of old. Fact, I owned him once."

So they changed the subject.

The reader is left to infer the old man's opinion of O'Dwyer's worth as a bushman and as a judge and rider of horses, as well as the previous history of Moses. This is pure Furphy, and not at all bad, but the rest of the story, or the fragment of it here (there may be more elsewhere, though I suspect this is as far as Furphy got), does not quite come up to the standard of these passages. Nonetheless, the story should be of interest to Furphy scholars for all of its typical and unusual features.

In giving an overview of Furphy's unpublished stories, Miles Franklin notes in the 1944 biography that

> this material could not have been collected by a minor or cursory observer: it has the Furphian charity for those defeated by fortune because of their inherent characteristics; but scarcely any of the stories are worthy of publication as they stand. They are in rough draft as to craftsmanship, and climactic focus is weak. They show fatigue on the part of the writer.[43]

This is true, perhaps, for many of the stories in the Howarth Collection. But it is a rather uncharitable characterization of the stories generally. A number of them deserved to be published on their own merits, and not just because they would be of interest as lesser works by the author of *Such is Life*.

Taken as a whole, the material in the Howarth Collection gives a behind-the-scenes look at an attempt to resurrect, or, if that is too strong a word, to reconfirm the reputation of the author of an acknowledged Australian classic. But since *Such is Life* is a classic which few, even in Australia, ever read, such a project was not one destined for great success. Although Howarth was never able to get *Here Be Truths* into print, he was able to secure the publication of acceptable texts of *Rigby's Romance* and *The Buln-buln and the Brolga*. In the process, he says, "I did all that was humanly possible, and apparently

[43]Franklin and Baker, p. 173.

exceeded my function, in the opinion of the editorial department, in doing so."[44] Throughout the collection run the tracks of the editor and the scholar at work. In addition to the correspondence, there are Howarth's notes and drafts for forewords and articles and his corrections in the typescripts of the stories. As far as they go, the tracks are worth pursuing for anyone interested in the workings of literary scholarship in Australia and in Joseph Furphy as a working author.

[44]R.G. Howarth, unpublished textual note on *Rigby's Romance*.

Photograph of Alice Henry, n.d. *HRHRC Photography Collection.*

Alice Henry: "Building for the Harmonist" in Australia and America

BY DESLEY DEACON

> Last sea-thing dredged by sailor Time from Space,
> Are you a drift Sargasso, where the West
> In Halcyon calm rebuilds her fatal nest?
> Or Delos of a coming Sun-God's race?
> Are you for Light, and trimmed, with oil in place,
> Or but a Will o'Wisp on Marshy quest?
> A new demesne for Mammon to infest?
> Or lurks millenial Eden 'neath your face?
> The cenotaphs of species dead elsewhere
> That in your limits leap and swim and fly,
> Or trail uncanny harp-strings from your trees,
> Mix omens with the auguries that dare
> To plant the Cross upon your forehead sky,
> A virgin helpmate Ocean at your knees.
>
> Bernard O'Dowd, as quoted
> by C. Hartley Grattan as the frontispiece
> to his *Introducing Australia* (1942)

"You remind me that the Australian scene is unnecessarily cluttered with men," wrote Miles Franklin to C. Hartley Grattan early in the latter's second visit to Australia in 1936–38.[1] Paradoxically, however, three Australian women—Nettie Palmer, Miles Franklin, and Alice Henry—played a principal role in encouraging the interest Grattan had developed somewhat accidentally in Australia in 1927, paving the way for his return nine years later. The interest of these women in the percipient young American is not surprising. At a time when W.K. Hancock in his 1931 *Australia* was

---

[1] Undated letter from Miles Franklin to C. Hartley Grattan, Box 32/folder 1; reference to the recent death of Walter Burley Griffin suggests it was written soon after 11 February 1937. Box and folder numbers refer to manuscripts in the C. Hartley Grattan Collection of Southwest Pacificana, Harry Ransom Humanities Research Center, The University of Texas at Austin. I am grateful to Laurie Hergenhan, Frank Poyas, and Cathy Henderson for guidance in locating this correspondence.

describing a contented, and mindless, citizenry ready to claim "the right to work, the right to fair and reasonable conditions of living, the right to be happy" from a State "whose duty it is to provide the greatest happiness for the greatest number," Australian women were ruefully aware that the great promise of the "social laboratory of the world" had not been fulfilled for them.[2] Young and critical like Nettie Palmer or older and disappointed like Miles Franklin and Alice Henry, these three women welcomed Grattan as a representative of a country that took its culture seriously and as a link to the American Progressive tradition for which Australasia had, in many ways, been an exemplar.

As Laurie Hergenhan and Frank Poyas each point out elsewhere in this publication, Hartley Grattan's interest in Australia was completely fortuitous, resulting from a nine-month visit in 1927 when, as a young man of twenty-five, he accompanied his first wife, the singer Beatrice Kay, on her Australian tour. When he published his article on "Australian Literature" in *The Bookman* of August 1928, alongside a story by D.H. Lawrence and articles by Katharine Anthony and Upton Sinclair, Grattan was beginning to make his mark as one of the "young critics," a group that included Kenneth Burke, V.F. Calverton, and Jean Toomer.[3] In 1929 Grattan published a monograph on Ambrose Bierce and a revisionist history of America's role in World War I, contributed extensively to a volume on William Jennings Bryan, and edited a collection of writing by Burton Rascoe. The following year he edited *The Critique of Humanism*, which included articles by Kenneth Burke, Edmund Wilson, and Malcolm Cowley. In 1932 he issued his major intellectual history, *The Three Jameses*, along with another edited volume, *Recollections of the Last Ten Years*; and in 1936 he published *Preface to Chaos*.[4] Amongst this flurry of

[2]W.K. Hancock, *Australia* (London: Ernest Benn, 1931; New York: Scribner's sons, 1931), p. 72. For the situation of women in 1930, see Desley Deacon, *Managing Gender: The State, The New Middle Class, and Women Workers 1830-1930* (Melbourne: Oxford University Press, 1989).

[3]Grattan was in Australia from February to October 1927. For his standing in 1929, see Gorham B. Munson, "The Young Critics of the Nineteen-Twenties," *The Bookman* 70, no. 4 (December 1929): 369-73, esp. 372. The author of "Australian Literature" is described as follows in *The Bookman* 67, no. 6 (August 1928): iv: "Shortly after his name had become known through critical articles in several magazines, C. Harley [*sic*] Grattan left New York for an extended trip around the world. The longest halt in his journey was in Australia, where he made a study of local life and culture which has resulted in several articles eventually to be incorporated in a book. Mr. Grattan's first article appeared in the *American Mercury* in 1924. It dealt with James Russell Lowell as a critic, and is now assured immortality by being referred to in a footnote in Parrington's 'Main Currents in American Thought.' Most of Mr. Grattan's articles deal with some aspect of American literature or international politics."

[4]*Why We Fought* (New York: Vanguard, 1929; reprinted New York: Bobbs-Merrill Company, 1969); *Bitter Bierce: A Mystery of American Letters* (Doubleday, Doran and Co., 1929; reprinted New York: Cooper Square Publishers, 1966); *The Peerless Leader: William Jennings Bryan*, with Paxton Hibben; introd. by Charles A. Beard (New York: Farrar and Rinehart, 1929; reprinted New York: Russell & Russell, 1967); Burton Rascoe, *A Bookman's Daybook*, ed. with introd. by

activity, Grattan's Australian article, and his interest in that part of the world, might have sunk into oblivion had it not been received enthusiastically by Australian writer and critic Nettie Palmer, who immediately recognized in this young American a sympathetic and potentially influential voice.

Living at Caloundra, a small seaside town north of Brisbane, Nettie Palmer wrote enthusiastically to Grattan as soon as she heard of his work through her husband's summary of an article he had read and committed to memory while on a trip to Brisbane:

> Your article in the August *Bookman* has attracted much astonished attention among writers in Australia: and now someone sends on a New York *Tribune* with some notes of yours on the conditions and difficulties of "colonial" writers in general. May I say, as one of the toads beneath the harrow, that you're incredibly right in your summaries. . . . I can't imagine how you know so much without being an Australian: & even Australians don't know it. . . .[5]

Within months Nettie Palmer and Hartley Grattan had established a working friendship that continued, though in somewhat attenuated form, until her death in 1964. The publication in 1929 of Grattan's essay on Australian literature in monograph form, with a foreword by Nettie Palmer, coincided with a burst of interest in the subject, due to the unexpected American success of Henry Handel Richardson's novel, *Ultima Thule*.[6] Thereafter, Grattan began to be in demand as an authority on matters Australian. Katharine Susannah Prichard, one of the few Australian writers considered by Grattan as "hopeful," sent her *Haxby's Circus* (1930) to Richardson's publishers, Norton, and a favorable review by Grattan resulted in publication of the book as *Fay's*

C. Hartley Grattan (New York: Horace Liveright, 1929); *The Critique of Humanism: A Symposium* (New York: Brewer and Warren, 1930; reissued Freeport, New York: Books for Libraries Press, Essay Index Reprint Series, 1968); *The Three Jameses: A Family of Minds* (London: Longmans, Green, and Co., 1932; reprinted New York University Press, 1962); *Recollections of the Last Ten Years*, with Sylvan Hoffman (New York: Knopf, 1932); *Preface to Chaos* (New York: Dodge, 1936).

[5]Letter from Nettie Palmer to C. Hartley Grattan, 24 October 1928, Box 35/folder 4. Permission to quote from the Nettie Palmer correspondence has been granted by the Palmer estate. Nettie Palmer was the literary executrix of Alice Henry's estate.

[6]C. Hartley Grattan, *Australian Literature*, ed. Glenn Hughes (Seattle: University of Washington Chapbooks, No. 29; reprinted in *Antipodes* 2, no. 1 [Spring 1988]: 20-24). For correspondence on Palmer's foreword, see Palmer to Grattan, 3 and 17 February 1929, Box 36/folder 1, and Louis Esson to Palmer, 11 February 1929, Box 35/folder 4. *Ultima Thule*, published on 10 January 1929, was an American Book-of-the-Month selection in September 1929; see H.H. Richardson to Vance Palmer, 6 August 1929, in Karl-Johan Rossing, ed., *Letters of Henry Handel Richardson to Nettie Palmer* (Uppsala: Essays and Studies on English Language and Literature XIV, 1953), pp. 13-14. An indication of new interest in Australian literature is the advertisement for M. Barnard Eldershaw's *A House Is Built* (1929) in *The Bookman* for November 1929 (p. xxiv).

123

Circus in 1931.[7] By the end of that year, when an open letter by Nettie Palmer about the 1928-29 essay, and Grattan's reply, were published in the Brisbane *Telegraph*, Grattan's position as the American expert on, and savior of, Australian literature was well-established, at least in the minds of its practitioners.[8]

The *Telegraph* articles also prompted Miles Franklin to begin her long correspondence with Grattan. She had already written to him, probably in 1930, in her guise as "Brent of Bin Bin,"[9] but early in 1932 she wrote to Grattan from London, this time under her own name. A friend in America, Miles said, had drawn her attention to his December article, and she was keen to enter the debate with a long reply, a copy of which she enclosed, along with her latest book.[10] This led to a meeting in the United States on Franklin's return trip to Australia and her attempts, over the next few years, to help Grattan himself to return for a more comprehensive study of the country to which he was now increasingly linked in the eyes of both Australians and Americans.[11]

II. ALICE HENRY AND C. HARTLEY GRATTAN

The "friend in America" who had drawn Miles Franklin's attention to Grattan's work was no doubt Alice Henry, the third of the women who eagerly drew him into the Australian orbit. Born in Melbourne in 1857, Alice Henry had gone to the United States in 1905 as an established journalist, feminist, and social reformer, and had quickly been absorbed into the main currents of Progressive America. After a long career with the Women's Trade Union League, where she was joined from 1906 to 1915 by Miles Franklin, she retired in 1927.[12] When Grattan published his article on Australian literature

[7]For the beginning of correspondence, see Prichard to Grattan, 2 April 1930, Box 35/folder 1b. Grattan reviewed the American edition of *Fay's Circus* in *Current Reading* (June 1931): 369-375. Prichard was already known in America for her *Working Bullocks* (1926) and, to a lesser extent, *Coonardoo* (1929).

[8]*Telegraph* articles July and December 1931; see Miles Franklin to C. Hartley Grattan, 18 March 1932, Box 32/folder 1.

[9]Undated letter, "February (some date or other)," Box 32/folder 1. Since it mentions *Up the Country* (1928) and *Ten Creeks Run* (1930), the letter was probably written in 1930.

[10]Letter from Miles Franklin to C. Hartley Grattan, 18 March 1932, Box 32/folder 1. The book was probably *Old Blastus of Bandicoot* (1931), which was the first book she had published under her own name since 1909. Franklin tells Grattan in her teasing way that she had intended to call it *Old Barry of Bin Bin*, but the name "Bin Bin" was "used ahead of me."

[11]Letters from Miles Franklin to C. Hartley Grattan, 5 May and 24 July 1933; 14 March 1935; and 18 August 1936, Box 32/folder 1.

[12]The only major study of Henry is the unpublished dissertation by Diane Elizabeth Kirkby, "Alice Henry, the Women's Trade Union League of America and Progressive Labor Reform in

in 1928, Henry was seventy years old, retired, and living in California. She had always been interested in music, literature, and the arts, and shared Grattan's appreciation of the poet Bernard O'Dowd, whom she had introduced to the American public in 1912.[13] Responding no doubt to the new interest in Australian literature, Henry published an intimate and sympathetic portrait of Henry Handel Richardson in *The Bookman* in December 1929.[14] It is not clear how and when Alice Henry and Hartley Grattan met, but it was inevitable that they would do so. As a Progressive and a feminist in Melbourne in the early years of the century, Henry had been a friend of Nettie Palmer's aunt, Ina Higgins, and her famous brother, Henry Bournes Higgins, the Arbitration Court judge responsible for the concept of the "living wage." During her years in the American trade union movement, Henry had been a major interpreter to the American public of the Australian industrial arbitration system and the work of Henry Higgins. In 1929 Nettie Palmer was beginning work on a biography of Higgins, which would be published in 1931,[15] and she was a close friend of Miles Franklin, who had worked with Henry on the WTUL's *Life and Labor* during her American sojourn.[16] Alice Henry was a link, therefore, between the socially innovative Australia whose vestiges Grattan admired and the new culturally conscious generation of writers he encouraged.

The evidence suggests that Alice Henry and Hartley Grattan met in 1932 during Miles Franklin's visit to the United States. If they did not actually

Australia and the United States, 1906-1925," University of California, Berkeley, 1983. Kirkby provides a briefer account of Henry's American years in "Alice Henry and the Women's Trade Union League: Australian Reformer, American Reform," in Margaret Bevage, Margaret James, and Carmel Shute, eds., *Worth Her Salt: Women at Work in Australia* (Sydney: Hale & Iremonger, 1982), pp. 244-56. See also Diane Kirkby, "Alice Henry," *Australian Dictionary of Biography 1891-1939*. Nettie Palmer gave a brief outline of Henry's career in "Who Was Alice Henry?," in *Australian Women's Digest* 1, no. 9 (April 1945): 19-20; and there is an article on Henry by Kate Baker in the Baker Papers, National Library of Australia, MS 2022/2/98. The bulk of Henry's papers are in the National Library of Australia, MS 1066 (Alice Henry Papers), which contains 59 folders of material, and MS 1174 (Vance and Nettie Palmer Papers). Additional articles and cuttings are in the Mitchell Library, Sydney, MSS 364, 3639, and 3659 (Miles Franklin Papers). For Franklin's American career, see Verna Coleman, *Miles Franklin in America: Her Unknown (Brilliant) Career* (Sydney: Angus & Robertson, 1981).

[13]Alice Henry, "Bernard O'Dowd," *Twentieth Century Magazine* (May 1912): 33-39.

[14]Alice Henry, "Who Is Henry Handel Richardson?," *The Bookman* 70, no. 4 (December 1929): 355-359.

[15]Alice Henry, *Union Labor Advocate* 8 (March 1908): 30; Nettie Palmer, *Henry Bournes Higgins: A Memoir* (London: G.G. Harrap & Co., 1931). For Higgins, see John Rickard, *H.B. Higgins: The Rebel as Judge* (Sydney: George Allen & Unwin, 1984), esp. p. 197 for visit to Henry in Chicago in 1914.

[16]Coleman, *Miles Franklin in America*; Kirkby, "Alice Henry, the Women's Trade Union League of America and Progressive Labor Reform," 1983.

meet, at least Franklin put them in touch with each other. In any case, the two women must have discussed the subject of Grattan's return trip to Australia, for Miles Franklin applied herself to the task of organizing support for such a trip after she returned to Australia at the end of 1932, and when Alice Henry finally decided to return to Australia the following year, the question of Grattan's projected visit was one of her first priorities.[17] In October 1933, only two months after her departure from the United States, Henry was writing to a prospective financial supporter:

> One of the first thing [sic] that impress me on my arrival is the wonderful—and as yet hardly touched possibilities that lie before Australian writers, existent, and to be. Very little of this is yet understood in Australia itself, and nothing at all outside. And it is, of course, outside, and particularly in the United States that the world market exists. And besides there is always the powerful effect of foreign opinion, back upon Australian opinion, and its stimulus upon Australian literature and Australian writers. . . . There is, however, one man in America who is an enthusiast on this very subject, and he is C. Hartley Grattan, of New York.[18]

There is no further record of Henry's efforts to facilitate Grattan's visit. However, she was in regular contact with Nettie Palmer, one of Grattan's chief Australian supporters, working with her on a bibliography of Australian women writers and a chapter on suffrage for the *Centenary Gift Book* edited by Palmer in 1934.[19] When Grattan finally arrived in Australia at the end of 1936 with a two-year grant from the Carnegie Corporation, Henry, by then eighty years old, did everything she could to help him get to know the country. Her beloved brother had been a surveyor in western Queensland, and one of her principal interests since her return had been in the efforts of the Australian Inland Mission to improve the lives of the isolated settlers in the outback. One of her first suggestions, therefore, was for Grattan to investigate the work of this uniquely Australian organization, and throughout his visit she supplied him with information on its activities and mode of operation.[20] She also emphasized the importance of the Australian Worker's Union, pointing out its difference from the American Federation of Labor, which had ignored the problems of the migratory workers, a group for whom she had always been particularly concerned. As she told Grattan, the A.W.U.'s efforts had received little scholarly attention, yet:

[17]Letters from Miles Franklin to C. Hartley Grattan, 5 May and 24 July 1933; 14 March 1935; and 18 August 1936, Box 32/folder 1.

[18]Letter from Alice Henry to Arthur O'Connor, 9 October 1933, Box 32/folder 2.

[19]See "Marching Towards Citizenship," in Frances Fraser and Nettie Palmer, eds., *Centenary Gift Book* (Melbourne: Robertson & Mullens, 1934).

[20]Letters from Alice Henry to C. Hartley Grattan, 14 March, 4 April, and 14 October, 1937; 15 August 1938, Box 32/folder 2.

126

Alice Henry and Miles Franklin, n.d. In Verna Coleman's *Miles Franklin in America: Her Unknown (Brilliant) Career* (Angus & Robertson, 1981). From the library of Desley Deacon.

It has always seemed to me a great achievement; and a contrast in its relation to the Federation of Trade Unions, to the attitude of the A.F.L. towards the migratory worker, an attitude either of helplessness or of scorn. And the strength of the A.W.U. has been, as far as I know the outgrowth, not of legislation, but of organization. And there is in it an element of industrial, as distinguished from craft organization. . . . My brother was surveying in Queensland, before there was anything of the sort, and he used to say conditions as to lodging, food and terms of all sorts were shocking, except with an exceptional employer.[21]

Still keenly interested in feminist and progressive reform, Alice Henry also supplied Grattan with the names of women active in the women's movement and prominent in professional and social welfare activities. Among the women she suggested he meet in Sydney were Jessie Street, Mrs. Muscio, Dr. Constance D'Arcy, Margaret Harper, and Sister Spencer.[22] When Grattan visited Melbourne in October 1937, Henry also pointed out innovative child care programs, and did everything she could to smooth his access to the collection of "Spenciana" in Adelaide covering the life and work of her old friend, Catherine Helen Spence.[23] Her main interest was, of course, the women's trade union movement. Bringing to his attention Muriel Heagney's pamphlet, *Do Women Take Men's Jobs?*, she noted:

It . . . contains a great deal or [*sic*] original matter, never before collected. The Women's Bureau thinks most highly of it. I hope you have been in touch with the writer, who is one of the best informed labor authorities in this country, having also had experience abroad. I'm sending you some material touching the new organization she has just launched, analogous to the National Women's Trade Union League of America, on the only sound basis—a federation of the different labor bodies—trade unions—concerned in the establishment of fair wages.[24]

Later that year she reported the appointment of "an exceedingly active and progressive labor woman," Mrs. May Brodney, as "secretary of the Labor College of the Trades Hall here."

I have known her personally for many years. Now she is in a position to use American news of all sorts and I am working with her to that

[21]Letters from Alice Henry to C. Hartley Grattan, 14 and 18 October 1937; 7 January 1938, Box 32/folder 2.

[22]Letter from Alice Henry to C. Hartley Grattan, 4 April 1937, Box 32/folder 2.

[23]Letters from Alice Henry to C. Hartley Grattan, 14 and 18 October 1937, Box 32/folder 2.

[24]Letter from Alice Henry to C. Hartley Grattan, 18 October 1937, Box 32/folder 2.

end. She is very unlike the labor officials here, and is determined to make a change in her own section.[25]

Two years later, though ill and exhausted, Alice Henry was still acting as a go-between for American and Australian feminists. Grattan had written to her about Mary Beard's project to establish a World Center for Women's Archives.[26] Beard's aim, "the projection of women's personality out of the shadows of time into the living force which is women in fact, into written history," was highly congenial to Henry.[27] She promised Grattan to interest people in Australia in the project, and to provide Beard with material on Catherine Helen Spence and "some modern movements in which Australian women are playing an active part," such as the correspondence schools for isolated children and the bush nursing system. Amongst the material collected for this now-defunct archive were materials from Australia dealing with the Centenary Council of Melbourne in 1938, probably provided by Nettie Palmer at the suggestion of Alice Henry.

Alice Henry was also active in supplying Grattan with information and materials about Australian literature. Early in his tour she sent him a copy of what she called "The Miles Franklin Country."[28] After he had visited her in Melbourne, Henry sent Grattan one of her copies of the original edition of Joseph Furphy's *Such is Life* to replace the copy which had disappeared from the Library of Congress.[29] She urged him to see Professor Morris Miller of the University of Tasmania, who was completing a survey and bibliography of Australian literature begun by Sir John Quick and Mr. H. Rutherford Purnell of the Adelaide Public Library.[30] On Grattan's second visit to Melbourne in August 1938, Henry organized a meeting with the elderly poet they both admired, Bernard O'Dowd, whose work supplied the prologue to Grattan's first book on Australia.[31] Henry was herself in declining health at this time, writing rather sadly after the event, "I wish I had not been so eager over Bernard O'Dowd. We could very likely have had Maurice Blackburn too, and then we should have lived in the present instead of the past. He is up-to-date."[32]

Grattan's presence in Australia provided Alice Henry with the stimulation she needed to embark on her autobiography. They had obviously spoken of it during his last visit to Melbourne, as Henry mentions it in her farewell letter

[25]Letter from Alice Henry to C. Hartley Grattan, 15 December 1937, Box 32/folder 2.

[26]Letter from Alice Henry to C. Hartley Grattan, 28 November 1939, Box 32/folder 2.

[27]Ann J. Lane, ed., *Mary Ritter Beard: A Sourcebook* (New York: Schocken Books, 1977), pp. 33-42, 210-14, esp. 34, 37.

[28]Letter from Alice Henry to C. Hartley Grattan, 14 March 1937, Box 32/folder 2.

[29]Letters from Alice Henry to C. Hartley Grattan, 14 and 18 October 1937, Box 32/folder 2.

[30]Letter from Alice Henry to C. Hartley Grattan, 18 October 1937, Box 32/folder 2.

[31]Letters from Alice Henry to C. Hartley Grattan, 19 February and 15 August 1938, Box 32/folder 2. C. Hartley Grattan, *Introducing Australia* (New York: The John Day Company, 1942; reprinted Sydney: Halstead Press, 1944).

[32]Letter from Alice Henry to C. Hartley Grattan, 15 August 1938, Box 32/folder 2.

to Grattan of 28 August. Giving him names of American friends, including Frances Bird, Carroll and Dorothy Binder of the *Chicago Daily News*, and Paul Douglas of the University of Chicago, she notes, "They would want the autobiography."[33] Although the stimulus came from Grattan, the idea of the autobiography was very much Nettie Palmer's. Writing to Grattan on 31 August, Palmer made it quite clear that she saw the book as an important part of her own larger project of recording and disseminating Australian culture:

> Miss Henry has unique memories: Melbourne in the 'eighties & 'nineties, journalism as a woman on the *Argus* who somehow managed to refuse mere fashion notes, organisation of the Women's Franchise League in the 'nineties, affecting the Federal Convention ... I haven't asked her bluntly, but I'm very much afraid she may leap over these things. *Subconsciously*, at least, like so many of our writers, she has her mind on an English publisher. As for Australian memories (as Dr. Cumpston said) who will want to read them! You know the vicious circle. No one will write about Australia because it isn't interesting : & it isn't interesting because no one has written about it.[34]

Nettie Palmer therefore enlisted Grattan in her effort to encourage Henry, and to influence the direction of the memoirs:

> Alice Henry was here today, & spoke of you: to say goodbye to you was like saying Goodbye to America over again.... Can you put a word in, edgewise or straight? She will take a great deal from you. She was delighted, by the way, with your final talk. Vance said it was very full & valid too.[35]

In May of the following year Palmer again prompted Grattan to support her efforts to preserve Alice Henry's memories. "This is not a letter," she wrote, "simply, if you'll forgive me, an injunction: Write to Miss Henry."

> She may not live very long, though she's full of vitality in mind, as you know... She has a romantic passion, not to say a well-founded devotion, to America and what it stands for : and you have somehow brought it all back to her, given her a faith in herself as a woman valued in America. (I can't quite forget that the last time I saw her she was recovering from an attack of exhaustion after moving to the new house, and admitted to several nightmares that suggested her life had been wasted or ill-spent).[36]

[33]Letter from Alice Henry to C. Hartley Grattan, 28 August 1937, Box 32/folder 2.
[34]Letter from Nettie Palmer to C. Hartley Grattan, 31 August 1938, Box 36/folder 1.
[35]Ibid.
[36]Letter from Nettie Palmer to C. Hartley Grattan, 3 May 1939, Box 36/folder 1.

Grattan responded quickly to Nettie Palmer's urgent request. On 22 June he wrote to Alice Henry, emphasizing to her that she belonged to "that Australian generation that did so much to make Australia important to . . . the world." He concluded: "I can think of no other Australian woman of your generation who has more of importance to tell."[37]

Grattan's encouragement came too late, however. In November 1939 Alice Henry wrote to him for the last time: "I am still getting on, though very slowly, with the autobiography. With the present upset condition of the world I find it quite difficult to concentrate upon a world so very different as that in which I grew up. But I'm trying."[38] She moved to a nursing home in 1940 and died on 14 February 1943.

In July 1944 Nettie Palmer wrote to Grattan about Henry's memoirs, which she had had duplicated and bound in an edition of 100 copies. "Don't expect too much of the MS," she wrote. "Alice Henry undertook it very late in life & in any case she was an organiser & co-ordinator [more] than a subtle or sensitive observer. It's the memoir of a great warrior at least."[39] She planned to distribute 50 copies in Australia and 50 in the United States, and "to squeeze a few for Margaret Bondfield to place in England."[40] Mary Beard had agreed to place 12 copies in key libraries in the United States as part of her efforts to improve research resources on women. Nettie Palmer asked Grattan if he would do the same. Grattan immediately wrote to Mary Beard, who told him she planned to keep one copy for herself and distribute the others to universities and individuals who were establishing research programs on women—to Radcliffe College for its National Center for Women's Archives, to Smith College, which already held her correspondence with Alice Henry and other Australian women, to Syracuse University and the Kappa Alpha Theta sorority house there, to Chapel Hill, Duke, Scripps, the University of Wisconsin, and Hunter College. Two copies were to go to Mrs. Eva vomBauer Hansl, "who feeds programs about women over the air and even ideas to Hollywood," and to Miss Marjorie White, Mary Beard's close friend, "who is collecting sketches of women for insertion in the Encyclopedia where

[37]Letter from C. Hartley Grattan to Alice Henry, 22 June 1939, Vance and Nettie Palmer Papers, National Library of Australia, MSS 1174/1/5559-62.

[38]Letter from Alice Henry to C. Hartley Grattan, 28 November 1939, Box 32/folder 2.

[39]Letter from Nettie Palmer to C. Hartley Grattan, 26 July 1944, Box 38/folder 5.

[40]Margaret Bondfield was a longtime friend and correspondent of Henry's. A "fiery and fearless speaker" associated with the Women's Trade Union League in England, Bondfield was Minister of Labour in the first Labour Government after World War I. She now worked in Adult Education. See Nettie Palmer to C. Hartley Grattan, 14 November 1944, Box 38/folder 5; 15 December 1945, Box 36/folder 1; Mary Anderson, *Woman at Work: The Autobiography of Mary Anderson as Told to Mary N. Winslow* (Westport, Conn.: Greenwood Press, 1951), esp. pp. 126, 220, 237.

United States of America

The Library of Congress.

Washington, D.C., October 18, 1945

The Library has received from you a copy of the

"*Memoirs*
of
Alice Henry."

Melbourne, 1944, (Limited ed. 100 copies).

a valued addition to its collections for which I have the honor to return grateful acknowledgments.

Very respectfully,
Your obedient servant.

To
Mr. C. Hartley
Grattan

Luther H. Evans

Librarian

Certificate from the Library of Congress acknowledging receipt of a copy of Alice Henry's *Memoirs. HRHRC Grattan Collection.*

Alice Henry deserves a place."[41] The following March, Nettie Palmer sent another copy to the United States, to "Miss Pesetta, who ran the Women's Garment-Worker's Union, 1933-43," whose book she had seen advertised in the *Saturday Review*.[42]

We do not know where Grattan sent some of the memoirs. The University of Michigan is mentioned in one letter,[43] and an acknowledgement of the receipt of two copies from the Library of Congress dated 18 October 1945 is among Grattan's papers. Nettie Palmer was pleased, however, with his distribution, writing to him, "I think you have made splendid use of the book."[44] In December 1945 she was still receiving requests for the memoirs from the United States (one from Arnold Dresden of Swarthmore College), and sent Grattan two additional copies to use as he saw fit. These are probably the two copies now in the Grattan Collection in the Harry Ransom Humanities Research Center at The University of Texas at Austin.

Nettie Palmer gave copies of the memoirs to all public and academic libraries in Australia, and to "special bodies" such as the Council for Civil Liberties and the Trades Hall, and sent some to New Zealand. In December 1945 she had 13 copies left. These she intended to "go gradually to Labour libraries here, on specific request." As she told Grattan, "I've found the book has meant a good deal to people, some taking an interest in one part of it, some in another."[45] Fifteen months later she sent Grattan an indication of that interest—a "firm little personal pen-picture of AH in her old age—as you knew her, too, written by an ex-librarian to whom I showed the memoir."[46] Unfortunately the pen-picture has not yet been found among the unsorted papers of the Grattan Collection.

II. THE MEMOIRS

The Memoirs of Alice Henry, published in Melbourne in 1944 in a limited edition of 100 copies, is a slim volume of 101 pages, simply bound between buff-colored covers. Twelve pages are devoted to her childhood and educa-

[41]Letter from Mary Beard to C. Hartley Grattan, 18 September 1944, Box 27F/folder 3. See also Mary Beard to Grattan, 23 August 1945, Box 32/folder 2. Marjorie White worked with Mary Beard on a feminist critique of the *Encyclopedia Britannica*; see Lane, *Mary Ritter Beard*, pp. 44-50, 215-24.

[42]Letter from Nettie Palmer to C. Hartley Grattan, 9 March 1945, Box 35/folder 4/3.

[43]Letter from Mary Beard to C. Hartley Grattan, 23 August 1945, Box 32/folder 2.

[44]Letter from Nettie Palmer to C. Hartley Grattan, 15 December 1945, Box 36/folder 1.

[45]Ibid.

[46]Letter from Nettie Palmer to C. Hartley Grattan, March 1947, Box 36/folder 1.

tion; thirteen to her career as a journalist, feminist, and reformer in Melbourne; ten to her visit to Britain in 1905; fifteen to her work in the Women's Trade Union League in the United States from 1906 to 1922; and thirty-five to pen-pictures of men and women she had worked with in the United States labor movement. A short postscript by Nettie Palmer summarizes the rest of Henry's career and describes her life and interests during her last years back in Melbourne. The memoirs close with a chronological résumé of Alice Henry's life and a list of her published books, both prepared by Palmer.

As the work of a woman in her last years, it is not surprising that one of the most delightful parts of the *Memoirs* is Henry's description of her childhood in the early days of Victoria. Her Scottish parents met on board ship on the voyage from Glasgow to Melbourne—considered a "good voyage" because it only took three months. Her father, an accountant, and her mother, a seamstress, married shortly after their arrival in 1852. Melbourne was swollen by gold-seekers, and the couple had to set up house in Canvas Town, a collection of tents on what is now upper St. Kilda's Road. Later they moved to the suburb of Richmond, where Alice Henry was born in 1857, her brother Alfred in 1859, and another sibling who died.

When the American Civil War ruined the cotton industry and the soft goods importing firm for which Charles Henry worked, the family took up a selection near Berwick.[47] Like many others who tried their luck on the land in this period, they were hopelessly poor, living in a tiny timber cottage with an earth floor, and almost wholly self-sufficient. Yet life on Gurny-Gurney Farm (named after the creek where platypus could be heard jumping) was very satisfying to the young Alice Henry, moulding her love of her strange new country. "Most of our selection was as yet uncleared," she wrote:

> so we really lived in the wild bush on the edge of the great Gippsland forest, surrounded by magnificent eucalyptus under their many guises, from rough bark to spotless creamy satin, and so tall that when I first saw oaks and elms and plane trees, they looked quite tame and domestic compared with my imposing giants.[48]

Almost a century later one of the last things she tried to arrange for Hartley Grattan was "a real day off, in the beautiful fern gully country in the Melbourne surroundings." "Have you yet been told," she asked Grattan, "that the South-East corner of Australia is the only region in the temperate zone, where exist and flourish the tree-ferns, cycads, grass-trees and other primitive forms of vegetation, belonging to the carboniferous age."[49]

[47]A selection is a small block of land for homesteading.
[48]Alice Henry, *Memoirs*, ed. with postscript by Nettie Palmer (Melbourne, 1944), p. 3.
[49]Letter from Alice Henry to C. Hartley Grattan, 19 February 1938, Box 32/folder 2.

Rural life also inculcated a strong sense of female independence and efficacy in the young Alice Henry, as it did in other Australian feminists such as Rose Scott and Miles Franklin.

> The distinctions between qualities and standing between boys and girls were literally unknown to me, though it was in my hearing that my mother remarked upon it, when a visitor offered a ride upon his pony to my little brother and took no notice of me. That was perhaps my first lesson in feminism.[50]

She saw her mother "making the best of it," efficiently running the dairy, raising poultry, making soap and candles, and giving the children their first lessons, despite the illness that was to kill her ten years later.[51] Luckily this rural interlude lasted only three years, and Alice Henry's feminism was not tinged by the bitterness of Miles Franklin, who saw her mother crushed by the burdens and disappointments of the "cow-cocky's" wife.[52]

Back in Melbourne, Alice Henry passed the matriculation exam at Richard Hale Budd's Educational Institute for Ladies. "It was quite certain that I was to earn my own living," she wrote.[53] As women were not yet admitted to the University of Melbourne, she became a pupil teacher at her old school, one of the few options open to educated women.[54] Several other educational experiences were significant enough for her to mention them in her memoirs. The first derived from her father, a serious, cultivated man who belonged to the Swedenborgian Church and passed on his love of music and opera to his daughter.[55] The second was a literature class conducted by an American friend of her mother's, Mrs. Florence Williams, the daughter of the popular novelist G.P.R. James.[56] Finally, there were Harriet Elphinstone Dick, the long-distance swimmer who introduced the Ling gymnastic system into Australia, and Thomas Hare, whose *Representative Government*, read in the Mechanics' Institute Library at the age of twenty, gave her a "vision of the possibility of

[50]Henry, *Memoirs*, p. 3.

[51]Ibid.

[52]For Australian feminists and rural life, see Desley Deacon, *Managing Gender* (1989); "Her Brilliant Career: The Context of Nineteenth-Century Australian Feminism," paper presented to Texas Women Scholars: Contemporary Perspectives Symposium, The University of Texas at Austin, 1986; and "The Importance of Context: Some Speculations About the Effect of Economic and Political Change on the Development of Feminism in New South Wales," paper presented to Crucible of Feminism: Women in the Nineteenth Century, conference organized by the Research Centre for Women's Studies, The University of Adelaide, South Australia, 1985.

[53]Henry, *Memoirs*, p. 8.

[54]Ibid.

[55]Ibid.

[56]Ibid., p. 7.

releasing and utilizing the vast political energy of the whole people, to give them their proper share in governing themselves."[57]

The routine of teaching did not appeal to this active young woman. In 1884 she began her career in journalism with the *Argus* and the *Australasian*, two "safely conservative" papers on which she was well-trained by their Scottish editor, David Watterston.[58] She became involved in the care of mental patients and epileptics, keeping abreast of the latest American developments in their treatment, and in 1903 helping to establish a Farm Colony for Epileptics with the aid of the National Council of Women.[59] She also supported the establishment of Queen Victoria Hospital, where systematic pre-natal advice could be dispensed by women doctors for the first time.[60] Despite the conservatism of the papers she wrote for, Alice Henry was involved in a number of radical causes. Along with Dr. Charles Strong of the Australia Church and Henry Bournes Higgins, she opposed Australia's participation in the Boer War.[61] She worked for women's suffrage and the local progressive leagues which dealt with "any question touching the social and civic welfare of the home and the family"—the "suffering women," as the son of one suffragist called them.[62]

When Alice Henry went to England for the first time in 1905, at the age of forty-eight, she found herself a "stranger in a strange land." The editor of a "good provincial paper" opened the dinner conversation one evening with: "We don't like the way you do things in Australia, Miss Henry, your tariffs and your white Australia and all the rest of your queer legislation."[63] Despite the attractions of Bernard Shaw and the new feminism led by the Pankhursts, it was America rather than England that welcomed and captivated her.[64]

"It was as a middle-aged woman that I made acquaintance with America," Alice Henry wrote. Like many who came in contact with the "great people in the social workers' world" of the United States, she was able to testify: "I was singularly fortunate in the welcome I received."[65] Henry had introductions to this world from her old friend, fellow feminist, and supporter of the Hare system of proportional representation, Catherine Helen Spence, who had visited the United States in 1893, meeting Charlotte Perkins Gilman in San Francisco, staying at Hull House in Chicago, and visiting Anna Garlin Spencer in New England. Spence took Gilman's first published book to

[57]Ibid., pp. 10-11, 25; Thomas Hare, *A Treatise on the Election of Representatives, Parliamentary and Municipal* (London: Longman, Brown, Green, Longman & Roberts, 1859).

[58]Henry, *Memoirs*, p.13.

[59]Ibid., pp. 14-17.

[60]Ibid., p. 16.

[61]Ibid., p. 20.

[62]Ibid., pp. 22-23.

[63]Ibid., p. 29.

[64]Ibid., pp. 30-33.

[65]Ibid., p. 37.

WOMEN AND THE
LABOR MOVEMENT

❂

ALICE HENRY

THE WORKERS' BOOKSHELF
Volume IV

Cover of Alice Henry's *Women and the Labor Movement* (Doran, 1923). *HRHRC Grattan Collection*.

England with her, where it was published in the edition which made Gilman's British reputation.[66] Alice Henry was welcomed, therefore, as part of the transpacific and transatlantic sisterhood that encircled the world at the turn of the century. In words reminiscent of Florence Kelley's description of her own welcome to Hull House on a snowy Christmas day in 1892,[67] Henry wrote of the New York Settlement House of which Anna Spencer was a member: "I was taken in at once and made welcome. At once! At first! A favored visitor from far-away Australia!"[68]

Like Florence Kelley, Alice Henry was immediately put to work. "Oh dear! they were in a hurry to have something from me. . . . An appointment had been made for me to address the New York School of Social Workers the very next morning." Henry soon found that

> Australia was a word to rouse interest in all that circle and I arrived at a moment when Australia was beginning some of her most notable experiments in social legislation. . . . My ready passport at that moment was my familiarity with "votes for women" . . . so for the rest of that lecturing session I was passed on from one small paying engagement to another.[69]

Alice Henry's familiarity with women's suffrage took her to Chicago, to which she was summoned by Jane Addams and Anna Nicholes to assist them in securing the municipal vote for women. She lovingly describes the city in which she was to live and work for the next twenty-two years, and Hull House, the center of the network of reformers with whom she was to be intimately associated.

> You have heard of Hull House as the very heart of Chicago, the spring of so many young activities, where met budding trade unions; where so many thousands of foreign immigrants first made the acquaintance of civilized America; whence came demands for street cleaning and proper lighting in the poorest districts; where held suffrage meetings, while "votes for women" were still unladylike. Its lighter side, so friendly to this stranger, was a joy.[70]

She arrived in Chicago on a warm summer morning in 1906 after sitting up all night on the train from Minneapolis. Scheduled to speak that evening, she "promptly nestled into [her] little bed at Hull House, first asking for

[66]Susan Magarey, *Unbridling the Tongues of Women: A Biography of Catherine Helen Spence* (Sydney: Hale & Iremonger, 1985), pp. 165-168; C.P. Gilman, *The Living of Charlotte Perkins Gilman* (New York: Harper & Row, 1975).

[67]Florence Kelley, *The Autobiography of Florence Kelley: Notes of Sixty Years*, ed. and introd. by Kathryn Kish Sklar (Chicago: Charles H. Kerr Publishing Company, 1986), pp. 77-79.

[68]Henry, *Memoirs*, pp. 37-38.

[69]Ibid., pp. 38-39.

[70]Ibid., p. 44.

something to read, only bargaining that it be not anything about reform. And the jolly resident only laughed and promptly produced several magazines and a novel."[71] Of Jane Addams—"America's First Citizen," as Henry calls her—she writes perceptively:

> It is difficult to describe a very great person and Jane Addams was extremely simple; she had no corners; she carried on a great public career without thinking much about herself at all.[72]

The American sisterhood, with its large, well-organized women's groups, its settlement houses, and its independent influence in the proliferating networks of reformers and pressure groups, provided American women with a "baptism of power and liberty" not enjoyed by Australian and British women.[73] Alice Henry was quickly assimilated into this active female political world. At Sunday dinner at Hull House she met Margaret Dreier Robins and her husband Raymond Robins. The next day Mrs. Robins invited her to become the office secretary of the Chicago branch of the Women's Trade Union League, of which she was president.

Alice Henry and her office boss, veteran trade unionist Emma Steghagen of the Boot and Shoe Workers Union, had deskroom in the office of the *Union Labor Advocate*, the Chicago labor monthly. From 1908-10, Alice Henry edited the women's page of the *Advocate*, assisted by her friend Miles Franklin. Warmly welcomed "as another arrival from that distant and most interesting country, Australia," Franklin had come to Chicago in 1906 and become one of Mrs. Robins's private secretaries.[74] From 1910 to 1915 the two Australian women edited *Life and Labor*, the Women's Trade Union League's own monthly publication, where Miles Franklin put her flirtatious abilities to work for the cause. As Henry says:

> With the Labor men she was always popular and could be depended upon to draw them out and obtain from them opinions and information, which they could never have put so attractively themselves.[75]

Although she had little direct contact with labor organizations in Australia, Alice Henry was familiar, as all Progressive Australians were, with her country's experiments in trade union organization, wages boards, and industrial arbitration. In addition, she was a close friend of one of the industrial system's chief theorists and practitioners, Henry Bournes Higgins. Her expertise was useful, therefore, to the burgeoning American labor movement and its middle-class supporters, especially in the fight for the minimum

[71]Ibid., p. 43.
[72]Ibid., pp. 61-63.
[73]Ruth Bordin, *Frances Willard: A Biography* (Chapel Hill: University of North Carolina Press, 1986).
[74]Henry, *Memoirs*, p. 89.
[75]Ibid., pp. 45-48, 89.

wage.[76] Much of her memoirs are taken up with portraits of the men and women she worked with and admired in this movement—Sydney Hillman, that "great, constructive labor organizer" who became at the age of twenty-seven president of the Amalgamated Clothing Workers of America at its inception in 1914;[77] Margaret Dreier Robins and her sister Mary Dreier, the vice-president of the New York branch of the WTUL, whose friendship Alice Henry prized "exceedingly";[78] Mary Anderson, the immigrant shoe factory worker who became Director of the Women's Bureau in the U.S. Department of Labor;[79] Elizabeth Christman, the former glovemaker who was the secretary-treasurer of the National WTUL;[80] and Agnes Nestor, another glovemaker who became an "A1 lobbyist" in Congress and among the women's clubs.[81]

One of Alice Henry's favorite characters from her Chicago period seems to have been James Mullenbach, whose career covered many of her own concerns—care of the homeless and mentally ill, support for striking unionists, education, and labor mediation. Mullenbach succeeded Raymond Robins as Superintendent of the Chicago Municipal Lodging House, where he was "intensely interested in what went into the making of tramps and was all the while trying to unmake them."[82] He handled relief aid for the WTUL during the clothing workers' strike of 1910; became Superintendent of Cook County Charitable Institutions; acted as impartial chairman of the Labor Board of Hart, Schaffner and Marx, the main clothing employers of Chicago; was on the Chicago Board of Education from 1924 to 1931; and was an important labor mediator during the New Deal, working on the Petroleum Labor Policy Board, the National Steel Labor Relations Board, and the Textile Labor Relations Board before his death in 1935.

Alice Henry was always enthusiastic about the arts. She devotes several pages, therefore, to two aspects of the work of the Hull House circle that are rarely discussed. The first is the Hull-House Players, a theater group run by former actress Laura Dainty Pelham, which staged experimental and controversial plays by Shaw, Ibsen, Lady Gregory, and Galsworthy.[83] The second is the movement to bring music to the people through Sunday concerts in the parks in workingclass areas. This successful Chicago experiment, in a city Henry characterizes as generous with music, was run by Arnold Dresden, the

[76]Ibid., p. 87.
[77]Ibid., p. 55.
[78]Ibid., pp. 66-69.
[79]Ibid., pp. 70-73.
[80]Ibid., pp. 74-75.
[81]Ibid., pp. 85-86.
[82]Ibid., pp. 56-57.
[83]Ibid., p. 76.

old friend from Swarthmore College who would request a copy of her memoirs in 1947.[84]

In 1920 Alice Henry became secretary of the WTUL's educational department, and from 1920 to 1922 she was responsible for organizing and coordinating the Bryn Mawr Summer School for Working Women.[85] The final section of the memoirs is, fittingly, devoted to her description of the first years of this experiment in workers' education, which "offer[ed] to working women an interpretation of their own problems on the one hand and, on the other, [gave] them access to the world of literature and science."[86]

III. Postscript

Nettie Palmer's postscript briefly fills in the rest of Alice Henry's full life. In 1925 she returned to Australia for a visit, during which she was "received by many friends and societies as one who had been abroad on a lengthy and distinguished ambassadorship."[87] After living in retirement in Santa Barbara, California, she returned to Australia permanently in 1933. "Indignant at the Australian lack of interest in the US and the New Deal," she was "a tired and rather lonely woman, lonely not because she had no friends, but because so few of her friends understood what life had been for her in her best years." As time went on, Palmer continues, "she came to draw her life from the books, papers and letters that came by the American mail." When the Council of Civil Liberties was formed in Melbourne in 1936, she joined this Australian version of the organization her friend Roger Baldwin had begun in the U.S. (though, as she pointed out, the Australian organization was an offshoot of the British rather than the American Civil Liberties Union). She interested herself in the League of Nations Union, the YWCA, and the newer organizations for correspondence schools and the Flying Doctor. Finally, she welcomed Hartley Grattan, the young American who reminded her of the quest she had shared with her American colleagues—a quest encapsulated in a quotation from Bernard O'Dowd's *Dawnward?*, which she used on her card of farewell to her American friends when she left California to return home in 1933:

> Building, for the Harmonist,
> The City of His Dream.[88]

---

[84]Ibid., pp. 44, 82.
[85]Kirkby, "Alice Henry and the Women's Trade Union League" (1982), p. 255.
[86]Henry, *Memoirs*, pp. 90-95.
[87]Ibid., pp. 96-99.
[88]Ibid.

Iris Milutinovic and her husband Milor, from the xeroxed copy of an article entitled "Pen Portrait of a Migrant," with a handwritten notation: "Herald 7/12/78." *HRHRC Milutinovic Collection.*

Iris Milutinovic—Between Two Worlds

BY JOHN MCLAREN

Born in Tasmania in 1909, Iris Osborne Milutinovic began her career of writing and broadcasting late in life in Albany, a small and isolated town on King George's Sound, towards the southwesternmost point of the Australian coast. Her 60 radio broadcasts, delivered between 1958 and 1975 through the Australian Broadcasting Commission, contained accounts of her life in Albany and reminiscences of her family, while her stories, collected in *I'm Still Here, Aren't I?* (1985), and two novels, *Talk English Carn't Ya* (1978) and the unpublished "The Street of Seven Tongues," written during the 1950s and 1960s, were partly fictionalized autobiography.[1] The Iris Milutinovic Collection at the Harry Ransom Humanities Research Center at The University of Texas at Austin comprises draft manuscripts of "The Street of Seven Tongues"[2] and *Talk English Carn't Ya*,[3] as well as manuscripts of her short stories;[4]

[1]Iris Milutinovic, *I'm Still Here, Aren't I?* (Lenah Valley, Tasmania: Shearwater Press, 1985); *Talk English Carn't Ya* (Melbourne: Hyland House, 1978).

[2]The uncatalogued Iris Milutinovic archive in the HRHRC collections totals thirteen numbered boxes. In the first two boxes are four typescript versions of the unpublished novel, "The Street of Seven Tongues": an early version, labeled "First Draft" and dated by the author as being written between 1954 and 1963; and three later versions: one labeled by the author, "File Copy—2nd Completed Version," a second renamed *Not Far From Nowhere* (including a partial manuscript version), dated 1975, and described in a note by the author as the "File Copy of Final version of Street of Seven Tongues with additions & deletions & new title," and a bound copy labeled "File Copy of Completed Book (First Version)." The bound copy is housed in Box 2; all other drafts are in Box 1.

[3]In Box 13 of the Milutinovic Collection is the draft manuscript to *Talk English Carn't Ya*, written by hand in fifteen notebooks, each of which comprises a separate chapter, as well as two typescript versions and two carbon-copy typescripts. One of these versions, apparently the earliest, bears the title "Give a Poor Bastard a Go," crossed out with "Talk English Carn't Ya" written above it. The original title later became the title of the first chapter of *Talk English Carn't Ya*. Evidently, Milutinovic originally intended to publish under a pseudonym, since on three of the four manuscripts she has indicated the author as "I. Maggie Ostin." Page proofs to the book are contained in Box 12.

[4]Milutinovic's short stories can be found in Boxes 3, 4, and 7.

typescripts of Milutinovic's radio talks;[5] correspondence with editors, publishers, friends, and relatives; personal notebooks; and assorted memorabilia, all apparently arranged by Milutinovic herself and donated to the HRHRC over a period of time from 1976 to 1985.[6] Taken as a whole, the Milutinovic Collection affords a valuable historical record of domestic life during the period when European emigration to Australia reached a peak, and of the cultural clashes produced in Australia by this influx of postwar European immigrants.

In particular, the Iris Milutinovic papers reveal a woman caught between the conflicting cultures of her Anglo-Celtic establishment family and of her Serbian second husband, Milor Milutinovic. The expectations peculiar to both cultures, particularly with respect to the roles of men and women in the family, in addition to the obvious language differences, contrived to separate the couple from their respective cultures and created difficulties for the marriage. Iris's upbringing within her largely conservative and middle-class family, the Osbornes and Burnells of Tasmania, prepared her for a life of frugal but comfortable domesticity amid a wide circle of family and friends. Yet her family also bred in her a strain of rebellion, which led her into her first and wildly unsuitable marriage to an Irish guardsman in the 1920s and then in 1951 into her second and successful marriage to Milutinovic. By a previous marriage, Milor had sons in Yugoslavia, where he had been a comfortable landowner before enduring the war and arriving in Australia as a penniless immigrant. After his marriage to Iris, he took his new wife to Albany in pursuit of his dream of establishing another farm of his own. There, the Milutinovics found themselves isolated by penury and distance from family and friends, by Milor's difficulties with the language, and later by illness. While Milor tackled his problems through constant toil, Iris began writing, and her radio broadcasts and short stories brought additional income to the couple. At the same time, Iris escaped the isolation of her life in the bush through correspondence with family, friends, and admirers.

Although Milutinovic was a busy professional writer whose work included regular articles on cooking for the *Epicurean* and short stories published in literary journals such as *Overland* and popular publications such as *Australian*

---

[5]A list of Milutinovic's radio talks, compiled by the author, can be found in Box 2, along with a package of radio talks. Other radio scripts are contained in Boxes 5 and 6; a package of rejected radio scripts is in Box 3. Milutinovic's radio talks were broadcast mainly on "All Ways on Sunday," a women's program for the rural network of the Australian Broadcasting Commission (ABC) in Western Australia. Some 40 of Milutinovic's scripts for "All Ways on Sunday" are held by the former producer of the show, John Barnett, of Channel 10 in Perth, WA, Australia. It has not been possible to compare these with the holdings in the HRHRC collections.

[6]Correspondence, notebooks, diaries, financial statements, and other miscellaneous materials are housed in Boxes 8-11. Among her memorabilia are souvenirs of arts festivals in Toowoomba and Bendigo, where Milutinovic won prizes for short stories in 1972 and 1975, rejection slips from various editors, and a cassette tape of unpublished reminiscences.

Women's Weekly and *Woman's Day*, during her life she published only two books, the novel *Talk English Carn't Ya* and the short story collection *I'm Still Here, Aren't I?* Like her published novel, the unpublished "The Street of Seven Tongues" is a slightly fictionalized autobiography based on Iris's life with her husband, Milor, but whereas in *Talk English Carn't Ya* the first person narration purports to be the words of the husband as dictated to his wife, in this book the wife speaks in the first person. Thus, while Milutinovic gave to her husband a fictionalized voice to address the Australian community that had otherwise refused to hear him, she left unpublished her own narration. "The Street of Seven Tongues" documents the attempts of the husband to establish himself in a new land and his wife's attempts to reconcile her own ambitions with his dreams and insecurities. The conflicts between husband and wife, and between the two of them and their neighbors and the authorities, repeat those of the original Australian drama of settlement within the new circumstances created by the postwar wave of immigration. The unpublished book, unstructured though it is, records the emergence of a multicultural community and consciousness.

Set in Albany, "The Street of Seven Tongues" reports on life on Ulster Road, where, in the words of the unnamed narrator, "My Serb migrant husband [Tomic] and I arrived in 1951."

> Along its lower side have settled people from many lands, who have, as we have, struggled to establish themselves, to adapt themselves, and probably, as seems to be one of humanity's greatest concerns, to justify themselves.[7]

In this environment, the Australian Aboriginal past remains only in the remembered images of the "children [who] used to sell boronia, the sweetest scented flower in the State,"[8] and the bush track, now become a "recognizable road," beside the "small swampy creek."[9] The present is being forged through the adaptation of the immigrants to the strange land and their adaptation of it to suit their way of life. From within this process the narrator writes her book and offers her story as a history of "Migration in Miniature," which is the title of her second chapter.

The couple's pioneering venture starts with their life together in the uninsulated one room "flat" or apartment owned by the eternally cheerful Mrs. Chester, the ultimate exploitative landlady who gladly shifts any blame for the shortcomings of her accommodation to the tenants themselves. Soon after their arrival, Tomic, driven by his "intense longing to own, without

---

[7]Milutinovic, "The Street of Seven Tongues," p. 1 of "File Copy–2nd Completed Version," Box 1. Permission to quote from the unpublished writings of Iris Milutinovic has been given by Stephen Murray-Smith, her literary executor.

[8]Ibid., p. 4.

[9]Ibid., pp. 1-2.

encumbrance, one's own land and living quarters," buys a block of land on the outskirts of the town and builds his own home.[10] Small as it is, it represents his claim on the new country. "I have always been proud of that first small home, built with such difficulty by a man who not only disliked anything to do with carpenter's tools, but whose every instinct called him outside where the land waited to be cleared and cropped," the narrator explains.[11] But this achievement leaves untouched the deeper conflict arising from the different origins of husband and wife. Tomic likes watching people, but his difficulty with the English language leads him to shun company. As a consequence of her husband's attitude, the narrator, brought up in a small town with the constant company of family and friends, is forced to deny her own gregarious instincts. The cultural backgrounds and personalities both husband and wife bring to their new life seem to collude with the situation in heightening the sense of isolation each feels.

After the building of the house, the story widens from the paradigmatic experience of Tomic and his wife to encompass the lives of their neighbors, in a variation on the theme of isolation. The first to come are members of a Polish family, whose mother remains even more isolated than Tomic through her total inability to learn English. Next is the Slav, Milan, who dislikes Australians for their failure to appreciate his wavy hair and handsome moustache and resents their national predilection for controlling production through government marketing boards, which set compulsory limits on production in order to market goods on the government's own terms. "In Europe," he complains, "often things are very bad. Too much some years, not enough others. But on his own land a man can plant as he likes."[12] Then come a Czech and his German wife, who cause trouble by leaving their poultry free to roam and to invade their neighbors' territory. Eventually the street becomes home to Dutch, Australian, Italian, Yugoslav, Hungarian, Czech, and Polish families, some of which settle more successfully than others: the Hungarian takes his wife back to Germany because she cannot tolerate life in Australia; a German couple encounters marital trouble that leads eventually to their extending their household to accommodate the wife's lover. Visitors add to social life, but the little settlement remains concerned with cows and pigs, cats and dogs, the animals that still remain in the bush, the completion of building projects, and the maintenance of the assortment of motor vehicles on which their projects depend.

Although the settlers are united by their common struggle for security and their suspicion of the power of big business, unions, and bureaucracy, lack of a common language separates them and adversity divides them, as the impulse

[10]Ibid., p. 23.
[11]Ibid., p. 25.
[12]Ibid., pp. 30-31.

146

toward mutual assistance degenerates into exploitation of the more advanced by the less well-off, the latter trading on the generosity of their better-established neighbors. The narrator shows also how the community is split by the varying histories of the settlers and the national pride they shore up against their deprivations, focusing in particular on Tomic's sometimes idealized memories of his European past.

Tomic's earliest memories are of his mother's attempts during the First World War to save the family cow from the soldiers who were billetted among them and of her grief at her husband's death on Corfu after the heroic retreat from Bulgaria, when the Serbs exhumed and carried with them the sacred bodies of their medieval kings. Later, after the popular uprisings of Serbians and other Yugoslavians against King Paul's pact with Germany and Italy, Tomic spent four years as a prisoner of war. The narrator, Tomic's wife, reflects on his past tribulations.

> Hard, perhaps, but no harder than many others endured. . . . Many Europeans have suffered more. Like Tomic, their homeland is forever lost to them. Here they try to make new lives and some find it hard, a few, impossible. Many find us, the careless, laughing, generous, fictional Australians, the hardest part of it.[13]

Yet these experiences of suffering and deprivation do not necessarily make the settlers more tolerant of others. Czech visitors condemn the iniquities of Jews and Communists and praise the Aryans, but when invited to someone's home refuse to use Christian names with their host: "Oh, NO. In my country we only do this with friends."[14] Tomic cannot adapt his own customs to the expectations of a new society but neither has he any sympathy for the failure of the Aborigines to adapt to the ways of the society that has displaced them from their land and left them locked in a pre-European past. He resents his wife's attempts to engage a friendship with May Enders, the bright young Aboriginal girl who by the age of twenty-two is defeated, jobless, and left with three light-skinned children to support. Her fate, arising from the history of her people, leaves her to live alongside the immigrants without being connected to them in any way.

Poverty constantly frustrates Tomic's attempts to establish a satisfactory home on Ulster Road and his efforts to succeed on his own farm, a venture doomed from the start by his and his wife's ignorance of local farming conditions, by the duplicity of agents and bankers, and by the complete lack of advice or communication from the vendors, who resent the immigrants' changing the older Australia they have known. As the narrator describes an Australian vendor, "Neither Jack nor his middleaged wife liked what they

[13]Ibid., pp. 101-102.
[14]Ibid., p. 141.

didn't understand, and they certainly did not understand or try to understand Europeans."[15] The project fails and husband and wife retreat to Ulster Road, where eventually they are able to sell some of their property and build their dream home. By this time, however, the narrator has been struck by illness and has nearly died, and the story ends with an episode entitled "Back to a Beginning," in which Tomic and his wife sell the last of their land and use the money to travel to Tasmania to visit the narrator's ninety-year-old mother. The closing note is on the sadness of being old, but the husband and wife face their future with a strength drawn from the feeling that together they have overcome adversity and cultural differences and successfully established a home.

The reader shares the narrator's achievement as she and her husband steadily mold their physical environment and shape the pattern of their marriage to fit their separate needs and desires. The theme of diversity as a force for unity extends to the description of the various families of Ulster Road banding into a small neighborhood community which, in turn, gradually creates links with the town in which they live. Through this theme the narrative flows forcefully for the first ten of its twenty-one chapters, but the text then weakens and each successive chapter seems merely an episodic illustration of the daily life of the community rather than a stage in its development. The theme of unity becomes important again in chapter 16, when the narrator's illness brings her close to death, threatening the whole attempt at settlement and thus highlighting the mutual dependence that has grown between husband and wife. The story falls away again through two anecdotal chapters before story and theme are once again brought together in the final chapters, which by carrying the narrator back to her beginnings also seem to bring a sense of completeness to her life. However, the narrator's sense of resolution is with her own culture, not with that of her husband, who thus remains an outsider at the close of the story. Only when Milutinovic reworked the tale in her published novel, *Talk English Carn't Ya*, which includes an account of the husband's return to Serbia as well as the wife's to Tasmania, could the separate cultures and the separate lives be brought together into a single resolution.

In *Talk English Carn't Ya*, Iris Milutinovic deals directly with the confrontation of the two cultures. In essence this novel retells the story of "The Street of Seven Tongues," but concentrates on the experience of husband and wife rather than on observations of their neighbors. It has a more coherent structure, eliminating digressions and proceeding from the point of view of the husband rather than that of the wife. In the preface to the book, the author, speaking in her own name, explains:

[15]Ibid., p. 77.

148

. . . It is, to the best of my belief authentic. Most of it is about my husband and his life with me in Australia. Because one or two episodes concern others I have used the name "Borislav Mihailovic" for the composite, true but very real character of whom I have written. [16]

Despite the disclaimer, by providing fictitious names, Milutinovic fashions the book into a novel rather than a documentary, and it should be judged as a novel, by the truth it establishes rather than the truth it points to.

Most of the incidents in *Talk English Carn't Ya* appear in other forms in Milutinovic's talks and stories or in the typescript of "The Street of Seven Tongues," all found in the collected papers at the HRHRC. However, these incidents gain a different significance in the published novel by being shown from the husband's point of view. The story is ostensibly dictated by the husband to his wife and is told in his broken English, characterized by a preference for the present tense, with alternation between definite and continuous forms, omission of words—particularly articles—and with words or phrases used in places and senses different from those found in the idiom of the native speaker. Thus in a scene from the chapter "How High Is Up," in which Boris has been trying to supervise the building of the couple's large new house, he explains:

> We want table built on to one wall in very big room. This table will make place between the end of room where is cooking stove, sink, pantry and refrigerator. Other end has one big sofa and some armchairs and open fireplace. It is same size as ordinary table but is not moving. When Maggie sees it she is much cross. Table is 8″ higher and 8″ narrower than she asks. It is not table but bench. They pull it out and cut down but it makes hole in wall. To fix hole they put one big piece of black glass, and we are thinking this is no good but we find is best thing. [17]

The grammar and syntax may be unorthodox, but the words dramatize what Boris finds wrong—the lack of attention on the part of the Australian builder he has engaged.

At first this use of language seems to mock the immigrant's use of English, somewhat in the manner of the best-selling 1958 novel *They're a Weird Mob*, which was a joke in dubious taste at the expense of the immigrant finding

---

[16]Milutinovic, *Talk English, Carn't Ya*, [ix]. The pagination begins at page one of the novel, and so for easy reference I have supplied the roman numeral. All further textual references to *Talk English Carn't Ya* will be to the published version.

[17]Ibid., p. 70.

difficulty with the local idiom.[18] However, Milutinovic uses the language of the immigrant not as a joke but as a way of conveying the perceptions of the speaker and the difficulties put in his way by his own ignorance and by the obliviousness of the English-speaking society to his problems. As the book proceeds, the language grows more fluent, and the reader is made aware of the immigrant's speech not as something strange but as the embodiment of the cultural situation. Like the speaker in the novel, the immigrant's language is caught between two worlds. As Boris becomes more at home in Australia, his expression becomes clearer, but it never loses the sense of strangeness, of something alien to the native ear. Yet the very strangeness of the phrasing— "It makes hole in wall"—underscores the effort of the speaker to put the immigrant's situation into foreign words.

Talk English Carn't Ya highlights the difficulties as well as delights of the Milutinovics' marriage more clearly than any of the writer's talks or short stories. In particular, it shows the kind of thoughtless male arrogance that Boris brings from his culture and sheds only as he painfully comes to accept his responsibility to his wife, Maggie, and to see her as an independent person rather than merely a comfortable adjunct to his life. Unlike "The Street of Seven Tongues," *Talk English Carn't Ya* also shows the wife asserting herself to take charge of the couple's affairs.

The cultural and emotional aspects of the marriage and its fictional counterpart are dramatized by the contrast of the final chapters of the novel, when both Boris and Maggie return to their homelands. The incidents of the journey to visit Maggie's family in Tasmania had provided material for some of Milutinovic's radio talks, but their significance in the novel derives from Boris's increasing awareness of his responsibility for Maggie as a result of her physical weakness. On their return from Tasmania, Maggie suggests to Boris that he has finally become a patriot for Western Australia, his true home, although at first he does not recognize the reality of Maggie's remarks.

> Boris the way you kept telling those overseas tourists that West Australia is best state and Seaton best town in best state was too funny. Talk about a one man band. I had no idea you ever knew all those interesting things you told them about Australia and especially about Seaton.[19]

Boris must return to Europe before he can accept this truth, and in the last two chapters of the novel, he goes to visit his family in Yugoslavia, at Maggie's prompting. Here he takes his place in the same kind of extended family that

---

[18]John O'Grady ("Nino Culotta"), *They're a Weird Mob* (Sydney: Ure Smith, 1957). Ostensibly written by an Italian immigrant, Nino Culotta, *They're a Weird Mob* pretended to find Australians peculiar but in fact flattered our idiosyncrasies and excused our intolerance.

[19]*Talk English Carn't Ya*, p. 120.

MILUTINOVIC . . .

. . . So much so that she's used it for the title of a book which was published a fortnight ago.

The book has already received favourable comment with the obvious comparisons to John O'Grady's famous "They're a Weird Mob".

But it's more than that which gives it a special meaning to Mrs Milutinovic.

She was born at Cooee, the daughter of F. D. Osborne, but has spent the major part of her life in Western Australia.

Her husband, Milor, is from Serbia, and she said yesterday that in "Talk English Carn't Ya", she has tried to speak with a migrant's voice.

Based on experiences

The book is based on Milor's experiences.

"There's not one thing not true of this migrant (Milor) or any other migrant", Mrs Milutinovic said.

However, there are a few chapters not based on her husband's life — "But I'm not saying which ones they are", she said.

The book is described as a "cruel, sad, funny story" dealing with the culture-clash presented when a migrant comes face to face with Australian life.

The book's hero, "Boris Mihailovic", tells how it feels for an articulate, intelligent adult to be reduced overnight to the level of communication of a six-year-old, because he can't speak English.

In writing the book, Mrs Milutinovic said she had tried to get into her husband's mind, and therefore the mind of every migrant wrestling with the problems of a new homeland.

Although this is her first published book she has had many short stories published in magazines and anthologies.

One of them, "The Guppy", won a Victorian award and a collection of stories recently won the Jessie Litchfield Award for Literature.

Mrs Milutinovic has also contributed to the Australian section of the "Mrs Beeton's Cookbook".

East Devonport authoress Mrs Iris Milutinovic pictured at home yesterday.

Book spells out migrants' woe

"TALK English, carn't ya?" is a typical Aussie comment to a new migrant who obviously can't speak a word of English, let alone understand the Australian way of speaking.

But for migrants, the language barrier is usually their biggest problem in adjusting to the multi-national life-style in this country.

Top this off with a different culture, and you have a great rift.

So for the new Australian, life here at first, and quite often for some time, is difficult.

This is what Tasmanian-born author Iris Milutinovic, of East Devonport, writes in her recently published book "Talk English Carn't Ya!"

Old family

Mrs Milutinovic (nee Osborne) was born and brought up at Cooee on the North-West Coast.

She comes from an old Tasmanian family related to the Burnells and Dame Enid Lyons.

Last year she returned to Tasmania after 30 years in West Australia.

Mrs Milutinovic and her husband, Milor, now live in an old riverside cottage at East Devonport.

When interstate she met and married Milor, a Yugoslav migrant, and through him learned of a less homely Australia which presents itself to the migrant who speaks no English.

She has become a well-known writer of short stories.

Her work, "The Guppy", won the Victorian short story award in 1975, and she is highly respected for her radio broadcasting in Albany (WA).

Recently, she won the Litchfield award for services and contributions to Australian literature.

Her new book "Talk English Carn't Ya" was published this month.

"It is a tale which makes us laugh and makes us sad, give us pious, entertains us and baffles us by something about ourselves and our society," she said yesterday.

Clash

"It is a cruel, sad, funny story — for where there is culture clash there is misunderstanding, and therefore grief.

"The book is totally true, and tells of the story of a young migrant, Borislav Mikhailovic, arriving in Australia in 1949 without being able to speak a word of English," said Mrs Milutinovic.

"I thought the story might be valuable for people to read about what the life of a newly arrived migrant is like.

"I think it will show how very hard it is to settle in another country when you are uneducated," she said.

Iris Milutinovic speaks from her experience of marrying a non-English speaking migrant.

She has come to understand the difficulty migrants face and the anxiety of hoping to be accepted as an Australian.

"In this book I have attempted to speak with the migrant's voice," she said.

"Of course my story will not be true of all migrants, but surely it is representative of most.

"I hope it will help Australians to understand the problems of migrants, and maybe in the long run help them to accept their new countrymen as equals."

Mrs Iris Milutinovic in the garden of her East Devonport home . . . language is often the biggest barrier for migrants to Australia.

Habant Mercury 28/10/78

Xeroxed clipping of a review of Iris Milutinovic's *Talk English Carn't Ya*, with a handwritten notation: "Habant Mercury 28/10/78." *HRHRC Milutinovic Collection.*

Maggie had found in Tasmania. The ease with which both husband and wife rejoin their familial communities emphasizes the loneliness they suffer in their life together. Yet while Boris understands that the source of his being is European, he realizes also that he has now made his new life in Australia.

I am feeling I am being cut in two pieces. This is my country and here I can speak for myself and know always what is happening. But Maggie is my wife and I am liking her much and the country too. Australia does nothing bad to me. Some people are not trying to think what they will be like in my country, or some other place, and not good speaking. If they are in strange country and people are not good with them and slowly talk and listen, then I am thinking they are better dead. I am sometimes feeling this in Australia. Sometimes, when I am with Maggie and she is a little bit cross, I think of my own country and my heart cries too much. Then, even if it is middle of night I go out onto land and work. It is only thing helping. Wherever I

COUNTRY LIFE

The Albany Harbor, with whale chasers belonging to Australia's only remaining whaling station tied up at Town Jetty and, behind the silos, the land-backed wharf

View of the Albany Harbor, from the "Country Life" section of the *Bulletin* for 10 May 1969. *HRHRC Milutinovic Collection.*

am making my own land better and Maggie being kind and not cross any more is best thing.[20]

Husband, wife, and land are united through the struggle by which they have made the land theirs. Even while Yugoslavia remains his country, Boris can no longer live there. "I am much sorry that here, in my own country I am a stranger. My family have same blood but now I am different."[21] In the resolution of the final chapter and Boris's closing reflection, "Soon I will be home,"[22] Milutinovic achieves a unity of the two cultures that, in artistic terms, resolves the conflicts documented in the more directly autobiographical writings.

In her books, Milutinovic brought the conflict of the two cultures into an artistic whole as the fictionalized husband and wife were united by their joint struggle for existence. In the letters and radio talks, however, we see the personal conflicts that preceded this resolution and see also how in their actual lives the husband and wife apparently failed to achieve the mutual acceptance reached by Boris and his wife in the last two chapters of *Talk English Carn't Ya*. A comparison of Milutinovic's radio scripts of the 1950s with the accounts of the same period in her novels shows how little the events of the fiction differ from autobiography. Yet while the incidents are often identical, the tone and persona the writer assumes in her radio talks remain distinct from those in the fiction. Where the fiction emphasizes the indifference or hostility of the native Australian community, the scripts shape the author's experiences into comfortable anecdotes that assure the listeners that life is essentially the same for everyone. The letters, on the other hand, like the fiction, reveal the pain that Milutinovic could not resolve in real life.

In the radio scripts, the reader can see how Iris Milutinovic chose the kind of events in her own life with which listeners could identify, either directly or through their parents' lives before them. As she describes the scripts in an attached note, "Their main interest is that they were topical at the time or based on truth."[23] She talks about living in a construction camp at Loch 10 at the Murray-Darling junction with her first husband and about coming to Albany with her second husband, Milutinovic; about the whaling station at Albany; about train journeys, fishing, beer, and cats. She also recalls memories of childhood and family: train trips in her youth, and her grandparents' pioneering at the bleak and unproductive Misery Farm in Tasmania, where the lure of gold led her grandfather to select land that turned out neither to have substantial amounts of minerals nor to be arable. Throughout the talks, Milutinovic is sustained by memories of the warmth of a family such

[20]Ibid., p. 140.
[21]Ibid., p. 141.
[22]Ibid., p. 143.
[23]"List of Radio Talks with Some Letters, Contracts, Drafts Etc. dating from 1958 to 1975," Box 2.

as she had hoped to establish eventually for herself. She creates for herself the traditional Australian persona of "the battler," one whose skeptical sense of humor enables her to mix at all levels of society. The tone is whimsical and the sentiments are qualified by a lightly self-mocking irony, in itself typical of the rural idiom.

Although the theme of many of the talks is the family, often seen from the child's point of view, they are saved from coziness by a haunting sense of failure. This undertone is modulated by the unexpected beauty Milutinovic occasionally found in the land and people, as in the script "Let's Go by Train," in which she describes her journey to Balranald, across the bleakest stretch of the Riverina, the Murray-Darling plains of inland southeastern Australia.

> Ahead I could see what I thought was a small pool of water reflecting the blue sky. It was beautiful, shimmering like a sapphire in that burnt up country. But something was wrong. There was no green around the pool. It was brown right up to the water. By this time we were close to that wonderful blue patch and suddenly it rose into the air and flew into the lighter blue of the summer sky. The sapphire was hundreds, perhaps thousands of small blue parrots and while I live I will remember that intense cloud of blue flying into the sun. [24]

The bleakness is also masked by the kind of sardonic outback humor Milutinovic uses in describing local characters, such as one she met on her train ride.

> I also remember very well the old man whose luggage consisted of a big swag, three blackened billy cans, and a hat festooned with a cork edged fly net. He was a delightful old man who said not one word for the first half of the trip and couldn't stop talking and telling during that last 100 miles or so. [25]

The center of this talk, in fact, is Milutinovic's introduction, during the railway trip to Balranald, to a gallery of remittance-men, swaggies, runaways, and drunks, one of whom awakens on her shoulder.

> "You're a loverly woman, Mum," he said to me. "Now if a woman like you'd marry a bloke like me we could settle down real well." I'm not really sure if that was a proposal of marriage. What I am sure is that, at my then age of sixteen the Mum bit didn't flatter, and only youthful

[24]"Let's Go by Train," 18 September 1972, p. 2, Box 2. Unless otherwise stated, dates cited for the radio scripts are broadcast dates listed on the contracts. All radio scripts cited are from the HRHRC collections.
[25]Ibid., p. 2.

embarrassment stopped me from getting as far away from my
affectionate fellow traveller as possible.[26]

As in this anecdote, Milutinovic repeatedly portrays herself as an incompetent
but innocent bystander, an image reinforced in another radio script, an
account of an episode from her career as a civilian clerk in the Australian
Women's Army Corps.[27] Demonstrating splinting to a first-aid class,
Milutinovic hears a loud click and then the groan of the hapless patient,
"Gawd—You've put me b...knee out."[28] Similarly, in her tales of life in
Albany, Milutinovic describes herself as a bystander confined to the house by
illness and incapacity, while her husband deals with the serious matters of
building, growing crops, and earning a living.

Milutinovic's characteristic stance of the partially involved observer,
however, is somewhat shaken in the talks in which she approaches her own
defeats as wife and mother. In several of the scripts she refers to her "too
young, very unhappy first marriage," as she calls it in "The Street of Seven
Tongues."[29] "Matchless Future" tells of her marriage at eighteen to a former
Irish Guardsman from County Clare.[30] Then in a script titled "Faraway
Places," which ostensibly is about train journeys, she reveals how this
husband quickly became tired of his inexperienced wife.[31] In "Home Sweet
Home," she defines home in terms of the comfort it offered.

> Comfort meant fires and food and welcome; a place to hide when the
> going was rough, to play in when things were good. A pleasant place
> for all seasons and I'm not really talking about the climate.[32]

Other scripts suggest the difficulty she had in creating this ideal sense of
security in her own circumstances, whether because of inexperience, as
among the itinerants camped at Loch 10 in the late 1920s, or because of the
illness that prevented her from sharing in the building of her later home after
her second marriage.[33] But most moving of all is her talk, "A Dream of
Children," in which she speaks of her only child, who was born prematurely
and lived but briefly.[34] Left only with this memory, she recalls a dream family
she created, recording their birthdays, following their schooling, careers, and
marriages. This dream family not only provided compensation for her loss but

---

[26]Ibid., p. 3.
[27]"Mum's Army," 29 May 1973, p. 2, Box 2.
[28]Ibid., p. 2.
[29]"The Street of Seven Tongues," p. 15.
[30]"Matchless Future," no date, Box 2.
[31]"Faraway Places," 9 June 1970, Box 2.
[32]"Home Sweet Home," 26 August 1971, p. 1, Box 2.
[33]"Building a Home," 13 February 1967.
[34]"A Dream of Children," 10 November 1964, Box 2.

perhaps explains her stance as outsider, from which she longingly described the Australian dream she had inherited but failed to achieve.

Some of Milutinovic's talks go beyond her own history to give reminiscences of her family and so flesh out the background of the cultural conflict between husband and wife suggested in the novels. The author's grandfather was a farmer, albeit poor, and her father a brickworks manager. In "White Christmas," Milutinovic describes her family and a visit home to Tasmania,[35] and in "Lares and Penates" she describes her father, who became manager of the brickworks at Cooee, near Burnie in Northern Tasmania, after the collapse of the Van Dieman's Land Company Bank, for which he had previously worked.[36] In the same script, she discusses her mother's sister-in-law, Eliza Burnell, who stood unsuccessfully for parliament and whose daughter became Dame Enid Lyons, Milutinovic's first cousin, the wife of a Prime Minister, mother of a Deputy Premier, and, after the death of her husband, one of the first two Australian women to be elected to the Commonwealth Parliament.

Although Milutinovic's work deals with the social tensions of postwar Australia, its tone is rural and nostalgic. She did not care for those writers who had attempted to extend the boundaries of fiction, and in a talk, "How Could You, Mr. Joyce?," she blames the author of *Ulysses* and *Finnegans Wake* for causing "the decline in reading and the increase in magazines featuring pictures with short captions."[37] Milutinovic goes on to assert that

> Before Joyce, the best fiction writers aimed at a lucid, easily understood style. Like Shakespeare. Now there's a man who never strung words on words for nothing. His plots work, his characters live, and he is full of contemporary wise-cracks. Which cannot be said for other, later confusionists.[38]

Although Milutinovic clearly identifies where her sympathies lie, she does give Joyce credit for creating characters whose lives ("inner streams") "lead fairly quickly to the main river." Milutinovic admits that Joyce's characters are "true tributaries," while this is "Not so with most of his imitators."[39] Essentially Milutinovic found what she called "abstract art" ornamental and preferred art in any form that would "endure in the hearts and minds of those who need it, which is everyone."[40]

[35]"White Christmas," 24 December 1970, Box 2.
[36]"Lares and Penates," dated in Milutinovic's hand, "1956," Box 2.
[37]"How Could You, Mr. Joyce?," 3 April 1969, Box 2.
[38]Ibid.
[39]Ibid.
[40]Ibid.

In Milutinovic's own short fiction, she repeats a number of themes from her radio talks, including the comfort of childhood, youthful rebellion, and difficulties in communication across cultures, but her stories do not generally carry these themes further. An exception would be "Cottage Garden," which deals frankly with sexuality.[41] Although Milutinovic's writing is rarely overt, the overtones of childhood sexuality and incest in this story provoked an editor from D.C. Thomson and Co. in Dundee, Scotland, to comment that it was "salacious" and "lacked emotional depth."[42] The stories "A Day at the Old Farm" and "The Farm that Died" enlarge the picture given of her maternal grandparents in the radio talk "Misery Farm."[43] Milutinovic also wrote some speculative fiction, such as "Wholly City," a story dealing with coming to life in Sydney in the year 4001, after being frozen following a motor accident in 1971, and finding a world where sex has been abolished, where there are no men, and where no further evolution is possible. Milutinovic broached the same theme in her radio talk, "Deep Freeze–and All That," which she described in a note as speculation on possible outcomes of Women's Liberation.[44]

Apart from the scripts, Milutinovic's letters and contracts relating to the radio programs reveal another aspect of her life: the precarious economic state of a person trying to exist by her writings in Australia during the two decades after the Second World War. The contracts show that in 1965 Milutinovic was receiving £7 ($14.00) for a fourteen minute broadcast, including rehearsal time, and £4 ($8.00) for eight to ten minutes. At this time in Australia, the minimum weekly wage for males was £16.40 ($32.80), while average weekly earnings of employed males were £26.14 ($53.40).[45] Clearly, the weekly radio program provided only a small supplement to the family income, particularly since there was pressure on Milutinovic to reduce the length of her broadcasts to below ten minutes. Nevertheless, the letters from her producers suggest that Milutinovic's relationships with the ABC were good and that her programs were welcomed by their listeners.

[41]"Cottage Garden," 11 May 1970, Box 3.

[42]Letter dated 22 February 1974. See attachment to manuscript in Box 3. Milutinovic's own attitude toward sex is expressed in her talk, "How Could You, Mr. Joyce?," when she writes, "Some of us middleaged fuddy duddies have known about sex for years. Most of us enjoy it. . . . Thank heaven there are still people who, whatever they may do in bed or out of bed, in the line of sexual pleasure, prefer not to talk or write about it more than is necessary. Which means that sex should be an integral part of the plot or the character and not something dragged in to help sales. Anyway, reading about sex is a very poor substitute" (p. 2).

[43]"Misery Farm," 27 May 1974, Box 2. A copy of "Misery Farm" is also found in Box 4, along with "A Day at the Old Farm," which is retitled in Milutinovic's hand "Grandma Em'ly's Tasmanian Home" and bears Milutinovic's notation: "closely related to The Farm That Died."

[44]"Deep Freeze–and All That," 8 April 1969, Box 2.

[45]A.G.L. Shaw, *The Economic Development of Australia* (Melbourne: Longman, 1970), p. 200. The minimum weekly wage figure cited is for 1966; the average weekly earnings figure is for 1964.

Correspondence from editors and publishers, including rejection slips and suggestions for changes, indicates the diligence with which Milutinovic maintained her career as a professional writer. Her eventual success came through the support of Anne Godden, then of Nelsons and later of Hyland House, who accepted *Talk English Carn't Ya* and asked to see a book of short stories. Apparently, Godden was also interested in publishing "The Street of Seven Tongues" under its final title, *Not Far From Nowhere*, but this project came to nothing.[46] The last copies of *Talk English* were not sold until 1986, and such slow sales discouraged Hyland House from publishing another book by Milutinovic.[47] Perhaps the assessment of the reader at Rigby Publishing was correct when, in rejecting *Not Far From Nowhere*, he concluded, "Australians are not interested in reading about migrants."[48]

Through her letters, Iris Milutinovic kept alive the part of her personality that was denied by her marriage to a naturally reclusive husband who was further isolated from community by a language barrier. The letters in the collection show how, from her home by the Southern Ocean, Milutinovic continued to participate in both public and domestic activities around Australia. During 1975, in correspondence with Elizabeth Reid, then adviser on women's affairs in the Prime Minister's Department, Milutinovic complained of the injustices involved in geriatric care, of unsolicited advertisements she had received for cures for obesity, and of the ill consequences of unemployment benefits for the undereducated.[49] In 1970, she wrote to the Australian Broadcasting Commission to complain about the quality of Australian television—in particular about a music program entitled GTK, which she describes in the following terms:

> One group led by someone called Hendrix should never be shown to anyone under the age of ninety. . . . Unless my considerable experience has been of no value at all the whole performance was intended to be a sexual experience rather than a musical one. The leader appeared to be attempting to copulate with a guitar. . . . If it is desirable to encourage young people along these lines, surely proper copulation would be preferable.[50]

In a second letter, Milutinovic admitted to enjoying Hendrix on record, but insisted, "It seems to me that if the music is good enough, there is little need for such obscene cavortings."[51]

[46]See letters between Anne Godden and Iris Milutinovic dating from 10 May 1972 to 17 March 1975. Unless otherwise noted, all correspondence cited is from the HRHRC collections.

[47]Information from Anne Godden to author, 1986.

[48]Quoted in correspondence from Milutinovic to Al Grassby, Minister for Immigration, discussing language problems of immigrants, 4 October 1976 and 4 April 1977.

[49]Letter from Iris Milutinovic to Elizabeth Reid, 18 February 1975.

[50]Undated letter from Iris Milutinovic to the Australian Broadcasting Commission, [1970].

[51]Undated letter from Iris Milutinovic to the Australian Broadcasting Commission, [1970].

The more public issue of Aboriginal affairs is the subject of a series of letters Milutinovic received between 1971 and 1974. In the earliest of these letters, the Western Australian writer Mary Durack Miller comments that she, Miller, could make an excellent short novel from the story of a report she had prepared for the Coombes committee, the Commonwealth government committee then enquiring into Aboriginal policies, except that the characters could not be disguised,[52] a statement even more true of the letters to Milutinovic from Mrs. Kathy Strehlow and her husband Professor T.G.H. (Ted) Strehlow. The Strehlow letters, which discuss in some detail the controversy surrounding the use by other researchers of Professor Strehlow's papers on Aboriginal anthropology, provide fascinating insight into the passions aroused by academic and political infighting among anthropologists and scholars of Aboriginal culture.

A different aspect of public life is shown in a series of letters written to Milutinovic between 1971 and 1975 by her cousin, Dame Enid Lyons, whose husband, the Labor politician Joseph Lyons, had deserted his party in 1931 to lead a United Australia Party, which won the resulting elections, enabling him to become Prime Minister. The letters from Dame Enid Lyons to Milutinovic provide a glimpse of the family intimacy from which Milutinovic felt herself excluded and give some indication of her cousin's sense of public duty. In the letters Dame Enid talks mainly about family matters, but also of her efforts to tidy up her papers in order to give them to the country in gratitude for the fact that "so many privileges have come our way through public office."[53]

The writings and correspondence in the HRHRC's collection of Milutinovic's papers present a representative picture of a great deal of Australian life in the postwar years. Her position and interests provided connections between the older rural life of the pioneers, still felt to be characteristic of Australia, and the newer life coming into being, between public affairs and life in a small town, and between members of different language communities. While her health may have prevented Iris Milutinovic from fully realizing her talents, her perceptiveness and fine eye for detail and character enabled her to create through her books, talks, and stories a record of the two ways of life they describe. Her correspondence with public agencies and officials makes available a commentary on the issues that concerned her as well as the reactions of those more deeply involved. The bland responses of officialdom offer their own commentary on the nature of Australian public life. Finally, Milutinovic's accounts of life with her husband bring her own traditions and public concerns into direct confrontation with the very different history of Europe that during these years was working itself into new patterns on Australian shores.

[52]Letter from Mary Durack Miller to Iris Milutinovic, 7 March 1971.
[53]Undated letter from Dame Enid Lyons to Iris Milutinovic.

Christina Stead, from the dust jacket of her *Dark Places of the Heart* (Holt, Rinehart & Winston, 1940). *HRHRC Grattan Collection*.

Christina Stead's Encounter With "The True Reader": The Origin and Outgrowth of Randall Jarrell's Introduction to "The Man Who Loved Children"

BY ROBERT L. ROSS

When Christina Stead first opened the manuscript of "An Unread Book," the introduction Randall Jarrell had written in 1964 for her novel *The Man Who Loved Children*, she admitted in a letter to her longtime friend Stanley Burnshaw that she had done so with "the usual feeling of quiet nausea, fear too," which critical essays on her work always generated.[1] This time, though, she could not set aside the response to a novel published in 1940 and largely ignored for the next twenty-five years. It was through the efforts of Burnshaw, a New York editor and poet, that Holt, Rinehart and Winston had at last announced a reissue of the book, its second appearance scheduled for early 1965. To lend this publishing gamble credibility and prestige, Burnshaw had asked Jarrell to introduce the new edition, a task accepted eagerly by a poet and critic who called the novel "the best unknown book I know."[2] Burnshaw, fully aware of Stead's attitude toward any critical evaluations of her work, had sent Jarrell's manuscript to her for comment and approval. Although having initially faced the distinguished American poet's essay with "nausea" and "fear," Stead discovered within it a dazzling quality that she tried to capture in her letter to Burnshaw: "'How can it be? How can he love me? How puzzling!' ... Who does one write for? Oneself—and the true reader."[3] Stead had found Jarrell to be that "true reader." Wanting in some way to acknowledge him, but not knowing how, she told Burnshaw: "I'm not 'grateful' to Jarrell; I don't know what to say really; this is such a new and even pure sensation."[4]

---

[1] Letter from Christina Stead to Stanley Burnshaw, 7 December 1964. All correspondence can be found in the Harry Ransom Humanities Research Center. For permission to quote from Christina Stead's letters and related materials held by the HRHRC, I would like to thank her literary executor, Professor R.G. Geering, University of New South Wales, Sydney. Professor Geering is now editing a collection of Christina Stead's letters.

[2] Letter from Randall Jarrell to Stanley Burnshaw, undated.

[3] Letter from Christina Stead to Stanley Burnshaw, 7 December 1964.

[4] Ibid.

The manuscript that so moved Stead may well have been one of the most personally significant she would ever read; for it not only helped to revive her masterpiece but also to set her life and career on a new course. The story of the essay's origin and outgrowth forms a kind of *leitmotif* in the 156 letters from Stead to Burnshaw recently acquired by the Harry Ransom Humanities Research Center. Stead first met Burnshaw in 1935 when she and William Blake, her lifetime companion, visited the New York office of *New Masses*, a progressive journal for which Burnshaw was working.[5] The acquisition not only contains Stead's letters dating from 2 October 1936 through 19 December 1982 but also includes related letters to Burnshaw from Blake, correspondence from Randall Jarrell and others, several carbon copies of Burnshaw's letters to Stead, and two versions of a proposed play by Stead called "Letty Fox." (For a complete listing, see the Appendix at the end of this article.)

In an essay published by the *Kenyon Review* in 1968, Stead called the short story form a treasury, comparing it to the Indian anthology *Ocean of Story*. That book, she explained, was made up of "the sketch, anecdote, jokes cunning, philosophical, and biting, legends and fragments"; and in her view such diverse materials could appear in any piece of short fiction, which she defined as "a residue of the past and a record of the day."[6] So might Stead's letters to Burnshaw be described. Certainly, their "ocean of story" will give future scholars and biographers admittance into one writer's "workshop of the imagination";[7] however, the focus here will be on the events leading to and from that major juncture in Stead's career: the reissue in 1965 of *The Man Who Loved Children*.

I. 1934-1964: PRODUCTIVITY AND OBSCURITY

The Man Who Loved Children was Stead's fourth novel, her fifth book to be published. A short story collection, *The Salzburg Tales*, had appeared in 1934, followed a year later by her first novel, *Seven Poor Men of Sydney*, which had been written before the short stories; *The Beauties and Furies* was

[5]Stead recalls the details of this meeting in an article printed in the British journal *Agenda* and entitled "Some Deep Spell: A View of Stanley Burnshaw" (21.4-22.1 [Winter-Spring 1984]: 125-139). Originally commissioned by Hiram Haydn for *The American Scholar*, this essay was still unpublished at the time of Stead's death, appearing for the first time in the 1984 issue of *Agenda*, which was devoted entirely to Stanley Burnshaw. In addition to recalling their first meeting, Stead's "portrait" also traces Burnshaw's life and literary career, in part through a discussion of his poetry. Stead's writing of this essay is mentioned several times in letters during the 1970s.

[6]Christina Stead, "*England*: Christina Stead," *Kenyon Review* 30 (1968): 444.

[7]Letter from Christina Stead to Stanley Burnshaw, 14 August 1970.

published in 1936 and *House of All Nations* in 1938. This earlier work had been issued by both New York and London publishers, as was *The Man Who Loved Children*, which Simon and Schuster brought out in 1940 and London publisher Peter Davies issued a year later. Reviewed in major American publications, the novel seemed to confound the critics who sensed greatness but could not grasp its exact form; even while pointing out what they considered weaknesses—caricature, linguistic excessiveness, artificiality, monotony, and involuted structure—they admitted that these perceived defects somehow lent the work its power. Two prominent American critics, Clifton Fadiman and Mary McCarthy, were not altogether impressed, Fadiman faulting the authenticity of the American setting, and McCarthy noting how Stead's only "'original' and 'extraordinary'" qualities lay in "the fearful, disordered vindictiveness with which she pursues her character," a technique, according to McCarthy, that finally results in the reader's "numbed attention."[8] Overall more nebulous than negative, the reviews failed to recognize fully a book that would become twenty-five years later one of the most admired in twentieth-century world literature.

When the novel was published initially, Stead had been living in the United States for three years and was to remain for another six until she and Blake returned to Europe shortly after World War II. Later she recalled in one of her letters how "utterly despairingly miserable" she had felt in New York when writing *The Man Who Loved Children*: "I tore it out of me alive and I can still remember those awful feelings."[9] The novel's roots lie in the rich soil of her Sydney childhood, something which Stead often admitted. For example, two letters by Stead in other HRHRC collections reveal the work's autobiographical strain: In 1965 Stead wrote to J.D. Adams that she expected everyone knew she was the "'rebellious little girl'" called Louie in the novel;[10] to Robie Macauley, editor of the *Kenyon Review*, she explained that the Georgetown and Annapolis settings, even the geographical and botanical descriptions, were "for the most part...a transfer" from Sydney, adding, "I was brought up on such things."[11] Obviously, the pain, the "awful feelings," sprang not from recreating physical details but from dredging up memories so distant in time and place from the crucible of family life and the tangled course of self-realization. Jarrell proposed in his introduction that "A person is a process, one that leads to death," and "The process the book calls Louie is that of a child turning into a grown-up, a duckling turning into a swan, a being that exists in two worlds leaving the first world of the family for the world

[8]Clifton Fadiman, review of *The Man Who Loved Children*, *The New Yorker*, 19 October 1940, p. 104; Mary McCarthy, "Framing Father," *The New Republic*, 13 January 1941, p. 61.

[9]Letter from Christina Stead to Stanley Burnshaw, 19 February 1966.

[10]Letter from Christina Stead to J.D. Adams, 5 September 1965.

[11]Letter from Christina Stead to Robie Macauley, 20 September 1965.

outside."[12] Of course, this *Bildungsroman* has numerous counterparts in world literature, the most notable being Thomas Wolfe's *Look Homeward, Angel* (1929). Alike in their sheer intensity, synthesis of autobiographical materials, depiction of family, and their excesses that could never be excised, the novels stand as dramatic testaments to the development of an artist amid a bourgeois setting.

In Stead's next book, *For Love Alone* (1944), the "swan," who has left the family world for the larger one outside, goes on to pursue the process of which Jarrell spoke, this time as Teresa Hawkins. When Burnshaw asked Stead in later years for an accounting of her life, she provided an autobiographical sketch that in its entirety might serve as a plot summary of *The Man Who Loved Children* and *For Love Alone*, concluding with how in Sydney she "got various business jobs. Began to save up very hard to come abroad—it took me five years and then, 1928, I reached London (May)—two weeks later Bill [William Blake] gave me a job."[13] Granted, these last few lines cover several hundred pages of *For Love Alone*; but Stead was not writing the kind of bareboned autobiographical novel long popular in Australia. She eschewed what her only equal in Australian literature, Patrick White, dubbed "the pragmatic, the documentary approach" to fiction; instead, she fulfilled White's prescription for exploring the "autobiographical vein" by "launching into that admittedly disturbing marriage between life and imagination—like many actual marriages in fact—all the risks, the recurring despair, and rewards if you are lucky."[14]

The London office job that was offered to the young colonial—the fictional Teresa and the actual Christina alike—initiated a new life, one rich with the sought-after adventure, and love. For the Australian-bred author, the job soon led her to Paris, then to New York with the American Blake. In the United States, Stead wrote her three greatest novels, the two autobiographical works and *Letty Fox: Her Luck*, the latter published in 1946. Although *A Little Tea, A Little Chat* followed in 1948, and *The People With the Dogs* in 1952, neither reached the heights of the previous three. After leaving the United States in 1946, Stead and Blake lived in various parts of Europe for several years, then settled near London where they lived until Blake's death in 1968. From a literary standpoint, this period was not productive for Stead— at least outwardly. There are no letters in the collection from 1943 to 1959, and Blake wrote most of the single letter dated 1959, in which he provided the

[12]Randall Jarrell, "An Unread Book," *The Man Who Loved Children* (New York: Holt, Rinehart and Winston, 1965), pp. xxxii-xxxiii.

[13]Letter from Christina Stead to Stanley Burnshaw, 20 February 1975.

[14]Patrick White, "Patrick White Speaks on Factual Writing and Fiction," *Australian Literary Studies* 10 (1981): 100.

Burnshaws, who were coming to England, with directions to their house. Stead added a few lines saying that she was looking forward to their visit—and that she was writing.[15] In a sketch published in 1975 by the Australian journal, *Overland*, Stead recalls her and Blake's life in London during 1954 when they were living in a furnished room; she was working as a secretary in a hospital and Blake had found a job in an American television office.[16]

A Stead letter to Mrs. Guy Howarth in 1952—from the Guy Howarth Papers in the HRHRC—provides another glimpse into the years of obscurity that the reissue of *The Man Who Loved Children* altered so dramatically in 1965.[17] Stead notes her pleasure at having met Howarth, a University of Sydney professor and pioneer scholar in Australian literature, and his wife, and promises them some stories so they can choose one for *Southerly*, the highly regarded Australian literary journal then edited by Howarth. Their choice must have been "The Hotel-Keeper's Story," which appeared a few months later.[18] Stead also mentions having seen Florence James, a New Zealand writer, and Australian novelist Dymphna Cusack. Her main purpose for writing, though, was to solicit the Howarths' membership in an Australian-New Zealand Civil Liberties Council being organized by a London-based group from the two countries. This letter draws a tentative picture of the life led by Stead and Blake: one rich with literary activity, political and social causes, and friendship. It also shows that Stead had not broken connections with either her fellow Australians or her homeland, whose passport she still held, even though she had never returned.

Those must have been pleasant years in spite of persistent money problems. Stead had fallen happily into obscurity and does not give the impression that she held any bitterness or regrets over what some might have considered a failed literary career. After all, this "booksmith," as she once described herself,[19] never sought the public's approval, having confined her artistic ambitions to the art itself; as she told Burnshaw: "It's no use saying one writes for the public. (Well, I can't say it.)"[20] Whatever her attitude toward "the public," Stead was soon to exchange literary obscurity for recognition, neglect for attention, and seeming failure for acclaim.

[15]Letter from Christina Stead to Stanley Burnshaw, 1959.

[16]Christina Stead, "1954: Days of the Roomers," *Overland*, no. 62 (1975): 30-31.

[17]Letter from Christina Stead to Mrs. Guy Howarth, 16 January 1952.

[18]Christina Stead, "The Hotel-Keeper's Story," *Southerly* 22, no. 2 (1952): 74-82. In a note, the story is described as the opening chapter of a new novel, "Mrs. Trollope and Madame Blaise."

[19]Letter from Christina Stead to Stanley Burnshaw, 28 July 1980.

[20]Letter from Christina Stead to Stanley Burnshaw, 7 December 1964.

II. 1965: The Turning Point

Although Jarrell's introduction to *The Man Who Loved Children* has been credited in large part for the novel's rediscovery, it would be an oversimplification to say that the book lay altogether neglected before 1965. More than one "true reader" in the United States, in Australia, and in Great Britain had grasped its potency. During 1955, Elizabeth Hardwick published an essay in which she noted that *The Man Who Loved Children* "has a small but loyal band of friends."[21] Calling it "a genuine novel in the traditional meaning of the word," "a work of absolute originality," Hardwick lamented that such a book should be out of print while lesser novels "are pushed to the front of the counter like so much impatient, seasonal merchandise."[22] In 1962, *Southerly* devoted an entire issue to Stead, including a picture of her, a biographical sketch, R.G. Geering's essay "The Achievement of Christina Stead," a short story, and a chapter from an unpublished novel.[23] Geering opened his article by pointing out that none of Stead's work had been published in Australia and that imported copies of *Letty Fox: Her Luck* had even been banned as pornographic. While Geering acknowledged a few critics in Australia for recognizing Stead's genius, he felt that on the whole the Australian literary establishment paid her work scant attention.[24]

The efforts of *Southerly* notwithstanding, several years would pass before Australian critics fully accepted one of their greatest novelists. Nor did *Southerly* alter the situation overseas, even though Stead told Burnshaw about the special issue, which had pleased her.[25] But her good friend, by now a vice-president at Holt, Rinehart and Winston, had long nurtured plans of his own, and in 1963 Burnshaw wrote to tell Stead that his proposal for a clothbound edition of *The Man Who Loved Children* with an introduction by Jarrell had at last been approved by his publishing firm and that she would receive a token advance of $250.[26] This good news was the culmination of several years' work by Burnshaw. For instance, in his book, *Robert Frost Himself*, Burnshaw mentions asking the poet in 1959: "Did you ever hear of Christina Stead's *The Man Who Loved Children*? If not, you will. I may even ask for your help—help with 'the Holts,' whom I'm hoping to rouse to reissue the work. It's a rare novel. . . . We can rescue the book and resuscitate a truly

[21]Elizabeth Hardwick, "The Novels of Christina Stead," *The New Republic*, 1 August 1955, p. 17.

[22]Ibid., p. 19.

[23]*Southerly* 22, no. 4 (1962). *Southerly* has published two additional issues on Stead's work: vol. 38, no. 4 (1978), which contains articles; and vol. 44, no. 1 (1984), which contains unpublished writings, except for "A Little Demon," which appeared as "Fairy Child" in the *Harvard Advocate* 106, nos. 2/3 (Winter 1973).

[24]R.G. Geering, "The Achievement of Christina Stead," *Southerly* 22, no. 4 (1962): 193.

[25]Letter from Christina Stead to Stanley Burnshaw, 2 May 1963.

[26]Letter from Stanley Burnshaw to Christina Stead, 9 November 1963.

The Man
Who Loved
Children
**Christina
Stead**
**Introduction by
Randall Jarrell**

Dust jacket of Christina Stead's *The Man Who Loved Children* (Holt, Rinehart & Winston, 1940). Jacket design by Milton Glaser. *HRHRC Grattan Collection*.

remarkable writer." Frost replied: "You ought to know that I don't read novels these days—not many that is; but send me the book. Stead? Where does she come from?"[27]

Jarrell gladly agreed to write the introduction for the long-planned reissue of the 1940 novel and in letters to Burnshaw mentioned several other prominent admirers of Stead's work, including Elizabeth Bishop, Robert Lowell, and James Agee.[28] Lowell even furnished what he called a "blurb" in a letter to Burnshaw, and his remarks eventually appeared on the dust jacket of the 1965 edition.[29] Burnshaw received Jarrell's essay on 6 October 1964, accompanied by a letter in which Jarrell said that "it's heartbreaking to think of the world's treatment of the book and of Christina Stead."[30] He went on to thank Burnshaw for arranging the novel's republication and for asking him to introduce it, then added: "It really is a masterpiece—it's a joy just to know that it exists." Jarrell received $300 for his essay.[31]

On 23 February 1965, the new edition of *The Man Who Loved Children* arrived at the Blake household in England. The excitement aroused by the package of books is captured in the letter Stead wrote to Burnshaw that same day:

> The books arrived, all of them by airmail. . . . Thank you for all you did. One of them contained your card, which I have glued in with the words "sent by my old friend (printed Stanley Burnshaw) who did all this." And I am so grateful, so very grateful; it is a miracle to have a book reprinted after 25 years. May it happen to us all, too. . . . The BOOK, I, of course, cannot read and never could since it was printed; but I can read—or rather did read—R.J.'s wonderful introduction, with tears pouring out of my eyes, a regular fountain. That's his wonderful sympathy. I must write to that man. I sent him a Xmas card and said I would write, but I have such a curious feeling, as if he has written me the one letter of a lifetime, as if one was born to get one letter and I have got it. And then he understands me so well! It's not exactly difficult; it's delicate. You can't say, Thank you so much for wrapping me in rose and gold—as it were.[32]

Surely Stead could not have known that "The BOOK" in its striking new cover, with the introduction she so admired, would radically alter her life and career. Nor could she have imagined that if she were to write Jarrell she needed to do it soon, for he would not live out the year. When Stead learned some time

[27]Stanley Burnshaw, *Robert Frost Himself* (New York: George Braziller, 1968), pp. 178-79.
[28]Letter from Randall Jarrell to Stanley Burnshaw, undated.
[29]Letter from Robert Lowell to Stanley Burnshaw, 3 October 1964.
[30]Letter from Randall Jarrell to Stanley Burnshaw, undated.
[31]Letter from Mrs. Randall Jarrell to Stanley Burnshaw, 7 May 1966.
[32]Letter from Christina Stead to Stanley Burnshaw, 23 February 1965.

later from Burnshaw that Jarrell had apparently taken his own life, she recalled in a letter how she had bought a 1971 edition of his poems, and had been "shocked to feel, on reading many of them, how suicidal they are. I feel very bad about it. Of course, I suspected that his death was suicide."[33]

From time to time the Jarrell introduction has been denigrated, especially as more criticism on Stead's work appears. In fact, the HRHRC collection of letters includes one from a New England professor who told Burnshaw that "I, myself, have tried twice to describe the marvelous yet troubling talent of Christina Stead," then went on to say, "I *am* sorry about Jarrell's introduction, however, because by making hysterical claims for Miss Stead, I think it may have put as many people off as it attracted."[34] In his Twayne study of Stead, Geering disagrees with Jarrell on critical points and takes him to task for saying that *The Man Who Loved Children* was "a rejected masterpiece" when it first appeared and that its failure crippled Stead's future work. (Geering's chronology of important dates in Stead's life omits the reissue of the novel in 1965.[35]) But Stead, who had little regard for academic criticism anyway, never changed her original opinion of what Jarrell had written and continued to mention the introduction in letters to Burnshaw after 1965. For example, in 1978 she wrote: "I know that I owe much of TMWLC's reception the second time round to you and to your having asked the late and admirable R.J. to do the Introduction. But that was quite out of the way: there aren't any Intros like that!"[36] Again in 1981, when speaking of the novel's renewal, she assured Burnshaw: "But the success, in any case, I owe to you and Randall"; then added in parentheses: "And how many drear souls since have repeated his remarks or hinted at them!"[37]

However Jarrell's critical insights or assessments of Stead's career might be appraised in the future, the essay served its purpose and will likely gain a permanent place as a kind of Genesis within the growing volume of Stead criticism. As Burnshaw had hoped, Jarrell's prestige alone aided the book's reception in 1965; and most likely his introduction informed critics whose predecessors in 1940 had found themselves at least partially baffled. Literary fashions, too, had changed by 1965, thus admitting a work like *The Man Who Loved Children*—one that defied classification and overstepped all literary conventions.

No matter what the superficial reasons, an audience found a great novel. And Christina Stead, prepared or not at the age of sixty-two, was to gain the recognition so long withheld, so long deserved.

[33]Letter from Christina Stead to Stanley Burnshaw, 15 January 1981.
[34]Letter from Charles Thomas Samuels to Stanley Burnshaw, 16 December 1969.
[35]R.G. Geering, *Christina Stead* (New York: Twayne Publishers, 1969), pp. 121, 15-17.
[36]Letter from Christina Stead to Stanley Burnshaw, 26 September 1978.
[37]Letter from Christina Stead to Stanley Burnshaw, 15 January 1981.

Photograph of Christina Stead and William Blake, n.d. On back of print: "Gordon F. Fraser Birthday Photo." *HRHRC Burnshaw Collection.*

III. 1966-1983: FAME, LOSS, AND RETURN

"How does it feel to be 'famous'—my dear Stanley, I don't know, to tell you, would be to tell you a big secret, not fit for print. Though I will quite willingly tell you one day," Stead wrote to Burnshaw shortly after the reissue of *The Man Who Loved Children*, obviously in reply to a question he had posed.[38] If she ever did reveal the "big secret" to him, she must have done so in person as promised, or the letter has disappeared. Yet the correspondence with Burnshaw in the years to come insinuates that being "famous" did not always rest well with Stead. Reborn as a figure of consequence in the literary world, she soon faced the accompanying responsibilities and annoyances. The public wanted more writing. Publishers also expected cooperation in the promotion of her work. Interviewers, critics, would-be biographers, and those Stead called "thesis people," along with writers asking for advice, intruded as well.[39]

Surely she could have handled these demands had William Blake lived. But this man who for so long had been her mainstay, who had fulfilled all her dreams of "for love alone," died in 1968 after a long illness. Stead never fully recovered from the loss. A writer himself, Blake had failed to reach Stead's accomplishment—and knew it and accepted it. Apparently free of resentment or disappointment over his own limitations, he believed in Stead's work as passionately as their friend Burnshaw, and the letters in the collection from Blake to Burnshaw often touch on her writing. A letter written in 1960, for example, shows Blake's keen understanding and appreciation of *The Man Who Loved Children*:

> I am not surprised that "literary" women sometimes rebel against the book, it is for a good subjective reason. . . . Women have had little personal expression in letters to date: and, even those most gifted, Sand, Eliot, Gaskell, Austen, Colette, have not revealed too much of the feminine world. . . . It is Christina's gift and misfortune alike that in her books she bares the feminine needs and nature.[40]

The depth of the relationship between Stead and Blake reveals itself in part through a letter she wrote to Burnshaw shortly after Blake's death. She first told how in the last weeks of his illness she was hospitalized elsewhere and could not see him regularly but wrote each day:

> . . . And in those few letters I think I said to him the things that are not usually said between husband and wife in the usual daily conversation; and I think managed to give him some joy. There is something

---

[38]Letter from Christina Stead to Stanley Burnshaw, 2 April 1965.
[39]Letter from Christina Stead to Stanley Burnshaw, 17 March 1977.
[40]Letter from William Blake to Stanley Burnshaw, 20 September 1960.

about the life-embrace of marriage which prevents one from saying very often those things which one ought to say—which the partner wants to hear. (Though he was more loving this way than me, much more.) But I was able to say a few of those things. It was not much. He telephoned me every day from the hospital while he could and kept saying "I love you so much"; and I ask myself and I did ask then, who else ever was so good to me? Or ever will be? I didn't deserve it. But then I know that none of us deserves the gifts of that sort that are carelessly and without any reason thrown at our feet. No more. I am trying to avoid this kind of thinking, till I get to a place where I can be creative, which is what Bill liked, too.[41]

Over and again in subsequent letters, she expressed to Burnshaw the loss, the loneliness, and the love for Blake, sometimes addressing her discontent and unsettled life in a lighthearted manner: "Well, well—this is what happens to a girl without a husband."[42] In another letter, she placed herself in "the plight of all the old Mammas and Grandmammas in the world. . . once they have lost their man or men"; she then mentioned seeing a women's magazine that carried the headline: "'Why don't they burn us widows on the same pile as our husbands' bodies?'"—and added: "The same thought had occurred several times to me. *Not* in despair—just judging the situation."[43]

Yet however much Stead may have felt adrift, she met her obligations, even if the letters suggest that she often did so reluctantly and halfheartedly. Secure with her friend Burnshaw, she sometimes wrote in what might be interpreted as a mean and petty spirit about many of the people she encountered, a note absent from the earlier letters. Perhaps having no one else on whom to unload the kind of minor annoyances that often disappear once put into words, she turned to her old confidante, whom she reminded in 1982, "what a long time since we first have known each other!"[44] Still, she was generous with her time, granting numerous interviews; but she revealed to Burnshaw the pain of such experiences: "interviews make me sick. I go off into a palsied coma, more or less afterwards. They are dreadful."[45] In one letter she painted a vivid picture of an encounter with a feminist:

> Had an interview also with a dame from a privately sponsored radio station, who's interested in "current women's affairs" and all that horror, so I floundered and flopped—what am I doing in this *galere*? "I love men, for their beauty of character, their vigour, their

[41]Letter from Christina Stead to Stanley Burnshaw, 10 February 1968.
[42]Letter from Christina Stead to Stanley Burnshaw, 3 December 1979.
[43]Letter from Christina Stead to Stanley Burnshaw, 19 December 1982.
[44]Letter from Christina Stead to Stanley Burnshaw, 29 November 1982.
[45]Letter from Christina Stead to Stanley Burnshaw, 1 November 1974.

Photograph of Stanley Burnshaw by Lotte Jacobi, on dust jacket of Burnshaw's *Early and Late Testament* (Dial Press, 1952). Clipping supplied by author.

friendship, their compassion—" doesn't go! But I said some of it. What is wrong with the (quite decent) dames who don't like men?[46]

Needless to say, an obvious irony arises on considering the contradiction between Stead's repudiation here of the formalized feminist movement and the content of her writing.

Yet Stead found most of the criticism that was appearing on her work— whether feminist, Marxist, Freudian, or theoretical—a source of irritation, reacting in one instance rather violently to an article that Burnshaw had sent her:

> Thanks no thanks for the silly thesis by what's-her-name. Trouble with thesis people is that they HAVE to prove something. . . . I didn't read more than one and a half columns, realized she didn't give 2 cents for me; didn't care about my life wanderings, contacts—it's just the Paper World to her. She writes as if I'd stayed at home and kept my nose to the decapitated, basket-case of a Tree whose leaves I was scribbling upon—tree in the family backyard, too. Fooey and Pfui.[47]

Like many writers, Stead preferred not to talk about her work and avoided in particular critical discussions of it. The notable exception remained the Jarrell introduction. But he was, after all, a fellow artist, not one of the "thesis people." Jarrell may have explained why so much of the criticism on Stead's work fails to penetrate the text when he spoke of the "bewitching rapidity and lack of self-consciousness in her art" and of "How literary she makes most writers seem."[48]

The letters also refer on several occasions to a self-appointed biographer whom Stead believed was hounding her and taking advantage of the situation; eventually she managed to banish this ubiquitous person, only to be confronted by others. Too often, she believed, her admirers were motivated by self-promotion, not by an appreciation of her life and work, which she considered one and the same. And through the years Burnshaw must have asked her frequently if she were writing. To his queries she tended to reply with terse comments on her creative paralysis, not with excuses, saying at one point: "Why I don't work—will tell you maybe, some other time, but by some other time, perhaps I will be working a bit."[49]

Still, the time following 1965 was not altogether void, for Stead published in 1966 *Dark Places of the Heart* (titled *Cotter's England* in Great Britain), and in 1967 *The Puzzleheaded Girl*; nothing more appeared except for two minor works, *The Little Hotel, A Novel* in 1975, and *Miss Herbert (The Suburban*

[46]Letter from Christina Stead to Stanley Burnshaw, 25 January 1973.
[47]Letter from Christina Stead to Stanley Burnshaw, [1977].
[48]Jarrell, "An Unread Book," p. xxviii.
[49]Letter from Christina Stead to Stanley Burnshaw, 3 December 1979.

Wife) in 1976. Geering, whom Stead appointed as her literary executor, has edited two posthumous books: *Ocean of Story* (1985)—a collection of previously published short stories whose title the editor borrowed from the Indian anthology that Stead admired; and a novel, *I'm Dying Laughing* (1987).[50]

During 1969 Stead returned to Australia for the first time since leaving over forty years before. After serving as a Fellow in the Creative Arts at the Australian National University, Canberra, she went back to England, but in 1974 she moved to Australia permanently, where she lived with her brother in a Sydney suburb, an unlikely place for such a cosmopolitan woman. On 30 March 1983 Stead died in Sydney, where she had been born, in 1902.

The letters to Burnshaw, continuing until December 1982, hint that the Australians treated Stead as something of a celebrity. Ironically, she had told the *Kenyon Review* editor in 1965: "I'm not sure Australians know how to honour people."[51] Such did not appear to be the case, however, in her report to Burnshaw telling how "The newspapers made a celebro" of her eightieth birthday; she then added with characteristic self-effacement: "which had me thinking of all the poor souls of 80 muttering to themselves 'And what about me? I'm eighty! Write about me, you sods! But no—of course not—no one cares about Mary Smith'."[52] In 1981 she informed Burnshaw that *The Man Who Loved Children* had become "a textbook (ugh!) in the highschools here and very wretched I was to learn it. . .''; she then related a story she had heard about a young girl telling her teacher that Stead's fictional home resembled her own:

> . . . That her father had raped her—oh, dear, oh, dear—and yet didn't Sam in effect "rape" Louie—the symbolic pushing of chewed food in her mouth,—it's horrid—but he really did that—well, I'm against it and I know they're going to hate me (the "textbook") for the rest of their lives.[53]

She also described her residencies in creative writing at various Australian universities where she always received gracious treatment, even if the kindness turned unintentionally suffocating at times. In 1974 she had been honored by the first Patrick White Award, the outcome of a fund White created with the money from the Nobel Prize for Literature he had received in

[50]Christina Stead, *Ocean of Story* (New York: Viking, 1985); *I'm Dying Laughing* (London: Virago Press, 1987). Geering has written an article on editing the novel: "*I'm Dying Laughing*: Behind the Scenes," *Southerly* 47 (1987): 309-17. In a letter dated 28 July 1980, Stead mentions this novel to Burnshaw: "haven't looked at it since the Year One—but I did so the other day looking for a possible story I could extract for someone I like. . . . But the MS. yielded nothing but gas, gas—and I'm sorry to say that I wrote it too fast—up to 20,000 words a day."

[51]Letter from Christina Stead to Robie Macauley, 20 September 1965.

[52]Letter from Christina Stead to Stanley Burnshaw, 19 December 1982.

[53]Letter from Christina Stead to Stanley Burnshaw, 15 January 1981.

Pictured from left to right are winners of the 1960 National Book Awards: William L. Shirer, Conrad Richter, and Randall Jarrell. Photograph taken 14 March 1961. *HRHRC "New York Journal American" Collection.*

1973. Stead was an appropriate choice, considering that when the Academy recognized her fellow novelist some Australians argued that she should have been the recipient.[54] Attention kept up from abroad as well, including an offer from Hollywood to film *The Man Who Loved Children*, an opportunity she bypassed, explaining to Burnshaw how "they impudently say that if I don't like the shooting script, they will take my name off. Think you will do anything for their Geld, they do."[55]

Asked by Burnshaw shortly after her move in 1974 if she were becoming accustomed to living in Australia, Stead replied: "I left my life lying on the shore of other countries and I came to Australia. No question of coming back— you can't come back. . . . I am not home."[56] At the conclusion of *The Man Who Loved Children*, Louie leaves Spa House, and believes the others will decide that she has just gone for a walk; she then smiles to herself, thinking, "'So I have. . . . I have gone for a walk round the world'."[57] Like Louie, Christina Stead made such a choice, explaining to Burnshaw near the end of her life: "I am a wanderer. Or I like to be away."[58]

Those wanderings—sometimes literal, other times emotional, creative, and intellectual—are well-recorded in the HRHRC's collection of letters from Christina Stead to Stanley Burnshaw. From this correspondence and the related materials, there emerges a picture of a real woman, altogether human, even ordinary at times in her responses to the process of living. More significantly, though, the letters reveal much about the artist—apart from the woman, yet a part of her. Perhaps a line from one of the letters exemplifies the sort of realness that can only be conjured up by a writer's correspondence to a close friend; for only to a friend would the author of novels like *For Love Alone* and *The Man Who Loved Children* write: "It's 8:10 a.m. and I already have the house tidy and am sitting down to the typewriter, and with lipstick on, too."[59]

Certainly the examination of Randall Jarrell's role in the revival of *The Man Who Loved Children* comprises but one aspect of the HRHRC correspondence, yet it may help to clarify what has come to border on myth. Some would belittle Jarrell's role, others overplay it. Had the novel been published in 1965 without "An Unread Book" introducing it, the acclaim might well have been accorded Stead anyway, in spite of her lifelong belief that Jarrell's introduction had established her reputation. But that can be a subject only for conjecture: Jarrell's essay did appear, its origins owing to the devotion of William Blake and Stanley Burnshaw, its outgrowth stemming from the singular talent of Christina Stead.

[54]See, for example, Dorothy Green, "Patrick White's Nobel Prize," *Overland*, no. 57 (1973-74): 23-25.

[55]Letter from Christina Stead to Stanley Burnshaw, 15 January 1981.

[56]Letter from Christina Stead to Stanley Burnshaw, 4 April 1975.

[57]Stead, *The Man Who Loved Children* (1965), p. 527.

[58]Letter from Christina Stead to Stanley Burnshaw, 28 July 1975.

[59]Letter from Christina Stead to Stanley Burnshaw, 12 April 1943.

Appendix: A Listing of the Christina Stead Letters and Related Materials in the Harry Ransom Humanities Research Center

A. CHRISTINA STEAD'S LETTERS TO STANLEY BURNSHAW:

Unless indicated otherwise, the letters are typed on aerograms, the pages full, sometimes with notations and corrections of the poor typing—something for which Stead often apologized. Her correspondence is listed here by year, number of letters, and the country from which she wrote.

1936, 1 letter, Belgium
1937, 1 letter, United States
1938, 3 letters, United States
1939, 1 letter, United States
1942, 2 letters, 1 postcard, United States
1943, 1 letter, United States
1959, 1 letter, England
1960, 4 letters, England
1963, 4 letters, England
1964, 5 letters, England
1965, 17 letters, England
1966, 3 letters (2 handwritten), Puerto Rico; 4 letters, England
1967, 5 letters, England
1968, 17 letters, England
1969, 9 letters, England
1970, 13 letters (1 handwritten), 1 postcard, England
1971, 7 letters, England (1 with photograph, 1 with newspaper clippings)
1972, 5 letters, England
1973, 19 letters, England
1974, 4 letters, England; 2 letters, United States; 1 letter, Australia
1975, 6 letters, 1 postcard, Australia
1976, 6 letters, Australia
1977, 3 letters, Australia
1978, 5 letters, Australia
1979, 3 letters, Australia
1980, 1 letter, Australia
1981, 3 letters, Australia
1982, 2 letters, Australia
    1 undated letter from Australia
    1 unidentified second page of a letter
    1 telegram from Stead to Burnshaw, 1981, Australia

B. LETTERS TO STANLEY BURNSHAW FROM:

1. William Blake
    1942-1967, 44 letters
2. Randall Jarrell
    4 letters (handwritten), undated,
    written during 1963-64
3. Mrs. Randall Jarrell
    1966, 1 letter
4. Robert Lowell
    1964, 1 letter
5. Charles Thomas Samuels (professor)
    1969, 1 letter
6. Ruth Blake Hall (William Blake's daughter)
    1968, 1 letter
7. Cyrilly Abels (Stead's literary agent)
    1970, 1 letter
8. Charlotte Mayerson (editor)
    1978, 2 letters
9. Markie Benet (a Stead admirer)
    1978, 1 letter

C. LETTERS FROM STANLEY BURNSHAW TO:

1. Christina Stead and William Blake
    1963, 2 letters
2. Christina Stead
    1973, 1 letter (carbon)
3. Christina Stead
    1975, 1 letter (carbon)
4. Christina Stead
    1983, 1 page of a longer letter (carbon)
5. Markie Benet
    1978, 2 letters (carbons)
6. Charlotte Mayerson
    1978, 1 letter (carbon)

D. RELATED MATERIAL BY CHRISTINA STEAD:

1. 1941, two versions of a play to be called "LettyFox," including sketches
    for the setting; sent to Stanley Burnshaw
2. 1963, letter to Holt, Rinehart & Winston
3. 1970, letter to Clair Walsh (machine copy)

Harold E. Mertz (left) and Kym Bonython, from *The Australian Painters 1964-1966, Contempo-rary Australian Painting From the Mertz Collection* (Adelaide: The Griffin Press, Ltd., 1966). *HRHRC Collections.*

Australian Painting of the Sixties in the Mertz Collection

By John R. Clarke

When Harold E. Mertz, an American businessman, assembled paintings by Australian artists working between 1964 and 1966, he was creating a kind of time capsule. Housed in the University of Texas' Archer M. Huntington Art Gallery, the 148 paintings comprising the Mertz Collection reflect both the conditions of their making and the special character of Australian art at a time when New York claimed absolute cultural hegemony in the art world—a claim supported by the art market, the press, and cultural institutions worldwide.[1] Now, at a distance of more than twenty years, scholars are reevaluating the rarefied New York culture that stole the idea of modern art,[2] and the Australian paintings in the Mertz Collection provide an ideal opportunity to rethink the cultural climate of the art of the West at the beginning of the Space Age.

During the sixties, Australian painters found themselves in a similar position to their Canadian or Latin American colleagues: they were defined by their exclusion from the New York scene. Their relative isolation paradoxically gave them much greater freedom in choosing styles and masters than the Americans had. Free of the polemics of formalist criticism that created cultural war zones in New York, the Australian painters as students could choose to study with Italian, British, or French masters, and as professionals they could freely choose styles (like Social Realism or Surrealism) that were anathema in New York.

Kym Bonython, the art dealer who assisted Harold Mertz in assembling his collection, worked hard to choose representative works not only from the older, established artists like Sir William Dobell, Sir Russell Drysdale, Albert

[1]Eight of the paintings are on long-term loan to the Australian National Gallery, Canberra. All but three are illustrated in the exhibition catalogue, *The Australian Painters 1964-1966, Contemporary Australian Painting From the Mertz Collection*, text by Ross K. Luck (Adelaide, Australia: The Griffin Press, Ltd., 1966). I wish to thank James Mollison, director of the Australian National Gallery, Canberra, for his valuable comments on this article in manuscript.

[2]Serge Guilbaut, *How New York Stole the Idea of Modern Art: Abstract Expressionism, Freedom, and the Cold War* (Chicago: University of Chicago Press, 1983).

Tucker, Arthur Boyd, and Sidney Nolan, but also from the just-emerging new generation still in their thirties when the collection was assembled. Whereas the earlier generation had fought cultural battles that ended in the belated acceptance by the 1960s of modernist painting in Australia, the newer generation was able to take the more tolerant cultural climate for granted. The Australian avant-garde was heralded in 1937 in Melbourne by the formation of the Contemporary Art Society, the appearance in the following year of the journal *Angry Penguins*, and the exhibition in 1939 of over two hundred works by the French and British masters of modern art. The 1939 exhibition at the National Gallery of Victoria included works by Cézanne, Chagall, Gauguin, Léger, Matisse, Modigliani, Picasso, Van Gogh, and Dalí. Although late in coming, these events set the stage for modernism in Australia and resulted in the acceptance, first in art schools and then by the public, of new art that broke with a by now dated and provincial (if still very competent) art influenced by nineteenth-century English romanticism.

Today the modernism of the older masters seems rather tame, but contemporary reaction from both the public and the art-world establishment was often violent. When William Dobell's painting shifted from realism into modernist expressions, he became embroiled in a lawsuit that reveals much about the conservatism of Australian art in the forties. Dobell had received his training at the Slade School in London and had traveled in Europe in the thirties, but in 1944 he won a national prize for his portrait of artist Joshua Smith. Two enraged fellow contestants, claiming that the Giacometti-like portrait was a caricature rather than a portrait, brought Dobell to court with the charge that the painting was ineligible for the prize under the terms of the original bequest. Although eventually dismissed after a long hearing, the case made public the modernist debate.

The six Dobells in the Mertz Collection provide a representative sample of his mature style. Painted in oil on canvas, all of the Dobells in the Mertz Collection are small, ranging in size from the tiny study of *Helena Rubinstein* (1960, 4½ x 4 in.)[3] to the *Study for Self Portrait* (1966, 9 x 14¼ in.).[4] *Romping in the Rain, Vietnam* (1964, fig. 1) is the most Dionysian of the six, rendered in calligraphic brushstrokes. Dobell uses a subdued palette of grays, dark blue, and green to set nature's somber tone, just the opposite of the human presence in the landscape. Quick, curvilinear huts and two nude rompers in the foreground—one cartwheeling in the lower right, the other throwing his buttocks back and his arms up in an exuberant dance—give the picture a giddy feeling that borders on the eerie. Although Dobell's technique in all of the Mertz paintings allows details to dissolve in wispy brushwork and milky transparencies, his selective vision heightens, rather than diminishes, expression.

[3] *The Australian Painters*, p. 34, fig. 7 (color plate).
[4] Ibid., p. 36, fig. 12.

Dobell, like his contemporary Russell Drysdale, often documents human beings at the margins of society. His *Woman at Trash Bin* (1966) reveals a kinship with Daumier in its composition and technique.[5] The woman's bulky form, lit in stark chiaroscuro, balances the transparent trash she eyes so voraciously. Her dishevelled hair and dress (held together with a safety pin between her breasts) and her hungry stare emphasize her marginality. With her the viewer focuses on the object of her longing gaze, a newspaper ad reading "Home for Sale."

Russell Drysdale's modernism lies in his application of Social Realist techniques to the study of the people in the small bush towns of central New South Wales. But if *The Ruins, Lake Callabonna* (1965) "documents," in the manner of an American Social Realist like Thomas Hart Benton, the sere landscape of the bush country, Drysdale's vision borders on the dream imagery of Surrealism.[6] More than merely recording the activities of the characters who live in the outback, like *Brandy John* (1965)[7] or the inhabitants of the *Rabbiters' Camp at Tilcha* (1965),[8] Drysdale makes his figures ghostly dwellers in both the land and their bodies. The staring eyes, resigned demeanors, and omnipresent isolation of his human subjects show the imprint of the wasteland on its denizens in a kind of symbiosis of the land and human beings. Social critique is implicit in Drysdale's work. Although lady- or queen-like in her classic three-quarter length pose, his *Half-Caste Woman* (1961, fig. 2), her head turned stiffly to the viewer, derives her energy from her otherness, her estrangement from the viewer.[9] It is not inaccurate to read in the awkwardness of her pose the awkwardness of her position in white Australian society.

In terms of technique, *Half-Caste Woman* reveals Drysdale's expressive use of heavy impasto to achieve effects of pure, unblended color. The scumbled bright yellow at the bodice, bounded by heavy black outline, is reminiscent of Rouault's handling. Here Drysdale's technique is more heavy-handed than in his soft, impressionist treatment of *Billy Grace at Cattle Creek* (1966) with its careful landscape details.[10] Beyond mere technique, Drysdale's forte is the evocation of outback characters, people on the fringes of society who peer out at us in seeming incomprehension. Drysdale usually succeeds in upsetting the viewer's expectations of his characters, drawing power from the

[5]Ibid., p. 36, fig. 11.

[6]Ibid., p. 44, fig. 23 (color plate) and cover.

[7]Ibid., p. 45, fig. 24.

[8]Ibid., p. 45, fig. 25.

[9]Russell Drysdale's *Half-Caste Woman* (1961) is also illustrated in Geoffrey Dutton, *Russell Drysdale* (London: Thames and Hudson, 1964), fig. 119; originally in the collection of Mrs. Rose Skinner under the title of *Portrait* (1961). Another painting, also entitled *Half-Caste Woman* but dated 1960, is illustrated in color plate XXVIII, p. 89.

[10]*The Australian Painters*, p. 46, fig. 27.

seemingly mundane, "straight" portrait or genre scene. Drysdale's subjects remind the city dweller of the harshness of the land and the toughness of those who were living on its primitive edges in the sixties.

Like Drysdale, Arthur Boyd explores the landscape and its folk, particularly those of central Victoria. Arthur Boyd, who came from a family of painters and ceramicists, was an important figure, along with his sister Mary Boyd and her husband John Perceval, in the premier avant-garde group in Melbourne during the forties. Whereas Arthur Boyd's best work from this early period is his series of landscapes of the Wimmera district, his paintings in the Mertz Collection recall the art of Marc Chagall, with its buoyant, large-eyed figures and symbolic, serial imagery.[11]

Albert Tucker, who was the most outspoken founding member of the Contemporary Art Society of Australia, found reinforcement for his ideas in the work of literary figures like poet Max Harris and lawyer and publisher John Reed. But when Australia returned from World War II, Tucker discovered that the efforts by his group to gain a public audience and a modicum of acceptance had seemingly no effect at all. R.K. Luck observes that "In many cases the public were openly hostile, and several influential gallery directors joined the reactionary groups in a stand against what one of them termed 'the monstrosities of the devotees of ugliness'."[12] In 1947 Tucker left Australia for a twelve-year stay in Europe, his own self-imposed exile part of what appeared to be a mass exodus of Australian painters, among them Sir Sidney Nolan, James Gleeson, Donald Smart, and many others who worked in London, Paris, and Rome.

The most interesting outcome of Tucker's expatriatism is that being away from Australia increased the power of his "Antipodean Heads," both in their composition and their technique. Postwar Europe was struggling to build an identity in the face of the dramatic shift of the international art scene to New York. European artists in this period were experimenting with the new synthetic polymer resins, which were much faster drying than oil paints and could be mixed with heterogeneous materials such as sand and glass to produce rich, sculptural textures. Because painters using these materials had to work rapidly, their paintings had the characteristics of *alla prima* techniques: ragged, gestural brushstroke, transparency, and the celebration of accident. In *Masked Faun* (1964, fig. 3) Tucker uses polyvinyl acetate to build physically heavy textures rather than rendering them illusionistically. In this respect his painting closely approaches sculptural relief. Here Tucker paints his faun in the image of the masked shaman, with square and rectangular blocks constituting the faun's upper chest (hair indicated by commas scratched into the textured paint), neck, head, and fantastic headdress. A

[11]Ibid., pp. 31-33, figs. 1-5, 6 (color plate).
[12]Ibid., p. 18.

184

Fig. 1. William Dobell, *Romping in the Rain, Vietnam* (1964), oil, 9 ½ × 11 ½ ins. Archer M. Huntington Art Gallery, The University of Texas at Austin, Gift of The Mertz Art Fund, 1972.

Fig. 2. Russell Drysdale, *Half-Caste Woman* (1961), oil, 29 × 23 ins. Archer M. Huntington Art Gallery, The University of Texas at Austin, Gift of The Mertz Art Fund, 1972.

Fig. 3. Albert Tucker, *Masked Faun* (1964), polyvinyl acetate, 31 ½ × 23 ½ ins. Archer M. Huntington Art Gallery, The University of Texas at Austin, Gift of The Mertz Art Fund, 1972.

Fig. 4. John Passmore, *The Bite* (n.d.), oil, 27 × 35 ins. Archer M. Huntington Art Gallery, The University of Texas at Austin, Gift of The Mertz Art Fund, 1972.

Fig. 5. Clifton Pugh, *Depredations of a Wild Dog* (1956), oil, 36 × 45 ins. Archer M. Huntington
Art Gallery, The University of Texas at Austin, Gift of The Mertz Art Fund, 1972.

Figs. 6 & 7. James Gleeson, *Odysseus* (1964, details), enamel, 7⅛ × 5⅝ ins. Archer M. Huntington Art Gallery, The University of Texas at Austin, Gift of The Mertz Art Fund, 1972.

Fig. 8. Jeffrey Smart, *Steps, Palma* (1965), oil, 24 ½ × 30 ½ ins. Archer M. Huntington Art Gallery, The University of Texas at Austin, Gift of The Mertz Art Fund, 1972.

triangle of chin or beard points downward, echoed by the deep curve of the headdress. The only illusionistic shading is in the white horns surmounting the headdress, revealing the light which bathes the image from the left. This same light source reveals the canals and craters of the faun's tortured face, in brownish flesh tones, while burnt umber and black dominate the whole. Tucker has scraped and wiped the background paint to utter thinness, providing maximum contrast to the figure's heavy impasto surfaces, whose craggy textures are not present in only one place, around a black hole in the headdress: the smooth, sinister, and unique area where one's eye inevitably comes to rest. Tucker has orchestrated texture and form around this mysterious black pool, perhaps standing for the faun's "eye" or savage consciousness.

The same paradoxical intensification of Australian imagery occurs in the work of nearly all the painters in exile during the fifties. Before leaving for London in 1950, Sidney Nolan had completed a series on Ned Kelly, an Australian bush ranger and folk anti-hero. Nolan had visited the scenes of Kelly's exploits, recording details of the landscape but creating a hybrid, Surrealist image of Kelly. In the *Death of Constable Scanlon* (1954), Kelly's

Fig. 9. Sam Byrne, *Mt. Robe Silver Mine 1896* (1964), oil, 23 ½ × 30 ins. Archer M. Huntington Art Gallery, The University of Texas at Austin, Gift of The Mertz Art Fund, 1972.

homemade suit of armor is a spectral black construction with a square mask-like face, his eyes gazing out at the viewer.[13] The good constable floats upside-down with his rifle in hand. The buoyant, floating quality of the figures, along with the magical illumination of the landscape, once again recalls more than any the work of Marc Chagall. Like Tucker, Nolan used the new synthetic emulsions, but for their transparency and rapid drying speed rather than for their textural possibilities.

John Passmore represents a more orthodox approach to modernism, particularly in the expressionist works of his later career, represented in the Mertz Collection by *The Bite* (n.d., fig. 4). Passmore frequently hides his figures within seemingly abstract marks or patches. These hidden figures fit with a tradition of abstraction going back to the early works of Kandinsky.[14] They also appear in the work of many Abstract Expressionists (such as the American Willem De Kooning), who merge with the late-Cubist conception of the flattened figure with gestural brushstroke, varied paint handling, and conventional, rather than realistic, color.

In *The Bite* Passmore hides his figures in chunks of color that form his classically-composed figural groups. This camouflaging has the effect of slowing down the viewing process. The artist rewards the hard-working eye with animated forms and unexpected color passages. The left half of the canvas holds seven or eight figures, hidden because they share their colors with those of the foreground, horizon, and sky, and because Passmore defines each in a different way. In the center, two figures are defined principally through black outline around their lavender forms; a bulky male form, on his knees, bows toward the viewer as a child crawls up to him. A thin standing figure in profile echoes the curves of the male form's back and shoulders. Dark values of green, blue, and brown define the figures massed around the key to the picture's title: a hand clenching a (biting) creature that terrifies a squatting figure who raises (her) right hand skyward. The standing figures behind to right and left are foils that frame this drama. Passmore's deliberate merging of figures with landscape and with each other creates a mirage-like transmutability of forms that forces the viewer to see both abstractly and concretely. Is the dark egg-like form in the left foreground a seated nude seen from the rear or a smooth rock? At right center a brown figure on its back seems to blend with the horizontals that establish the sere landscape. In the final analysis, Passmore's painting occupies a position between figural expressionism and abstraction. His concealed figures read as a narrative, while his gestural brushstroke and paint handling connect with the abstract tradition in European and American twentieth-century art.

[13]Ibid., p. 39, fig. 16 (color plate).

[14]Rose Carol Washton-Long, "Kandinsky and Abstraction: The Role of the Hidden Image," *Artforum* (June 1972): 42-49.

Characterized as a nature painter, Clifton Pugh owes much to the abstract tradition. Although twenty years younger than Passmore, Pugh constructs his flat images in abstract shapes reminiscent of synthetic Cubism. His *Depredations of a Wild Dog* (1956, fig. 5) includes elements of Aboriginal bark paintings in its insistent flat geometry and linear patterns. The dog assumes demonic forms as it crouches over its pale prey. Pugh abandons naturalistic color for the triad of orange-red, black, and white. Sawtooth patterns mirror each other throughout. One Aboriginal design is the banded snake that joins the dog's spine with that of his prey, while the sawtooth or zig-zag that touches its curve is mirrored in the structure of the tree rising on the right. Infilling patterns of parallel hatched lines and reticulate cross-hatching also borrow from the primitives. The only contradictory notes are struck in the conventional landscape passages behind this violent group: leafless trees in the middle ground and a hint of sparse greenery in the far background.

Donald Laycock's *Gilgamesh* (1962),[15] like Tucker's *Masked Faun*, places a premium on texture, but is more radically modern in dispensing with the figure-ground relationship. Whereas Tucker's faun is separated from his background, Laycock's image occupies the whole, flattened, pictorial surface. Laycock juxtaposes hot red stripes of varying hue to form the flattened, mask-like icon of the Assyrian god. Lawrence Daws's *Mandala IV* (1962) carries Laycock's textured abstraction a step further, dispensing with figural allusions entirely in favor of a single, flat form, the circular mandala of the title.[16] Both paintings have in common the large size and monochrome treatment of texture that came to dominate avant-garde painting of the fifties and sixties. As such, they are more in step with contemporary European and American developments than the works of the older generation like Dobell, Passmore, and Drysdale.

In contrast to the Australian painters who took their cues from European abstraction, two paintings represented in the Mertz Collection are more closely tied to Surrealism. Surrealist connections can be seen particularly in the works of James Gleeson and Jeffrey Smart. Like Tucker, Gleeson has combined critical writing with painting (he published a 1964 monograph on William Dobell).[17] His *Odysseus* (1964, figs. 6 and 7) marries the precisionist illustrator's art with the automatic techniques of the Surrealists to evoke the cosmic forces of the epic poem. If the precise incidents of Homer's narrative elude the viewer in the eight miniatures that make up the work (four verticals measuring 7¼ × 5⅝ inches and four horizontals measuring 4¼ × 5½ inches), Gleeson's turbulent settings convey the savage beauty of the natural forces Odysseus battled. The most explicit and legible in its symbolism is the

[15]*The Australian Painters*, p. 55, fig. 47.
[16]Ibid., p. 61, fig. 60 (color plate).
[17]James Gleeson, *William Dobell* (London: Thames and Hudson, ca. 1964).

cave of Polyphemus (fig. 6). Four men in the center foreground stand unaware of the limbs of the one-eyed figure in the oval opening of the cave behind them. Above, a single eye with green iris shines from the darkness. The full moon in the sky above rhymes with that eye. Gleeson's academically-drawn nudes contrast strikingly with the fantastically striated rock formations and the spongelike networks of water and rock in the foreground.

In the twenties and thirties Surrealist Max Ernst explored so-called "automatic" methods that produced random arrangements of paint on the canvas: "decalomania" consisted of rubbing paint between two canvases sandwiched together; in "frottage" Ernst impressed textures, like wood grains, on the canvas by rubbing; in "grattage" he manipulated the paint surface, scratching it with a comb so that it produced landscape-like features. Ernst is also credited with inventing a machine for spattering paint at random on the canvas.[18] Gleeson's method in arriving at the fantastic landscape forms seen in *Odysseus* owes a debt to Ernstian automatism. Gleeson has brushed on the enamel, blotting it with newsprint or other absorbent materials while still wet and tacky. The white of the gessoed ground shows through where the paint is removed, leaving rich, random patterns of color where the paint remains. Like Ernst, Gleeson uses the resultant patterns as a point of departure for his fugue on the heroic themes of *The Odyssey*. He converts seemingly random abstract patterns into fantastic backdrops for his heroic and academically correct nudes.

Jeffrey Smart's debt is to a different strain of Surrealism, that of the early De Chirico. In *Steps, Palma* (1965, fig. 8), he composes large, simple forms bathed in bright Mediterranean light. The largest form, an exaggerated kiosk, is a palimpsest of unreadable messages. Aside from the kiosk, color accents are few: bright blue banners fly against an ominous sky, and a string of red, yellow, and blue lightbulbs halve the picture plane at right. This reduction of elements increases the importance of the human figures: they contrast in age, gesture, and form. From the top of the stairs a girl gestures widely to an unseen viewer below, while a middle-aged woman leans against the stair wall, lost in her own reveries.

A characteristic of folk art is that it resists categorization in terms of style and influence. Although there are references to visual models even in the work of entirely unschooled folk artists, it is the immediacy of their naive visions that has captured the imagination of collectors and art lovers. Four self-taught folk artists are represented in the Mertz Collection: Sam Byrne, Pro Hart, Irvine Homer, and Henri Bastin.[19] Although Bastin and Byrne were both self-taught

[18]Barbara Rose, *American Art Since 1900* (New York: F.A. Praeger, 1967), p. 165.

[19]Like Byrne, Pro Hart, who was born in 1928, lived as a miner in Broken Hill, New South Wales. His *Eureka Stockade* (1964) is illustrated in *The Australian Painters*, p. 16, fig. 144. Irvine Homer, born in 1919, is represented in the Mertz Collection by *Approach of the Big Dust* (1962), illustrated in *The Australian Painters*, p. 14, fig. 142.

and near contemporaries, Byrne, who began painting at the age of 70, produced work that is more markedly naive than that of Bastin.[20] Byrne's *Mt. Robe Silver Mine 1896* (n.d., fig. 9) draws on his direct experience, since he worked all his life at the Broken Hill Mine in New South Wales. Here he paints a subject of considerable interest: the use of camel teams to transport silver ore over the rugged hills. Byrne places the sun where the viewer stands, so that the purple shadows form directly behind the camels—all in profile— and their white turbaned drivers—all seen frontally. His literalism surfaces elsewhere, for he has glued black mineral directly on the board to stand for the silver ore, and the cut-out camels tilt backward as they ascend the grade. The viewer's eye penetrates the depths of the striated rock to reveal two miners at work deep within.

Bastin's *Queensland Landscape* (cover), completed fourteen years before his death in 1979, announces its folk naivete in its use of conventional pattern, color, and paint handling. Bastin conceives deep space in successive, brightly alternating colored bands of bright blue and orange red. His keen eye for pattern, whether in the network of diagonal boulders in the mountains or in the trees that dot the landscape, transforms the pictorial space into that of a tapestry or quilt, where every element receives equal attention.

Bastin is not as true a primitive as Sam Byrne, for his command of linear perspective controls the patterns through a familiar system of foreshortening. The trees diminish in size from foreground to background. His medium of opaque watercolor allows him to lay in the bands of color first and add the meticulous repetitive details, like the ubiquitous bullrushes in the water that defy gravity as they slant downwards with the oblique lines of the river. Bastin transmits the magic reality of the place through his obsessive repetition of selected forms and colors.

This overview of three strains of Australian painting—expressionist, surrealist, and folk—has necessarily simplified questions of influence. Yet it is fair to say that most Australian painters of the mid-sixties looked to Europe rather than to the United States for painters they considered both their models and their colleagues. Conspicuous by their absence are two important American movements of the sixties: Pop Art and Minimalism. Louis James's work, especially *Don't Walk* (1966),[21] and Anthony Woods's *My World* (1964)[22] are exceptions, both owing a debt to Pop: James to painters like Larry Rivers and Alan D'Archangelo, and Woods to early Jim Dine. In place of the fully reductive Minimalist canvases of Americans like Frank Stella or Brice Marden, we find the European-inspired Neo-Constructivist work of Stanislaus Ostoja-Kotkowski (*Suspended*, 1965),[23] Sydney Ball (*Diagonal No. 1,*

[20]Byrne was born in 1883; Bastin in 1896 in Belgium.
[21]*The Australian Painters*, p. 63, fig. 65 (color plate).
[22]Ibid., p. 72, fig. 88.
[23]Ibid., p. 62, fig. 64.

1965, even though this work was painted after his New York experience),[24] Leonard Crawford (*Moonrise on Sounion*, 1963),[25] and Udo Sellbach (*Painting*, 1964).[26] These Australian painters were looking to the European advancement of the flat, planar color abstractions of the Nouvelle Tendence, a term used to denote painters and sculptors inspired by the pre-war purist art of de Stijl and the Bauhaus.

Several Australian painters show particular affinities for individual artists rather than for pan-European movements. Brett Whiteley, represented by five paintings in the Mertz Collection,[27] rethinks the art of Francis Bacon, paying homage to both his eccentric compositions and his peculiar distortions of the human figure. Peter Upward's *Sun in Libra* (1965)[28] builds on Adolph Gottlieb's *Blast* series of the late fifties, achieving a polar balance between calligraphic and expressionist elements. And Dusan Marek's *Scientific Priest* (1965)[29] owes a debt to Fernando Botero's big-headed, distorted, anti-clerical images.

The Mertz Collection's time capsule offers opportunities far beyond the scope of this essay, for studying not only the development of Australian painting by a few voices crying from the pre-World War II wilderness, but also its directions after 1966. Whereas this essay has attempted to show how those pioneer modernists formed one of the arts of Australia and brought it to international status by the time the Mertz Collection was assembled, another topic that has yet to be researched is the development of both the artists in the collection and the new directions taken in the intervening twenty-two years. The pioneering modernists who returned from exile in the early sixties were to find a receptivity and heightened cultural awareness in Australia that has propelled its arts beyond all provincial boundaries into world-class status in the eighties. But that is another story.

[24]Ibid., p. 73, fig. 91.
[25]Ibid., p. 58, fig. 53.
[26]Ibid., p. 65, fig. 73.
[27]Ibid., pp. 66-68, figs. 75 (color plate) and 76-79.
[28]Ibid., p. 86, fig. 129.
[29]Ibid., p. 85, fig. 128.

Books in the HRHRC Collections on Australian Art

Unless indicated by an asterisk, all books are in the C. Hartley Grattan Collection.

I. Individual Artists

Charles Blackman

Ray Mathew. *Charles Blackman*. Melbourne: Georgian House, 1965.

Arthur Boyd

Gavin Ewart. *The Select Party*. A poem by Gavin Ewart, with a drawing by Arthur Boyd. Richmond, Surrey: The Keepsake Press, 1972. An edition of 180 copies. HRC copy. 1 is no. 11, inscribed by the author and artist.*

Franz Adolf Philipp, ed. *Arthur Boyd*. London: Thames and Hudson, ca. 1967.

Noel Counihan

Max Dimmack. *Noel Counihan*. Carlton South, Victoria: Melbourne University Press, 1974.

Alan John Marshall. *Journey Among Men*. London: Hodder & Stoughton, 1962.

William Dobell

James Gleeson. *William Dobell*. London: Thames and Hudson, ca. 1964. Bibliography, pp. 207-208.

Sydney Ure Smith, ed. *The Art of William Dobell*. Introduction by Brian Penton. Sydney: U. Smith, 1946. Artist's inscribed copy.

Russell Drysdale

Art Gallery of New South Wales. *Russell Drysdale*. Retrospective Exhibition of Paintings from 1937 to 1960, with an introduction by Paul Haefliger. Sydney: U. Smith, 1960.

Allan Dawes. *"Soldier Superb": the Australian Fights in New Guinea.* Illustrated with drawings by Russell Drysdale and official war photographs. Sydney: F.H. Johnston, 1944.

George Russell Drysdale. *Paintings.* Reproducing 15 plates in color, with an essay by Joseph Burke. Sydney: U. Smith, 1951. 1000 copies of this first edition have been printed; signed: Russell Drysdale.

Geoffrey Dutton. *Russell Drysdale.* London: Thames and Hudson, 1964.

Leonard French

Leonard French. *The Seven Days.* Canberra: Department of the Interior in Association with the Australian National University, n.d.

Donald Friend

Robert Hughes. *Donald Friend.* With a foreword by John Olsen. Sydney: Edwards & Shaw, 1965.

Sali Herman

Daniel Thomas. *Sali Herman.* Australian Art Monographs. Melbourne: Georgian House, 1962.

Elwyn Lynn

Elwyn Lynn. *Contemporary Drawing.* The Arts in Australia. Victoria: Longmans, 1963.

Godfrey Miller

John Henshaw, ed. *Godfrey Miller.* An abridged chronology and an article and writings by the artist. Foreword by Peter Ballew. Sydney: Darlinghurst Galleries, 1966.

Sidney Nolan

Robert Lowell. *The Voyage, and Other Versions of Poems by Baudelaire.* Illustrated by Sidney Nolan. London: Faber, 1968.*

Elwyn Lynn. *Sidney Nolan: Myth and Imagery.* London: Macmillan, 1967.

Sidney Nolan [by] Kenneth Clark, Colin MacInnes, and Bryan Robertson. London: Thames and Hudson, 1961.

Sidney Nolan. Exhibition Catalog. January 1965. London, New York: Marlborough-Gerson Gallery, Inc., [1965].

Sidney Nolan. Exhibition January and February 1967, San Antonio Art League. Introduction by Alan Moorehead. San Antonio: Witte Memorial Museum, 1967.

Sidney Nolan. Leda and the Swan and Other Recent Work. 16 June-16 July 1960. London: Matthiesen Gallery, [1960]. Introduction by Stephen Spender. Artist's signed presentation copy to Spender; also inscribed in another hand on title page: "To J. Schwarz . . . June 21, 1960."*

Charles Osborne. *Swansong: Poems, Drawings by Sidney Nolan.* London: Shenval Press, 1968. Limited edition of 500 numbered copies; nos. 1-50 signed by author and artist. HRHRC has copy no. 70 signed by author and artist.*

Rudolph Stow. *Outrider: Poems, 1956-1962.* With paintings by Sidney Nolan. London: Macdonald, 1962.*

John Olsen

Virginia Spate. *John Olsen.* Australian Art Monographs. Melbourne: Georgian House, 1963.

Clifton Pugh

Noel Macainsh. *Clifton Pugh.* Australian Art Monographs. Melbourne: Georgian House, 1962.

Ivan Smith. *The Death of a Wombat.* With paintings, etchings and line drawings by Clifton Pugh. Melbourne: Wren, ca. 1972.*

Brian Seidel

Brian Seidel. *Printmaking.* The Arts in Australia. Melbourne: Longmans, 1965.

II. General Works

Kym Bonython. *Modern Australian Painting and Sculpture: a Survey of Australian Art from 1950 to 1960.* Foreword by Joseph Burke; Introduction by Laurie Thomas. Adelaide: The Griffin Press, 1960. Includes many of the painters represented in the Mertz Collection.

_____. *Modern Australian Painting, 1960/1970.* Introduction by R.K. Luck. London: Robert Hale & Co., 1970. Includes many of the painters represented in the Mertz Collection.

Great Australian Landscape Paintings. Melbourne: Lansdowne Press, 1973. 48 color plates, including works by Russell Drysdale, Ray Crooke, Lloyd Rees, and John Perceval.

Daniel Thomas. *Outlines of Australian Art; The Joseph Brown Collection.* Melbourne: Macmillan, 1973.

NOTES ON CONTRIBUTORS

JOHN R. CLARKE is a professor in the Department of Art History at The University of Texas at Austin. His publications include *Roman Black-and-White Figural Mosaics* (New York University Press, 1979) and a forthcoming volume entitled *Ritual, Space, and Decoration in the Houses of Roman Italy (100 B.C.-A.D. 250).* In the contemporary field he is a regular contributor to *Arts Magazine.*

DESLEY DEACON is an assistant professor in the American Studies Program at The University of Texas at Austin and codirector of the University's Center for Australian Studies. She is coauthor with John Higley and Don Smart of *Elites in Australia* (Routledge and Keagan Paul, 1979) and author of a forthcoming volume, entitled *Managing Gender: The State, The New Middle Class, and Women Workers, 1830-1930* (Oxford University Press at Melbourne).

LAURIE HERGENHAN is a reader in English at the University of Queensland in Brisbane, Australia, was foundation director of the Australian Studies Centre there from 1979 to 1982, and has been editor of *Australian Literary Studies* since its inception in 1963. His most recent publication is *The Penguin New Literary History of Australia*, for which he has served as general editor.

SUDHAKAR R. JAMKHANDI is an associate professor of English at Bluefield State College in Bluefield, West Virginia, and the editor of *Commonwealth Novel in English.* His *The Rhetoric of War: An Evaluation of Evelyn Waugh's Military Novels* is forthcoming from Peter Lang.

JOHN MCLAREN is head of the Department of Humanities at Footscray Institute of Technology in Victoria, Australia. A former editor of the *Australian Book Review*, he is now an associate editor of *Overland*, a literary and social journal published in Melbourne. His *Xavier Herbert's "Capricornia" and "Poor Fellow My Country"* appeared in 1981 from Shillington House.

FRANK B. POYAS is a doctoral candidate in the Department of History at The University of Texas at Austin. In addition to writing his dissertation on Australian diplomatic and political history from 1949 to 1954, he is presently working on a 25-year history of the international commission that directs the Roosevelt Campobello International Park.

JILL ROE is associate professor of history at Macquarie University in Sydney, Australia. She has written the entry on Miles Franklin in the *Australian Dictionary of Biography* and is currently editing the letters of Miles Franklin for publication by Angus & Robertson.

ROBERT L. ROSS is the editor of *Antipodes*, a North American journal of Australian literature, a publication of the American Association of Australian Literary Studies. His *Australian Literary Criticism–1945-1988* is forthcoming from Garland Publishing. He has written on a number of Australian figures, including Patrick White, Thea Astley, and Peter Carey (winner of the prestigious Booker Prize for 1988).

ROBERT ZELLER is an associate professor at Southeast Missouri State University in Cape Girardeau, Missouri. His article on Joseph Furphy's use of the yarn was published in the Spring 1988 issue of *Antipodes*.